THIRD EDITION

Creative Jazz Improvisation

SCOTT D. REEVES

The City College, The City University of New York

Prentice Hall

Upper Saddle River, New Jersey 07458

Library of Congress Cataloging-in-Publication Data

Reeves, Scott D.
Creative jazz improvisation / Scott D. Reeves.—3rd ed.
p. cm.

ISBN 0-13-088975-X
1. Jazz—Instruction and study. 2. Improvisation (Music) 3. Musical instruments—Studies and exercises (Jazz) I. Title.

MT68.R37 2001
781.65'136—dc21 00-023670

Acquisitions editor: Christopher T. Johnson
Editorial/production supervision
and interior design: Laura A. Lawrie
Copy editor: Laura A. Lawrie
Cover designer: Bruce Kenselaar
Prepress and manufacturing buyer:
Benjamin D. Smith
Editorial assistant: Evette Dickerson

This book was set in Aster by Prepare, Inc. and was printed and bound by Bradford & Bigelow.

Printed in the United States of America

10 9 8 7 6 5 4 3 2

ISBN 0-13-088975-X

Prentice-Hall International (UK) Limited, *London*
Prentice-Hall of Australia Pty. Limited, *Sydney*
Prentice-Hall Canada Inc., *Toronto*
Prentice-Hall Hispanoamericana, S.A., *Mexico*
Prentice-Hall of India Private Limited, *New Delhi*
Prentice-Hall of Japan, Inc., *Tokyo*
Pearson Education Asia Pte. Ltd., *Singapore*
Editora Prentice-Hall do Brasil, Ltda., *Rio de Janeiro*

To David Baker, *who first taught me about chords and scales, and serves as a role model as a jazz educator*;

Kenny Werner, *who helped me unlock my creative potential*;

Art Blakey, Michael Brecker, Will Marion Cook, Miles Davis, Duke Ellington, Bill Evans, Stan Getz, Tim Hagans, Dave Liebman, Joe Lovano, Bobby Mc-Ferrin, Jim McNeely, Pat Metheny, Dick Oatts, Sonny Rollins, Kenny Werner, and Randy Weston, *for their inspirational epigraphs*;

Louis Armstrong, Clifford Brown, John Coltrane, Chick Corea, Miles Davis, Bill Evans, Milt Jackson, J. J. Johnson, Thelonious Monk, Charlie Parker, Max Roach, Sonny Rollins, Woody Shaw, and Lester Young, *for the masterful improvisations transcribed in this text*;

all the other musicians and educators whose music and ideas have influenced the development of this book: Jamey Aebersold, Jerry Bergonzi, Jerry Coker, Todd Coolman, Joe Dailey, Hal Galper, Steve Grover, Lee Konitz, Gene Rush, Ed Soph, Clark Terry, and James Williams.

Contents

Preface

It is gratifying that, since the publication of the first edition in 1989 and the second in 1995, many college educators, private instructors, and students of jazz have found *Creative Jazz Improvisation* to be a valuable aid in their musical growth. This text is a direct outgrowth of over twenty-one years of experiences teaching jazz improvisation at the college level, as well as my own personal quest to develop as a jazz artist.[1]

I believe there is a direct parallel between life and art. The pursuit of understanding in any art form can teach us much about ourselves and serve as a catalyst for a lifetime of learning. My own musical perspectives have evolved since the second edition of this text was written, and much of this new information has been incorporated into the present volume. Therefore, I believe this edition to be much more than a minor reworking of the previous one. However, all of the same features that made *Creative Jazz Improvisation* a popular choice for classroom use are retained, including:

1. The philosophy that there are several paths to the same goal and that each student learns in his or her own unique way.
2. An orientation in difficulty toward college-level and intermediate-to-advanced musicians. For students at the high-school or community college level or adult beginners, I strongly recommend the entry-level companion to this text, *Creative Beginnings*, which comes with a play-along compact disc.[2]
3. The division of the majority of chapters into sections devoted to jazz theory, exercises over a specified chord progression, a list of relevant compositions, and a transcribed solo which has been transposed and edited for concert pitch treble clef, B♭, E♭ and bass clef instruments.
4. A thorough discussion of all facets of jazz theory, including major scale modes, forms and chord substitutions, melodic minor modes, diminished

[1] My college positions have included The City College of New York, the University of Southern Maine, Virginia Commonwealth University, the University of Memphis, and Western Washington University.

[2] Scott Reeves, *Creative Beginnings: An Introduction to Jazz Improvisation* (Prentice-Hall, Inc., Upper Saddle River, NJ, 1997)

and whole-tone scales, pentatonic scales, and intervallic and "free" improvisation.

5. The keying of the chord progressions to either the widespread Jamey Aebersold series or the compact disc accompanying *Creative Beginnings*.[3]
6. Exercises that include not only basic scales and arpeggios but also melodic ideas taken directly from cited recordings by master improvisers, arranged in order of relative difficulty.
7. The indexing of the list of compositions to legal fake-books, particularly the *New Real Book* and the Aebersold play-along series.[4]
8. The correlation of half of the transcribed solos with the widely available anthology, *The Smithsonian Collection of Classic Jazz*.[5]
9. The convenience of allowing a classroom of mixed instrumentation to work simultaneously from the text.

Differences between the second and third editions include:

1. The addition of a new chapter, "Whom to Listen To," which lists major innovators, important contributors, and women in jazz.
2. The expansion of the chapter on "Rhythm," with considerable new information and exercises.
3. Replacement of two transcriptions with more readily playable examples, including Miles Davis's "Solea" solo (in place of Wayne Shorter's "Masqualero" solo), and Bill Evans's "Autumn Leaves" solo (in lieu of Dizzy Gillespie's "Stardust" solo). In addition, J. J. Johnson's solo on "Aquarius" has been renotated in long meter to make it easier to read.
4. An expansion of the list of compositions in each chapter to reflect the ever-increasing number of play-along recordings by Jamey Aebersold. The third edition is now keyed to the first eighty-five volumes in his series, *A New Approach to Jazz Improvisation*.
5. An extensive reworking of all portions of the text to improve readability and reflect recent information.
6. A reappraisal of all exercises, with selected replacements and additions.
7. The incorporation of inspirational epigraphs at the beginning of each chapter.
8. A continued investigation of the how to bridge the gap between the technical and intellectual aspects of jazz with the creative and intuitive state of mind. Many of these ideas may be traced to my exposure to the concepts of pianist Kenny Werner, and I am indebted to his willingness to allow me to incorporate some of his ideas into this volume.[6,7]

[3] Jamey Aebersold, *A New Approach to Jazz Improvisation* (Jamey Aebersold Jazz, P.O. Box 1244, New Albany, IN 47151–1244)

[4] Chuck Sher, ed., *The New Real Book*, vols. 1, 2, & 3 (Sher Music Co., P.O. Box 445, Petaluma, CA 94953)

[5] Martin Williams, ed., *The Smithsonian Collection of Classic Jazz* (The Smithsonian Institution, in association with Columbia Special Products, Washington, DC, 1973, revised 1987. Distribution through W. W. Norton.)

[6] Those interested in Kenny's work should read *Effortless Mastery* by Kenny Werner, published by Jamey Aebersold Jazz, Inc., 1211 Aebersold Dr., New Albany, IN.

[7] Readers may also interested in hearing Kenny's performance on the author's compact disc, *You Are What You Think*, released in 1998 on the Brownstone label, Box 60163, Worcester, MA 01606.

This text reflects the influences of my previous teachers, particularly David Baker, Woody Shaw, and Kenny Werner, the many jazz artists whose work I have studied and transcribed, and the pedagogical concepts of Jamey Aebersold. I gratefully acknowledge these people, as well as the staff at Prentice Hall, particularly my acquisitions editor, Christopher Johnson and my production and copy editor, Laura Lawrie. I sincerely hope the readers of this text will find it a valuable aid in their growth as musicians.[8]

[8] Readers may contact the author through his Web site: http://www.creativejazz.com

PART 1 The Art of Improvisation

1

How to Practice, Creatively Improvise, and Teach Jazz Improvisation

"I keep notebooks and every time
I come up with something I like,
I write out the idea and date it...
I do these exercises in every key.
Then I forget it.
Usually in a couple of months,
the exercises that I practiced...
enter the subconscious pool
and come out in some way I never imagined."

tenor saxophonist Michael Brecker[1]

Learning to improvise involves developing the ability to hear the vocabulary of jazz *and* training your body to be able to play those sounds on your instrument in any key or tempo. Improvisation also means allowing that vocabulary to manifest itself in a spontaneous manner, with a minimum of premeditation. If you have to consciously think about what you are going to play, your music will not have a feeling of immediacy. Furthermore, the intellect cannot keep pace with some of the faster tempos at which jazz is commonly played, so an excess of intellectual thought may result in not being in sync with the rhythm section. Allowing your *trained* instincts to take over enables you to communicate your emotions and ideas through the music and interact with the other musicians in the group. Therefore, it is essential that the aspiring jazz musician not only practice various technical and stylistic exercises, but also learn to control the inner workings of the mind.

In developing the ability to improvise, there are many paths to the same goal. Most jazz musicians have practiced the following concepts, emphasizing those with which they feel the greatest affinity:

1. Assimilating the nature of jazz rhythms and the African-American rhythmic aesthetic.
2. Developing an understanding of jazz theory and the relationship between chords and scales.
3. Gaining facility with the basic vocabulary of jazz by practicing scales, patterns, or melodic quotes in all keys.
4. Ear-training exercises.
5. Transcribing and memorizing improvised solos by master jazz musicians.
6. Learning jazz compositions, with an emphasis on the memorization of the standard repertoire.

[1] Bill Milkowski, "Michael Brecker: Growth Investments," *Jazz Times* (June 1998) 37.

This text attempts to integrate these six approaches into one comprehensive method whose components can be emphasized at a pace that accommodates the needs and interests of the student of jazz.

How to Practice Rhythm

Rhythm is the most important component of jazz. No matter how inventive the melody and chords may be, they are meaningless unless they are played in tempo, with the correct interpretation. In the words of the Duke Ellington standard, "It don't mean a thing if it ain't got that swing."[2]

African-American musical styles, such as blues, gospel, rap, funk, and jazz, generally place a strong accent on the second and fourth beats of the measure, which are considered the weak beats in European musical traditions. When the rhythm is "swung," as in most styles of jazz, an uneven division of the eighth note is used. In medium to slow tempos, the eighth notes tend to be played like triplets with the first two notes tied:

As the tempo increases, the relationship between the notes tends to even out. Within these parameters, each artist finds their own unique interpretations.

In addition to this triplet relationship, consecutive eighths are usually played long (legato) and the offbeats are frequently accented:

Accenting the offbeats may seem difficult if one's primary experience is with European musical traditions. It may be helpful to think of the word "do-BAH," with the accent on "BAH." By accenting offbeats (with occasional accents on downbeats) and "ghosting" or de-emphasizing certain notes, an underlying polyrhythm and infectious sense of swing is created.

In Latin or fusion jazz styles, the eighth notes are played fairly evenly. Latin-American jazz styles that derive from Cuba and the Caribbean employ a pattern called the *clavé*. The "3–2" or *Son clavé* places an accent on beat 1, the "and" of 2, and 4 in the first measure, and beat 2 and the "and" of 3 in the second measure:

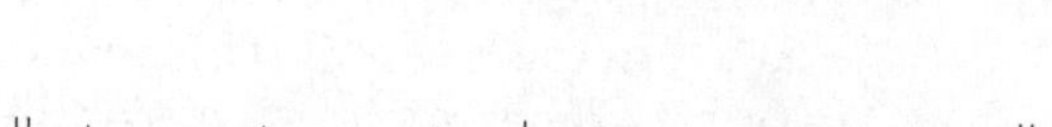

This pattern can also occur as a "2–3" or *reverse clavé*:

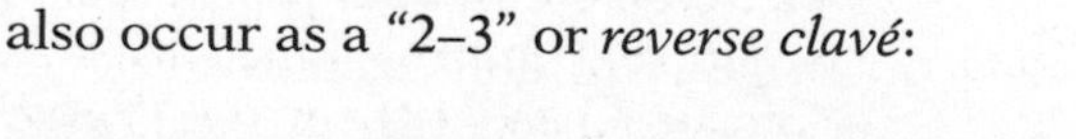

[2] Irving Mills and Duke Ellington, "It Don't Mean a Thing," published by Mills Music Inc., ASCAP.

Another variation on this basic pattern is the *rumba clavé*, which displaces the third note by a half-beat:[3]

Lapses in steady tempo tend to occur not when playing the notes, but during the rests. The notes we play serve to delineate the rhythm, but it is also necessary to feel the continuation of time when not playing. In fact, rests may be structurally more important than notes—they create a sense of phrasing (which is rhythm on a longer scale) and provide an opportunity for the rhythm section to interact with the soloist.

Listening to and playing with great jazz artists is essential in learning to internalize jazz rhythms. It is also helpful to practice with a metronome on beats 2 and 4, which emulates a drummer's hi-hat cymbal. In doing so, the musician defines the beat instead of simply following the metronome, and a wide range of tempos may be practiced. Tape recording one's practice sessions and critiquing the results will also aid in the development of a strong rhythmic concept. Additional concepts will be discussed in Chapter 3.

Jazz Theory

With the exception of free jazz styles, improvisations are based on a predetermined chord progression. For each chord in the progression, there is *at least* one scale that can be used in improvising over a given chord. The chord tones and scales provide the raw materials for the improvisation, but they do not create an interesting melodic line and should not rule out the possibility of effectively using "wrong notes" to add spice to the harmonic mix.

Knowing the chord-scale relationships will greatly simplify the harmonic demands of the tune. Many chord progressions, such as the I–vi–ii–V–I progression, utilize the same notes in their respective scales. By recognizing these relationships, you can reduce a multiplicity of chords to a few basic key areas. For example, the first phrase of "All Things You Are" is based on this chord progression:

Fmi7–B♭mi7–E♭7–A♭MA7–D♭MA7–Dmi7–G7–C MA7–C MA7

These chords can be analyzed as a vi–ii–V–I–IV progression in A♭, followed by a ii–V–I in the key of C. This reduces the harmonic demands from eight chords to only two key areas, A♭ major and C major.

It is also important to learn to *hear* these theoretical relationships, not just think about them. Frequently, musicians feel they play better when they do not look at the chord changes, as the theoretical part of the brain can "drown out" the part that controls inner hearing. As pianist Kenny Werner puts it, "The conscious mind is like the Armed Forces. You need the military to protect the country, but you don't want the generals to take over the government."[4]

[3] Gary Pack, personal conversation with author, Gorham, ME, 1999.

[4] Kenny Werner, private lesson, Scotch Plains, NJ, 1992.

Gaining Facility with Jazz Vocabulary

Repeatedly practicing scales, patterns, and melodic ideas by ear in all keys develops the ability to hear the harmonic/melodic vocabulary, strengthens the ear-to-body response, develops technical dexterity, and, when practiced with a metronome, helps create a surer sense of rhythm. However, care must be taken to keep this sort of practice from becoming mechanical. Some students of improvisation (including this author initially) often resist scale and pattern practice because of the unfounded fear that it will harm their creativity and spontaneity. Some of this resistance may also be due to a lack of disciplined practice habits and an unwillingness to devote the time and work required. However, *the practice of scales and melodic patterns need not interfere with the creative process as long as these materials are not viewed as "licks" to be inserted into an improvisation in a conscious manner*. Attempting to use previously practiced ideas in this way usually interrupts the spontaneous flow of ideas and rhythm. Instead, these materials should be practiced in a nonanalytical manner, as a means of developing an automated ear-to-finger response. Some of these scales and melodic patterns may spontaneously emerge during an improvised solo; others may never become part of the performer's improvisational vocabulary. Nevertheless, devoting a certain portion of one's practice time to this type of activity will definitely yield results. Werner describes the process: "I never try to play anything I'm practicing. I'm only interested in the effect practicing has on my playing."[5] The following concepts will prove helpful when practicing the scales, arpeggios, and melodic patterns found in this text:

1. Practice as slowly as necessary in order to play the most difficult passages cleanly and in rhythm. Most young musicians make the mistake of trying to play things too quickly. This simply reinforces bad technique and poor rhythm—problems that will persist until corrected by careful practice. Practicing with a metronome on beats 2 and 4 can be an effective tool in this process. Start slowly and gradually increase the speed, recording your results in the space provided below each pattern in the text: M.M. ______________. An alternative to this slow, gradual approach is to practice at fast tempos, but only play a small portion of the exercise, gradually adding more notes until the entire passage is learned.
2. Most of the technical studies in this text may be practiced with the play-along recordings from *Creative Beginnings: An Introduction to Jazz Improvisation* (by Scott Reeves, published by Prentice-Hall) or *A New Approach to Jazz Improvisation* (edited and published by Jamey Aebersold). Although play-along recordings do have the disadvantage of being noninteractive and confined to one speed, they are valuable in learning to hear the form, harmony, and rhythmic concepts being played by the rhythm section.
3. Extend the range, change the rhythm, or create your own variations of each exercise. A space in which to record your own ideas is provided at the end of the exercises in each chapter.
4. Experiment with a variety of rhythmic accents and expressive devices, such as pitch bends, half-valve effects, ghosted notes, and falloffs.

[5] Scott Reeves, "Two Conversations with Kenny Werner," *Jazz Educators Journal* (January 1999) 112.

5. Do not try to practice too many concepts simultaneously. It is better to thoroughly master a few patterns that appeal to you, rather than superficially practicing a large amount of material.
6. Once you are be able to play the basic scales and arpeggios, practicing short melodic ideas taken from improvised solos by major jazz artists will aid in making the transition from playing scales to creating interesting melodies. Jazz musicians do not simply play scales in their solos, they play rhythmic and melodic ideas; practicing a phrase by Sonny Rollins or John Coltrane will do more to help you assimilate the vocabulary than practicing numerous permutations of a mundane pattern.
7. Whatever you choose to practice, work on it until you can play it effortlessly, without having to think about it. Only when you have learned something at this deep level will it be able to emerge in an unpremeditated manner during an improvisation.
8. Try practicing away from the instrument, singing each exercise, while physically or mentally imagining yourself playing.

Ear-Training Exercises

Jazz has evolved fairly complex melodies and harmonic structures, and it requires a great deal of skill to recognize these sounds and play them on an instrument. There may be a genetic component that speeds up this process in some gifted individuals, but everyone can improve their ability to recognize melodic and harmonic relationships.

Practicing scales and patterns, playing transcribed solos and memorizing tunes all have the common goal of developing the ability to hear the jazz vocabulary. In addition, the following activities will also aid in your musical development:

1. Singing a phrase and trying to play it on your instrument.
2. Call and response between two musicians, with each musician trying to repeat what the other played.
3. Melodic, harmonic, and rhythmic dictation exercises.
4. Transcribing melodies, bass lines, chord progressions, and improvised solos from recordings.
5. Learning to play chord progressions on the piano.
6. Playing along with an unknown chord progression, using only your ear to pick out the desirable notes.

As your powers of inner hearing grow, there will be a marked change in the quality of your improvisations. Beginning improvisers may find that they do hear the chord changes internally, hence their melodic lines do not create tension and resolution with regard to the harmony. As one grows musically, you will develop the ability to improvise "inside" the chord changes and define the harmonic structure of the song. Professionals in the contemporary style may take this process one step further—they hear the chords in their head but choose to play "outside" of the harmonic structure. This approach works well when the improvised melodies have a strongly defined rhythm and periodically "touch base" with important chord changes, such as V–I relationships. An educated listener will hear the dissonance as intentional, and the results can be very exciting.

Transcribed Solos

Transcribing and practicing improvised solos by master jazz musicians helps the student of improvisation assimilate the vocabulary and style of these artists, in much the same way that children learn to speak by imitating their parents. In this way, the language and history of jazz is passed from one generation to the next. Many jazz musicians learned their craft using this approach almost exclusively. There are three ways to transcribe solos:

1. Learn the solo from a recording, committing it to memory by repetition. Do not write the solo down, but play along with the recording on a periodic basis to retain your memory of it. Try to express not merely the notes, but the inflections, dynamics, and rhythmic drive as well.
2. Transcribe the solo from a recording, writing it down on manuscript paper. Then memorize the solo, capturing the flavor of the improvisation. It can be helpful to slow the solo to half speed when transcribing, which will cause the pitch to be one octave lower. This can be accomplished by recording the solo on a reel-to-reel tape recorder at $7\frac{3}{8}$ i.p.s. and playing it back at $3\frac{3}{4}$. Some cassette decks and transcribing machines also feature a half-speed option.
3. Use a transcription from a book such as this text. If a recording is available, listen and sing along with it until the sound of the solo is in your ear. Play the transcription slowly, gradually speeding up until you can play it along with the recording, matching the nuances of the solo. Then memorize the solo.

After practicing a transcription, create your own improvisation on the tune, trying to incorporate elements of the artist's style. By emulating the masters, you will eventually find your own voice within the historical continuum of this art form.

Practicing Jazz Compositions

Improvising on jazz compositions is fun and immediately gratifying, whereas practicing scales and transcribing solos may seem more laborious. Nevertheless, students of improvisation should seek a balance between playing and practicing. Too much time spent on technical exercises can make the music lifeless, but simply playing tunes without learning any new vocabulary prevents the student from progressing to another level of mastery.

In each chapter of this text there is a list of compositions correlated to the specific theoretical concepts studied. These are provided to encourage the student to apply the theory they have learned to the standard jazz repertoire. These lists are not intended to be complete compilations but are restricted to a few of the most widely available sources of jazz repertoire: *The New Real Book* (legal fake-books published by Sher Music Co.) and the Aebersold play-along recordings, *A New Approach to Jazz Improvisation* (edited and published by Jamey Aebersold). These lists also include the songs found in the entry-level companion to this book, *Creative Beginnings: An Introduction to Jazz Improvisation* (by Scott Reeves, published by Prentice Hall). The goal of learning tunes should be to memorize and inwardly hear the melody and chords of each song. A good musician is expected to know the standard repertoire intimately, and the act of reading music often interferes with the listening process. Try the following procedures when practicing jazz compositions:

1. Internalize the melody.
   a. Learn the melody from recording by a major artist. If one is not available, use a fake-book or a play-along recording.
   b. Sing the melody, then play it on your instrument.
   c. After learning the melody, try playing it in different keys.
2. Study the harmony and form.
   a. Sing the roots of the chords, then play them on your instrument.
   b. Analyze the chord progression and form. Simplify the chords by reducing them to the fewest possible key centers. Look for sequences and familiar chord patterns from other tunes you already know.
   c. Outline the chord progression using guide-tone lines. (Guide-tones are pitches that define the sound of the chord, typically the 3rds and the 7ths.) Start by playing the 3rd or the 7th of the first chord, holding it for the duration of the chord. Then move to either the 3rd or the 7th of the following chord, whichever is closer.
   d. Outline the chords with the appropriate scales and arpeggios, using the harmonic rhythm of the chord progression. For instance, if the chord lasts two measures, play the scale in eighth notes up and down; if the chord lasts two beats, play only the first, second, third, and fifth notes of the scale.
   e. Play the chords on the piano.
3. Improvise on the composition, experimenting with these four approaches.
   a. *Playing With Recordings*: Play along with a recording of the song, trying to capture the style, energy, and rhythmic interpretation used by the musicians on the recording.
   b. *Melodic Development* (suggested to this author by saxophonist Lee Konitz):[6] Play the melody over and over, embellishing it slightly each time. Eventually, it will no longer sound like the melody but an improvisation devoid of obvious patterns or clichés.
   c. *Harmonic Outlining* (an approach exemplified by Coleman Hawkins' "Body & Soul" and John Coltrane's "Giant Steps" solos): Outline the chords with chord arpeggios and scales, but in a very free, improvisatory manner. Your melodic lines should define the harmony, without relying on the harmonic accompaniment.
   d. *Giving up conscious control* (suggested to this author by pianist Kenny Werner and elaborated on in the following section):[7] Improvise on the tune without thinking about the chords. Don't preconceive of anything you are going to play. Allow any sound to manifest itself without *you* having to make an effort.

Creative Jazz Improvisation

A musician must make the transition from the analytical state of mind used in studying the jazz language to the nonlinear state of mind used in making music. As Herrigel states in *Zen in the Art of Archery*: "The technically learned part of

[6] Lee Konitz, private lesson, Bellingham, WA, 1977.
[7] Kenny Werner, private lesson, Scotch Plains, NJ, 1992.

it must be practiced to the point of repletion. If everything depends on the (musician's) becoming purposeless and effacing himself (while playing), then its outward realization must occur automatically, in no further need of the controlling or reflecting intelligence."[8] The following are specific techniques that may aid in developing the ability to transcend controlling thought and tap into a state of awareness that may be called "the creative flow." Many of these concepts are derived from this author's private study with pianist Kenny Werner. For further elaboration on concepts relating to developing an intuitive approach to improvisation, I highly recommend Mr. Werner's book, *Effortless Mastery*.[9]

1. Learn to control your mind. Disciplines such as yoga, concentration exercises, breathing exercises, or meditation can help develop the ability to perform with fewer mental distractions and less "inner noise."
2. Do not consciously think about the chords and notes you are going to play. If you have done the necessary preparatory study, the notes will take care of themselves.
3. When practicing or performing, try to keep your thoughts still and your body relaxed. Don't force the music—*"let music, don't make music."*[10]
4. To aid in stilling your thoughts when performing, it may be helpful to concentrate on something outside of yourself, such as another person or an object, or to place your attention on maintaining a relaxed feeling in your embouchure, fingers, or airstream.
5. When practicing or improvising, imagine that you are not the one playing but a "silent witness" to the event.
6. Always listen and respond to the musicians with whom you are playing. Undue preoccupation with oneself will destroy the group's communication and rhythmic cohesion.
7. Focus on the emotional and rhythmic message you are attempting to convey. Use what you have practiced to say something meaningful.
8. Stage fright often results from ego-based thoughts such as "who's in the audience" and "what do the other musicians think of me." Believe in your intrinsic worth as a human being, and don't worry about what anyone else thinks of your playing.
9. View your music as a reflection of your personal growth and development of your consciousness. Ultimately, the way to improve your music is to improve yourself as a human being.

How to Teach Jazz Improvisation

Jazz improvisation not only can be taught; it is a skill that can be continually developed over a lifetime. All it requires is sufficient love of the music to provide the drive, perseverance, and self-examination necessary to continue to grow as a creative being. As one matures, the desire for quick achievement and

[8] Eugene Herrigel, *Zen in the Art of Archery* (Muenchen-Planegg, Germany: Otto Wilhelm Barth-Verlang, n.d.; USA: Pantheon Books, Inc., 1953; reprint ed., New York: Vintage Books, a division of Random House, Inc., 1989), p. 39.

[9] Kenny Werner, *Effortless Mastery* (Jamey Aebersold Jazz, Inc., New Albany, IN, 1996).

[10] Kenny Werner, private lesson, Scotch Plains, NJ, 1992.

recognition tends to fade, as one realizes that the real goal of this study is the joy that comes from the process of learning and growth.

Teaching is a natural outgrowth of the one's own experiences as a musician. I encourage all teachers to use this text as a means of organizing or supplementing their own concepts. Although improvisation is best taught in a class dedicated to the subject, it should also be addressed in private lessons and within the context of the jazz ensemble rehearsal. This book was designed as a text for college improvisation courses or for personal use by intermediate to advanced musicians. For the majority of high school students and adult beginners, *Creative Beginnings: An Introduction to Jazz Improvisation* may be a more appropriate text.[11]

The following supplementary materials are recommended for use with this book:

1. *Smithsonian Collection of Classic Jazz* (edited by Martin Williams; published by the Smithsonian Institution in association with Columbia Special Products, Washington, DC, 1973, revised 1987). A large portion of the transcribed solos in this text may be found in this collection.
2. *Creative Beginnings: An Introduction to Jazz Improvisation* (by Scott Reeves, published by Prentice-Hall, Inc.). This text and its companion play-along CD contains original compositions that may be used to supplement the "improvising on jazz compositions" section in *Creative Jazz Improvisation*. The play-along CD also contains rhythm section accompaniments to many of the "gaining facility" exercises.
3. *A New Approach to Jazz Improvisation* (by Jamey Aebersold, P.O. Box 1244, New Albany, IN 47151–1244). These play-along recordings can be used when practicing many of the exercises and compositions, if a rhythm section is not available.
4. *The New Real Book*, vols. 1, 2, and 3 (published by Sher Music Co., P.O. Box 445, Petaluma, CA 94953). These legal fake-books are good sources for repertoire and are available in C, E-flat, B-flat, and bass clef editions. Play-along cassettes are also available at an additional cost for many of the songs in volume 1. Sher Music also publishes *The Jazz Piano Book* by Mark Levine, which is excellent text for developing keyboard comping skills.
5. A library of representative recordings by major jazz artists, such as those listed in Chapter 2, as well as recordings of all the transcribed solos in this text. Listening to recordings is an indispensable part of learning to improvise.

The play-along recordings used for the "gaining facility" exercises and the sources for the transcribed solos are as follows:

Chapter	*Gaining Facility Exercises*	*Transcribed Solos*
3	*Creative Beginnings* of or Aebersold, vol. 24	Listening Section: Smithsonian Collection *Classic Jazz*; John Coltrane, *My Favorite Things*; Miles Davis, *My Funny Valentine*; Shelly Manne, 2-3-4
4	*Creative Beginnings* or Aebersold, vol. 21	*Smithsonian Collection*
5	*Creative Beginnings* or Aebersold, vol. 1	*Smithsonian Collection*

[11] Scott Reeves, *Creative Beginnings: An Introduction to Jazz Improvisation* (Prentice-Hall, Inc., Upper Saddle River, NJ, 1997).

6	*Creative Beginnings* or Aebersold, vol. 21	*Smithsonian Collection* or Miles Davis, *Kind of Blue*
7	*Creative Beginnings* or Aebersold, vol. 3	*Smithsonian Collection*
8	*Creative Beginnings* or Aebersold, vol. 3	*Smithsonian Collection* or Modern Jazz Quartet, *The European Concert*
9	No play-along available	Miles Davis, *Sketches of Spain*
10	Aebersold, vol. 2, 6, or 42	Charlie Parker, *The Verve Years*
11	Aebersold, vol. 47	*Smithsonian Collection*
12	Aebersold, vol. 16 or 68	John Coltrane, *Giant Steps*
13	No play-along available	no transcription
14	*Creative Beginnings* or Aebersold, vol. 3	J. J. Johnson, *J. J. Inc.*
15	No play-along available	*Smithsonian Collection*
16	*Creative Beginnings* or Aebersold, vol. 21	Miles Davis, *The Modern Jazz Giants*
17	*Creative Beginnings* or Aebersold, vol. 3	*Jazz Piano, vol. 4* (Smithsonian) or Bill Evans, *Portrait in Jazz*
18	No play-along available	*Smithsonian Collection* or Sonny Rollins, *Saxophone Colossus*
19	*Creative Beginnings* or Aebersold, vol. 3 or 21	Art Blakey, *Child's Dance*
20	No play-along available	Chick Corea, *Now He Sings, Now He Sobs* or *Jazz Piano, vol. 4* (Smithsonian)
21	No play-along available	Miles Davis, *Filles de Kilimanjaro*

Suggestions for Classroom Procedure

Although every teacher has their own individual classroom style, the following classroom techniques and pacing are suggested:

1. Do a variety of activities in the classroom and keep the pace lively. Alternate between theoretical discussions and analysis, group practicing, ear-training exercises, the study and performance of transcribed solos, as well as improvising on the chord progressions and tunes in a combo setting.
2. Encourage the students to play the exercises by ear, keeping analytical thought to a minimum.
3. Technical studies such as scales, arpeggios, and melodic patterns may be done in unison or individually. If the exercise is too difficult, have the students sing it, slow it down, or break the exercise into shorter fragments.
4. Introduce as many of the exercises as possible within the time constraints and ability level of the class. Then have the students focus on one or two melodic patterns that appeal to them, including ideas they may have discovered on their own. By limiting the amount of material, they should be able to thoroughly master it. It may take months for a new harmonic or melodic idea to become an unconscious part of an improviser's vocabulary, so they should be encouraged to continue the assimilation process long after the class is over.

5. Periodically assign transcription projects, beginning with simple melodies and chord progressions and working up to improvised solos.
6. When introducing new repertoire, play recorded examples of the composition. Encourage memorization of the standards by having the students learn as much of the song as possible by ear. Apply the scales, arpeggios, and patterns they have practiced, using them to outline the harmonic progression of the composition.
7. Use the chapters in this book in any order deemed appropriate to the needs of the students.
8. Tests may be given in the form of both written and playing exams. Playing exams will assess their ability to play the technical exercises, transcribed solos and memorized repertoire. Written exams may focus on theory, dictation, and analysis of musicians' styles.

Some Possible Course Formats (based on a 15-week semester)

One-semester course: Chapters 1, 2, 3, 4, 5, 6, 10, 7

Two-semester course:
First semester—Chapters 1, 2, 3, 4, 5, 6, 10
Second semester—Chapters 7, 11, 14, 8, 16, 17

Three semester course:
First semester—Chapters 1, 2, 3, 4, 5, 6, 10
Second semester—Chapters 7, 11, 12, 14, 8
Third semester—Chapters 16, 17, 19, 20, 21, 13

Four semester course:
First semester—Chapters 1, 2, 3, 4, 5, 6, 10
Second semester—Chapters 7, 11, 14, 8, 16
Third semester—Chapters 9, 12, 17, 15, 18
Fourth semester—Chapters 19, 20, 21, 13, Special Projects.

2
Whom To Listen To

"The music of my people is ...
now, which of my people?
I'm in several groups ...
I'm in the group of piano players,
I'm in the group of the listeners,
I'm in the group of people who
have a general appreciation of music,
I'm in the group of those who
aspire to be dilettantes,
I'm in the group of those who attempt
to produce something fit for the plateau ...
I'm in the group of those of those who
appreciate a good Beaujolais.
THE PEOPLE ... that's the better better word ...
because *THE PEOPLE* are *MY PEOPLE*

composer, pianist, band leader Duke Ellington, in response to a question asking him to define the music of his people[1]

In order to learn to play jazz, it is essential to listen to it—not just one particular style, but the entire breadth of the music. Long before books about jazz were written or schools began teaching it, aspiring musicians learned to play by listening to and imitating established artists. Eventually, the younger generation would add their own twists to the music, or perhaps even reconfigure its basic underpinnings.

Major Innovators Who Changed the Direction of Jazz

In the past one hundred years, jazz has undergone a rapid evolution in style, comparable to the last four hundred years of classical music. There are many great stylists on every instrument whose work has contributed to the development of the art. However, only a few of them were so innovative that they forever changed the way jazz was performed.

Improvisers

1920s: *Louis Armstrong*—acknowledged as the first great improviser in jazz, his trumpet playing and singing defined how jazz should be played in the '20s and '30s.

1930s: *Lester Young*—although he was initially ridiculed because of his light, relaxed approach to the tenor saxophone, his flowing eighth-note rhythms anticipated the Bebop style of the '40s, and his sound influenced many of the Cool artists of the '50s.

[1] "A Duke Named Ellington," *American Masters*, Public Broadcasting System, 1987.

1940s: *Charlie Parker*—the father of Bebop, his alto saxophone playing redefined the melodic, harmonic, and rhythmic underpinnings of jazz.

1950s and '60s: *Miles Davis*—relentlessly innovative, he was either a defining voice or the creator of several important stylistic trends in jazz. His warm, airy trumpet sound and his judicious use of space, broke with the traditional brassy approach to his instrument.

1950s and '60s: *John Coltrane*—his complex rhythmic groupings and rapid arpeggios (often called "sheets of sound"), exploration of pentatonic scales, and spiritual intensity stretched jazz to new vistas. Saxophonists from the acoustic post-bop and electronic fusion schools are indebted to his use of new timbres and expansion of the range of the soprano and tenor saxophones.

Composers

Although jazz is primarily an improviser's art, certain composers have defined the music of their era through their compositions. (Coincidentally, every composer on this list is a pianist, with the exception of saxophonist Wayne Shorter.)

1920s: *Jelly Roll Morton*—his orchestrations brought cohesion to the typically untamed collective improvisations of early jazz and set the stage for the large ensemble sound of the 1930s.

1930s–'60s: *Duke Ellington*—his pioneering work not only was instrumental in the development of the big band sound of the '30s, but with the help of his collaborator, Billy Strayhorn, his extended compositions raised jazz composition to the level of the greatest symphonic composers.

1940s–'50s: *Thelonious Monk*—his quirky, rhythmically unpredictable tunes not only defined the sound of Bebop, but pointed the way to freer forms as well.

1950s–'60s: *Horace Silver*—his well-crafted compositions combined memorable melodies with captivating rhythms, and came to personify the hard bop sound.

1960s: *Wayne Shorter*—his writing for Art Blakey, Miles Davis, and Weather Report extended the harmonic vocabulary of jazz composition.

Important Jazz Contributors

The following individuals have made important contributions to jazz. Although there are many emerging artists who are beginning to make substantial contributions, I have restricted this list to well-established figures, particularly those born before 1960.

Big Bands and Composers

Formulators and Contributors to the Swing Style of the '30s

Fletcher Henderson, Duke Ellington, Benny Carter, Chick Webb, Jimmy Lunceford, Benny Goodman, Tommy & Jimmy Dorsey, Charlie Barnet, Lionel Hampton

Big Bands in the Bop and Cool Styles

Woody Herman, Billy Eckstine, Dizzy Gillespie, Stan Kenton, Maynard Ferguson, Buddy Rich, Gil Evans, Claire Fischer

Harmonic Adventurers

Thad Jones/Mel Lewis, Toshiko Akiyoshi, Carla Bley, George Russell, Bob Brookmeyer, Bob Mintzer, Maria Schneider, Jim McNeely, Bob Belden

Saxophonists

The First Saxophonists

Sidney Bechet (soprano), Frankie Trumbauer (C melody sax)

Swing Era Saxophonists

Benny Carter and Johnny Hodges (alto), Coleman Hawkins, Ben Webster, Lester Young, Illinois Jacquet (tenor), Harry Carney (bari)

Transitional Figures to Bebop

Paul Gonsalves, Don Byas, Lucky Thompson (tenor)

Bebop: Bird and his Followers

Charlie Parker, Jackie McLean (alto), Sonny Stitt (alto and tenor), Dexter Gordon, Sonny Rollins (tenor), Cecil Payne (bari)

Second Generation Boppers and Cool Players

Cannonball Adderly, Lee Konitz, Phil Woods (alto), James Moody (alto, tenor), Stan Getz, George Coleman (tenor), Gerry Mulligan, Pepper Adams (bari)

Post-Bop: Trane and his Contemporaries

John Coltrane (soprano and tenor), Eric Dolphy (alto, flute, bass clarinet), Wayne Shorter (soprano and tenor), Joe Henderson, Archie Shepp, Pharoah Sanders (tenor)

Post-Coltrane/Post-Rollins Stylists

Gary Bartz, Kenny Garrett, Vincent Herring (soprano and alto), Charles Lloyd, David Liebman, Bob Berg, Steve Grossman, Michael Brecker, Joe Lovano, George Garzone, Joshua Redman, Chris Potter (soprano and tenor)

Ornette and the Free School

Ornette Coleman, Steve Coleman (alto), Dewey Redman, David Murray, Henry Threadgill (tenor), Hamiet Bluiett (bari)

Clarinetists

Early Jazz through Swing

Albert Nichols, Sidney Bechet, Johnny Dodds, Benny Goodman, Jimmy Hamilton, Artie Shaw

Bebop and Beyond

Woody Herman, Buddy DeFranco, Jimmy Guiffre, Paquito D'Rivera, Eddie Daniels, Don Byron

Trumpeters

Early Jazz Pioneers

Buddy Bolden, Joe "King" Oliver, Louis Armstrong, Henry "Red" Allen, Bix Beiderbecke

Duke's Men—Swing through Bebop

Cootie Williams, Ray Nance, Rex Stewart, 'Cat' Anderson, Clark Terry

Basie's Men—Swing through Bebop

Buck Clayton, Harry "Sweets" Edison, Snooky Young, Thad Jones

Other Swing and Transitional Players

Oran "Hot Lips" Page, Bobby Hackett, Charlie Shavers, Roy Eldridge

Dizzy and his Hard-Bop Successors

Dizzy Gillespie, Fats Navarro, Miles Davis, Clifford Brown, Kenny Dorham, Lee Morgan, Blue Mitchell, John Faddis

The West Coast and Cooler Stylists

Chet Baker, Miles Davis, Shorty Rogers, Art Farmer, Maynard Ferguson

Post-Bop Modernism

Miles Davis, Booker Little, Freddie Hubbard, Woody Shaw, Tom Harrell, Kenny Wheeler, Wallace Rooney, Tim Hagans, Nicholas Payton

Into Abstraction

Don Cherry, Lester Bowie, Dave Douglas

Electronic Experimenters

Miles Davis, Randy Brecker

Preservers of the Legacy

Wynton Marsalis

Trombonists

Early Tailgaters

Kid Ory, Jack Teagarden, Vic Dickinson, J.C. Higgenbotham

Swing Trombonists

Duke's Men—Joe "Tricky Sam" Nanton, Lawrence Brown
Basie's Men—Dicky Wells, Al Grey

Transitional Figures

Bill Harris, Benny Green, Jimmy Knepper

Beboppers, Cool Artists, and Post-boppers

J. J. Johnson, Kai Winding, Curtis Fuller, Slide Hampton, Steve Turre, Bob Brookmeyer (valves), Carl Fontana, Frank Rosolino

Freer Slip-horners

Roswell Rudd, Albert Mangelsdorff, Ray Anderson, Julian Priester

Pianists, Organists, and Keyboardists

Early Jazz and Stride Pianists

Jelly Roll Morton, James P. Johnson, Willie "the Lion" Smith, Earl "Fatha" Hines, Art Hodes

Swing Stylists

Art Tatum, Fats Waller, Duke Ellington, Count Basie, Teddy Wilson, Nat "King" Cole, Mary Lou Williams, Erroll Garner

Beboppers—The First Generation

Bud Powell, Thelonious Monk

Second Generation Boppers

Horace Silver, Oscar Peterson, Ahmad Jamal, Red Garland, Wynton Kelly, Cedar Walton, Hank Jones, Tommy Flanagan, Roland Hannah, Barry Harris, Jacki Byard, Kenny Barron, Jimmy Smith (organ)

The "Memphis" Connection

Phineas Newborn, James Williams, Harold Mabern, Mulgrew Miller, Donald Brown

Cool and West Coast Pianists

Lennie Tristano, John Lewis, Dave Brubeck

The Bill Evans Legacy

Bill Evans, Herbie Hancock, Chick Corea, Keith Jarrett, Kenny Werner

Post-Bop Modal: The McCoy Tyner School

McCoy Tyner, Larry Young (organ), Joanne Brackeen, George Cables

Freer Styles

Cecil Taylor, Sun Ra, Paul Bley, Ran Blake

Synthesists

Herbie Hancock, Chick Corea, Joe Zawinul, George Duke

Vibraphonists and Percussionists

Swing and Bebop Era Vibists

Lionel Hampton, Red Norvo, Milt Jackson

Beyond Bop

Gary Burton, Bobby Hutcherson, Double Image (David Friedman and David Samuels)

Percussionists in Jazz

Tito Puente, M'Boom (percussion ensemble), Airto Moriera, Mongo Santamaria

Violinists

Stephane Grappelli, Ray Nance, Svend Asmussen, Stuff Smith, Jean Luc Ponty, Michael Urbaniak

Guitarists

Pre-Bop Guitarists

Eddie Lang, Django Reinhardt, Freddie Green, Charlie Christian

Bop and Hard Bop Guitarists

Tal Farlow, Wes Montgomery, Jimmy Rainey, Johnny Smith, Kenny Burrell, Joe Pass, Jim Hall, Bruce Forman

Fusion and Post-Jim Hall Stylists

Pat Martino, John McLaughlin, Larry Coryell, Pat Metheny, John Abercrombie, John Scofield, Mick Goodrick, Bill Frisell, Mike Stern

Bassists

Early Jazz, Swing and the Transition to Bop

Walter Page, Slam Stewart, Milt Hinton, Jimmy Blanton, Oscar Pettiford

Bop Bassists

Charles Mingus, Ray Brown, Paul Chambers, Sam Jones, Percy Heath

Virtuosi of the '60s and Beyond

Scott La Faro, Ron Carter, Gary Peacock, Miroslav Vitous, Eddie Gomez, Dave Holland, Cecil McBee, Charlie Haden, Rufus Reid, Marc Johnson

The Electric Bass in Jazz

Steve Swallow, Stanley Clarke, Jaco Pastorius, John Patitucci

Drummers

Early Pioneers

Baby Dodds, Zutty Singleton, Big Sid Catlett

Big Band Swingers

Jo Jones, Gene Krupa, Chick Webb, Louis Bellson, Buddy Rich, Mel Lewis

Bop, Hard Bop, and Cool Drummers

Max Roach, Kenny Clarke, Roy Haynes, Art Blakey, Philly Joe Jones, Victor Lewis, Joe Morello

Contemporary Innovators

Ed Blackwell, Billy Higgins, Paul Motian, Elvin Jones, Tony Williams, Jack DeJohnette, Billy Hart, Bobby Moses, Rashid Ali

Fusion Stylists

Lenny White, Billy Cobham, Dave Weckl, Steve Gadd

Miscellaneous Instruments

Toots Theilman (harmonica), Howard Johnson (tuba), John Clark and Tom Varner (French horn)

Singers

The First Scat Singer

Louis Armstrong

The Blues Tradition—Early to Contemporary

Bessie Smith, Jimmy Rushing, Dinah Washington, Joe Williams

Swing and Early Bop Singers

Billie Holiday, Nat "King" Cole, Cab Calloway, Billy Eckstine, Anita O'Day

Four Divas

Ella Fitzgerald, Sarah Vaughan, Carmen McRae, Shirley Horn

Solo Reconstructionists (lyrics set to instrumental improvisations)

King Pleasure, Eddie Jefferson, Lambert/Hendricks and Ross

Song Deconstructionists

Betty Carter, Sheila Jordan, Mark Murphy, Leon Thomas

Singers of Diverse Inspiration

Al Jarreau, Bobby McFerrin, Milton Nascimento, Cassandra Wilson

Women In Jazz

Although jazz may appear to be a male-dominanted art, many women have made substantial contributions to the art form. Some names appear on the previous list, as well as the following. Notice how in recent decades, more women are gravitating to wind instruments and percussion, in lieu of the traditional pianist/vocalist roles.

The '20s

Lil Hardin Armstrong (pianist), Bessie Smith, Ma Rainey (vocalists)

The '30s

Mary Lou Williams (pianist, composer), Billie Holiday (vocalist)

The '40s

Ella Fitzgerald, Carmen McRae, Sarah Vaughn, Anita O'Day, June Christy (vocalists)

The '50s

Melba Liston (trombonist, arranger), Dorothy Donegan, Marian McPartland (pianists), Shirley Horn (pianist, vocalist), Betty Carter (vocalist)

The '60s

Alice Coltrane (pianist), Shirley Scott (organist), Annie Ross, Nancy Wilson (vocalists)

The '70s

Carla Bley, Toshiko Akiyoshi (composers, pianists, and big band leaders), Joanne Brackeen, Patrice Rushen (pianists), Jackie Cain, Sheila Jordan (vocalists)

The '80s and '90s

Maria Schneider (composer, big band leader), Jane Ira Bloom, Jane Bunnett (saxophonists), Ingrid Jensen, Laurie Frink (trumpeters), Renee Rosnes, Geri Allen, Marilyn Crispell, Claudia Amina Myers, Michelle Rosewoman, Lynne Arriale (pianists), Emily Remler (guitarist), Cindy Blackman, Terri Lynn Carrington (drummers), Marilyn Mazur (percussionist), Cassandra Wilson (vocalist)

3
Rhythm

"Jazz is not about flashy licks.
It's a story with a beginning, middle and end.
You must first learn the vocabulary
—scales, chords, etc ... then let it fly.
And be sure to listen inside the rhythm section
—that's the motor."

tenor saxophonist Stan Getz[1]

Rhythm is the most important element in jazz. If the rhythm is played well, the audience will react positively, even if the performer is having problems delineating the underlying harmony. Yet many developing musicians have problems with rhythm, perhaps due in part to a lack of exposure to artists with a well-developed rhythmic sense. Every student of jazz should listen closely to recordings and live performances by great musicians in order to assimilate their approach to rhythm.[2] Another source of rhythmic problems may result from tension in the body. Any method that teaches coordination and relaxation—yoga, physical exercise, dancing, meditation, and so forth—can be useful in getting rid of tension. A third source of rhythmic problems may be technical difficulties with the instrument. The more control you have over your instrument, the less of a barrier it presents to expressing yourself.

The way the rhythm is played is determined by the style of the music. What we call *swing* evolved around 1900 in New Orleans. African-American brass bands began playing the traditional marching cadence with a loose 12/8 feel, along with a strong accent on the off-beats (which were considered "weak beats" in European music).[3] The downbeats were often anticipated, creating *syncopation*. This led directly to the interpretation used in jazz, in which the eighth notes are played smoothly in a lopsided, "long-short" subdivision. In general, this subdivision can be thought of as triplets with the first two notes tied, and an accent on the last note of the triplet:

However, at faster tempos this ratio tends to even out, and every musician has their own personal interpretation. (Contrast the way drummers Tony Williams and Elvin Jones or saxophonists Cannonball Adderly and John Coltrane interpret eighth notes, to hear the range of possibilities.) The placement

[1] Herb Wong, "Stan Getz," *Jazz Educators Journal*, 24, no. 1 (Fall 1991), 59.
[2] This author's first exposure to swing was through recordings of the Count Basie Orchestra, an experience I still highly recommend.
[3] Todd Coolman and Ed Soph, personal conversation, 1986.

of the accents also can be varied between off-beats and downbeats, creating an underlying polyrhythm:

Ragtime, which evolved from a nineteenth-century dance known as the *cakewalk*, also employed syncopation (which was called "ragging" the melody). However, ragtime relied on straight eighth notes and dotted eighth–sixteenth note rhythms. Therefore, it did not swing in the same manner as the early jazz bands and is rhythmically closer to European music.

The swinging rhythms used by African-American marching bands such as the Excelsior, Tuxedo, and Onward brass bands later became the rhythmic basis for the earliest jazz bands, such as those led by Buddy Bolden, Joe "King" Oliver, and Ferdinand "Jelly Roll" Morton. More contemporary jazz styles such as *big-band swing*, *bebop*, and *post-bop* built upon this basic rhythmic style and refined it in different ways. For example, in the New Orleans marching bands, the rhythm section consisted of several percussionists, each playing a different drum or cymbal. In *early jazz* and *swing*, drummers such as Baby Dodds and Jo Jones became the entire percussion section, playing the bass-drum part with their right foot, the hi-hat cymbal with their left foot, and the snare, tom-tom, and other cymbals with their hands. The bass drum was usually played on all four beats to define the rhythm. In *bebop*, drummers such as Kenny "Klook" Clarke and Max Roach began using the bass drum for occasional accents, while the basic timekeeping function was relegated to the ride cymbal. This created a more fluid sound, although the less-than-explicit beat contributed to changing jazz from dance music into listening music, thus limiting its audience. *Post-bop* drummers such as Elvin Jones and Roy Haynes took this *bebop* style and added polyrhythms and complicated syncopations. Yet the essential quality of swing remained at the core of the music since its inception. Listening to recordings of artists with contrasting styles, such Louis Armstrong's recording with Duke Ellington, the Ellington/John Coltrane collaboration, and Coltrane's and Coleman Hawkins' joint participation on a Thelonious Monk recording, aptly demonstrates this continuum.[4]

Other cultures and styles of music also have had an impact on the development of jazz rhythms. South American, Central American, and Caribbean cultures evolved dozens of unique rhythmic styles. The ones that have had the biggest impact on jazz are the Brazilian *bossa nova* (a slower 4/4 rhythm) and *samba* (a faster 2/2 rhythm), and a Cuban pattern called the *clavé*, which is the underlying basis of the *mambo*, *cha-cha*, *meringue*, as well as other styles often lumped together under the title of *salsa* (see Chapter 1). Dizzy Gillespie, through his association with Cuban musicians Mario Bauza and Chano Pozo, was primarily responsible for bringing many of these Latin-American rhythms into the mainstream of jazz. The fusion of jazz with rock and funk styles was popularized by Miles Davis and his former sidemen, especially Herbie Hancock, Chick Corea, John McLaughlin, and Wayne Shorter. In both the *fusion* and *Latin* jazz styles, the eighth notes are played fairly evenly.

[4] Louis Armstrong and Duke Ellington, *"The Great Reunion,"* EMUS Records ES 12014; Duke Ellington and John Coltrane, MCA/Impulse Records MCA-29032; Thelonious Monk, *"Monk's Music"* (featuring John Coltrane and Coleman Hawkins), Riverside Records RS-3004.

Gaining Facility with Rhythm

Practice Exercises 1–5 over the following scales, using either a metronome or the play-along recordings from *Creative Beginnings: An Introduction to Jazz Improvisation* (track 2) or vol. 24, *Major and Minor* (disc 1, track 1), of *A New Approach to Jazz Improvisation* by Jamey Aebersold. (Note: exercises 1, 2, and 5, although arrived at independently, are similar in concept to exercises found in *Inside Improvisation, vol. 4: Melodic Rhythms*, by Jerry Bergonzi.[5] I highly recommend his book for further study.)

Treble clef C instruments

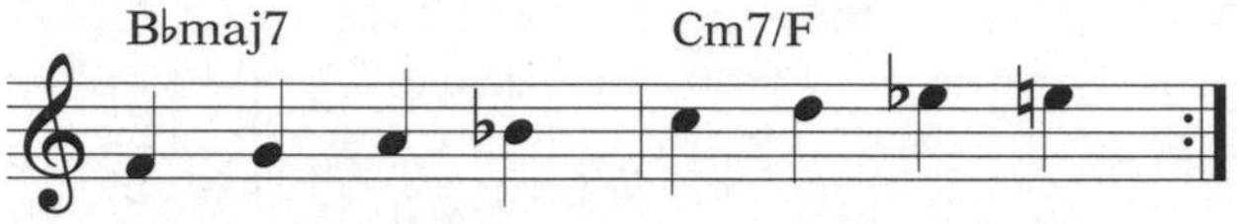

B♭ instruments

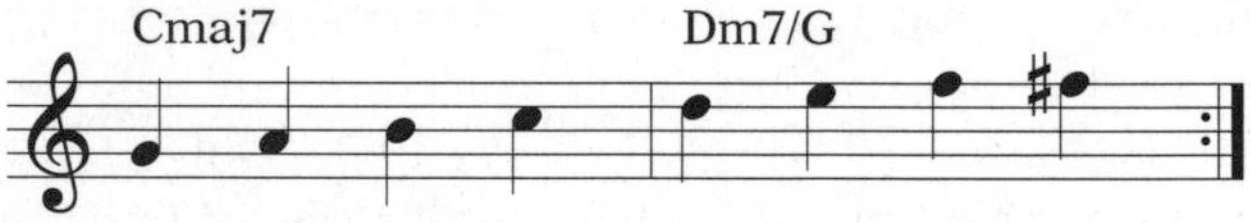

E♭ instruments

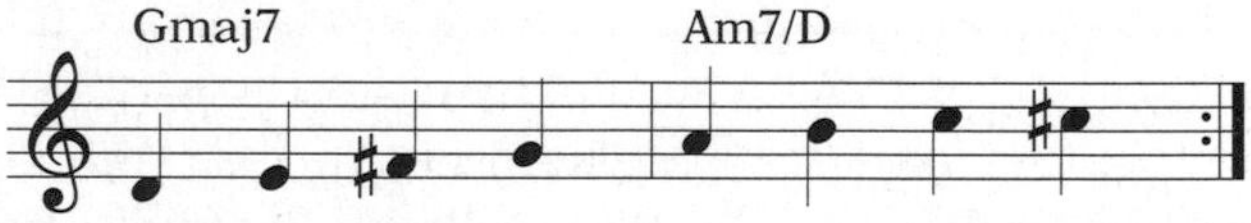

Bass clef instruments

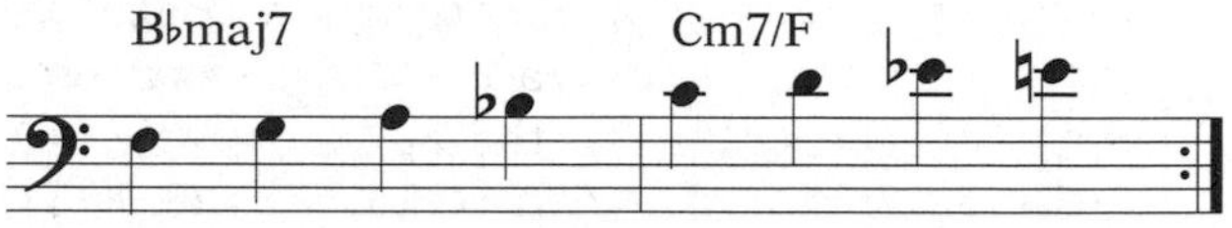

1. *Improvising on rhythms*: Improvise freely on the given scale, but limit yourself to the following rhythms. Don't worry about the notes, think only of the rhythms.

   a.

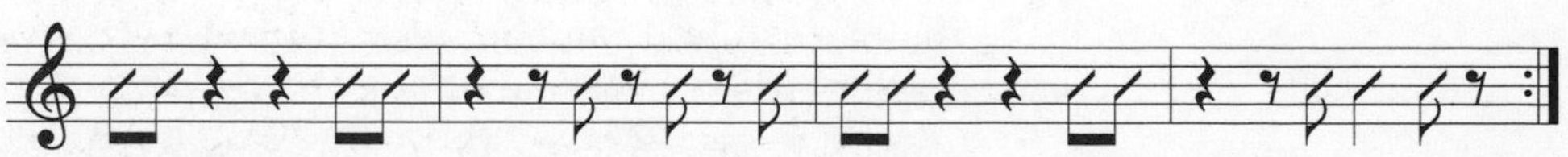

[5] Jerry Bergonzi, *Inside Improvisation, vol. 4: Melodic Rhythms* (Rottenburg, Netherlands: Advance Music, 1998).

b. Make up your own rhythmic patterns.

2. *Improvising with short rhythmic groupings*: Improvise freely on the given scale, but limit yourself to *motives* of one, two, or three notes, interspersed with rests. Use any combination of quarter notes, eighth notes, triplets, or sixteenth notes. Try to begin your ideas at different places in the bar.
a. Example: three-note motives.

b. Example: combinations of one-, two-, and three-note motives.

3. *Placement of the beat*: It is possible to place your notes consistently slightly behind, in the middle, or slightly in front of the beat, all while maintaining a steady tempo. Playing behind the beat creates a sense of relaxation, whereas playing in front of the beat creates a sense of urgency or excitement. Clap along with a metronome. If you are clapping right on the beat, you will not hear the metronome; if you are clapping slightly behind (called "laying back") or slightly in front (called "tippin'"), you will hear it. Now improvise on the scale given above, trying to play in front, in the middle, and slightly behind the beat. Observe the different moods each approach creates.[6]

4. *Phrasing*: Phrasing is rhythm on a longer scale. Instead of simply playing a series of notes, try to play melodies that make a complete statement. In general, most musicians and composers construct melodies in one of two ways (or a combination thereof): 1) *motivically*–using small rhythmic or melodic ideas which develop into complete phrases, or 2) *continuous melodic lines*–in which long melodic ideas, often in consecutive eighth notes, are continuously spun out. Improvise on the given scale, trying to create phrases using both the *motivic* and *continuous melodic line* approaches. Don't worry about the notes; think only about the phrasing of the melodic line.

5. *Polyrhythms*: Improvise on the given scale, but restrict yourself to rhythmic groupings not based on duple divisions such as quarters, eighths, or sixteenth notes. Instead, play over the beat using groupings of quintuplets, septuplets, or triplets accented in groups of twos. To avoid getting lost, focus your attention on the original tempo, while superimposing these polyrhythms.

[6] Todd Coolman, clinic, University of Southern Maine, Gorham, ME, 1989.

a. Example: scalar triplets, accented in groups of twos.

b. A Herbie Hancock idea that employs arpeggiated triplets, accented in groups of twos (Miles Davis, "My Funny Valentine," Columbia PC 9106).

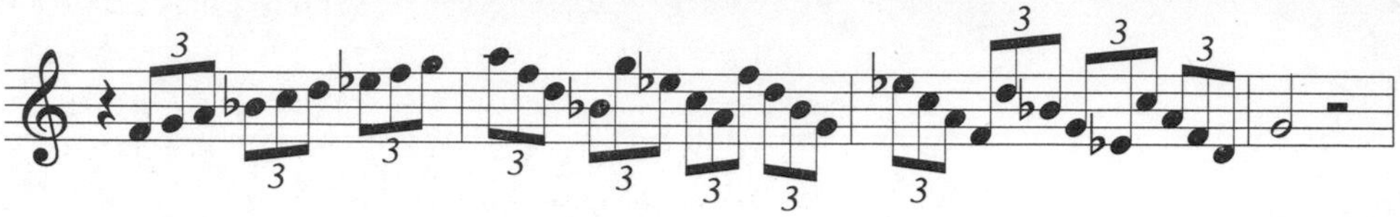

c. A Clark Terry idea based on arpeggios.

d. Example: the scale in quintuplets.

6. *Metric modulation*: Improvise on the given scale, but play in a meter different from that of the metronome or play-along recording. You can speed up and slow down, or play in a completely different tempo, but keep track of the underlying rhythm by dividing your awareness between listening to the accompaniment and concentrating on what you are playing. Periodically resolve what you are playing into the basic time.
7. *Bumps in the blues*: Tape record yourself playing or singing over the basic blues progression, without any accompaniment or a metronome (see Chapter 10). At the beginning of each of the three four-bar phrases, play an accented half-note "bump" on the first beat to clearly delineate the start of each new phrase. Play whatever you wish between the bumps. Listen to the tape and count the number of bars and beats to see if your time remained steady. You may discover a tendency to leave out beats during rests or rush the time when playing easier phrases.[7]
8. *Capturing the feeling*: Play along with recordings by major jazz artists, concentrating on assimilating their rhythmic concepts and emotional projection.
9. *Using different rhythmic styles*: With a rhythm section, improvise on a standard tune based on a sectional form, such as AABA (see Chapter 11). When a new section occurs, experiment with changing the style from swing to Latin or single- to double-time. Also trying varying the length of

[7] Joe Dailey, private lesson, Chicago, IL., 1969.

your notes, the range of the instrument, or the space between the notes. Notice the effect these changes have on the musicians in the group as well as the audience.

10. *Communication with the rhythm section*: Improvise with a rhythm section, listening closely to each member of the group. Try to play rhythms that the other musicians will respond to, and be ready to react to whatever they play. Play duets with the bass player, the piano player, or the drummer to develop a rapport with each member of the rhythm section. Learn to play different rhythm section instruments in order to gain an appreciation for their roles. Think of your improvisation as a group interaction rather than a solo. Do not depend on the rhythm section for your time; each person has to have his or her own inner metronome.

These exercises should be "revisited" periodically, after you have studied other chapters in this book.

Listening to Rhythms in Jazz Compositions

Listen carefully to the following recordings for the rhythmic qualities they demonstrate.

1. *Swing versus straight eighth notes*

a. Scott Joplin and Jelly Roll Morton, "Maple Leaf Rag," from *Smithsonian Collection*. Joplin's performance is syncopated but essentially straight, whereas Jelly Roll's version swings.

b. Miles Davis, "So What," from *Smithsonian Collection*. Although both Cannonball Adderly and John Coltrane play swinging eighth notes, notice how Coltrane's eighth notes are slightly more even than Cannonball's and often grouped five or seven notes to the beat.

2. *Placement of accents*

a. Coleman Hawkins, "The Man I Love," from *Smithsonian Collection*. Listen to how Hawkins tends to accent the notes on the downbeats.

b. Lester Young, "Lester Leaps In," from *Smithsonian Collection*. Notice how Lester varies his accents, often accenting the offbeats.

3. *Placement of the beat*

a. Count Basie, "Taxi War Dance," from *Smithsonian Collection*. Notice how Count Basie and most of the horn soloists play slightly behind the rest of the rhythm section. This approach to playing slightly behind the beat (but not dragging) became synonymous with the Basie style.

b. Dexter Gordon, "Bikini," from *Smithsonian Collection*. Dexter plays slightly behind bassist Red Callender. Dexter's tendency to lay back grew increasingly exaggerated in later recordings.

c. Sonny Rollins Plus Four, "Pent-Up House," from *Smithsonian Collection*. Sonny generally lays back, trumpeter Clifford Brown generally plays right in the middle (although at times he will lay back or push ahead a bit), and drummer Max Roach plays slightly on the front edge of the beat (see Chapter 7 for a transcription of Clifford's solo).

- **d.** Charles Mingus, "Haitian Fight Song," from *Smithsonian Collection*. Bassist Mingus plays on the front of the beat, pushing the entire band.

4. *Phrasing*

- **a.** Thelonious Monk, "Misterioso," from *Smithsonian Collection*. Notice how Monk conceives of his melodies, comping, and solos primarily in terms of motivic development.
- **b.** Charlie Parker, "Shaw 'Nuff," from *Smithsonian Collection*. Listen to how Bird builds his solo by unraveling a continuous melodic statement. (see Chapter 11 for the transcription).
- **c.** Sonny Rollins, "Blue Seven," from *Smithsonian Collection*. Sonny begins his solo with a motivic approach, but spins out continuous melodic lines during his double-time passages (see Chapter 18 for the transcription).

5. *Polyrhythms*

- **a.** John Coltrane, "My Favorite Things," from *My Favorite Things* (Atlantic 1361). Pianist McCoy Tyner and drummer Elvin Jones often imply a duple meter against the 3/4 time.
- **b.** Ornette Coleman, "Lonely Woman," from *Smithsonian Collection*. Drummer Billy Higgins and bassist Charlie Haden play in a fast 4/4 meter, while Ornette and Don Cherry play the melody in a slower tempo; yet the melody and the rhythm fit together perfectly.

6. *Using different rhythmic styles*

- **a.** Miles Davis, "My Funny Valentine," from *My Funny Valentine* (Columbia PC 9106). Within this one song, the rhythm varies from rubato, to a slow ballad, medium swing, and Latin styles. Textures range from unaccompanied solo–to duo–to the entire quintet, and the dynamics range from very soft to intense climaxes. Notice how effectively Miles uses space, and the impact this has on the audience during this live recording.
- **b.** Shelly Manne, "Cherokee," from *2–3–4* (Impulse 29073). Coleman Hawkins and the rhythm section vary the rhythmic feel from a slow ballad to double-time to a 3/4 waltz.

Max Roach's Improvised Solo on "Blue Seven"

Max Roach's improvised drum solo on the Sonny Rollins composition "Blue Seven" was transcribed from *Saxophone Colossus* (Prestige Records), and may also be found in the *Smithsonian Collection of Classic Jazz*. It was recorded in 1956 by Rollins's quartet, which included Sonny on tenor saxophone, Tommy Flanagan on piano, Doug Watkins on bass, and Max on drums. (This solo was transcribed by drummer/composer Steve Grover and given to the author for use in this text.)[8]

Along with Kenny "Klook" Clarke, Max defined the role of the drums in the revolutionary 1940s style called *bebop*. With its emphasis on the ride cymbal as the time-keeper, syncopated accents on the snare, and sporadic use of the bass drum, bebop drumming became more fluid and conversational. Max played with Charlie Parker's seminal group (which included Miles Davis) before coleading a highly acclaimed quintet with trumpeter Clifford Brown. He has

[8] Steve Grover is a drummer and composer who teaches in the Jazz and Contemporary Music Department at the University of Maine at Augusta. He was the winner of the 1994 Thelonious Monk Institute of Jazz/BMI Jazz Composers competition.

played and recorded with many of the major figures in the bebop, post-bop, and avant-garde styles, and continues to be highly active as a performer, leader, and educator.

"Blue Seven" is a 12-bar blues played at a medium tempo (♩ = 132). After Rollins's ingenious solo (a portion of which may be seen in Chapter 18), Max plays seven choruses of solo, which Grover describes as "alternating between 'time-keeping concepts' and episodes of drum set 'soloing'." Grover continues, "It is obviously a well-constructed and thoughtful improvisation using the form of the composition. Although other drummers, particularly Sid Catlett, had previously used the form of the song as a basis for soloing, Max called attention to the notion that it was an essential part of the artistry required of a jazz drummer. Furthermore, his soloing is not given to flashy displays of drum set technique. Although he possesses the ability and stamina to play fast tempos and has considerable control of the instrument, he is not a rudimental technician. Rather it is his compositional imagination that sets him apart. He has the attitude and musical bearing of an artist, and his highly musical playing is testament to that. Max found deep truths in the establishment of a personal vocabulary and the musical expression of it through his drum set. The vocabulary did not have to be technically impressive, although some of it is so. The interest for the listener is in its rendering of a complete musical statement."[9]

"Throughout most of his solo, Max accompanies his improvisation with a steady 4/4 beat on the bass drum and by playing on beats 2 and 4 with the hi-hat cymbal. The solo itself has an interesting arc, beginning in the fifth bar of the first chorus. Max spends a fair amount of time in an accompanimental mode, playing for a soloist who isn't there. He creates a dialogue with himself by the gradual introduction of left hand figures around the set and by playing an occasional roll placed in stark contrast to the prevailing harmonic rhythm. After developing these elements for four choruses, he initiates a series of double-time snare and tom tom figures in the first four bars of fifth chorus, then settles into playing time before playing a roll to crescendo into the sixth chorus. Here he introduces a new figure—a four stroke ruff—which implies a 3 against 2 polyrhythm. This is answered by a series of quarter-note and eighth-note triplets, before returning to the four stroke ruff idea. The climax of the solo occurs in the seventh chorus with an unrelenting series of sixteenth notes in a question and answer format. This double-time chorus is itself a recapitulation of the double-time passage he played in the first four bars of the fifth chorus. The last four bars of the seventh chorus imitate these four bars almost exactly, and provide a satisfying and stirring conclusion to the drum solo, as well as a fitting transition back to the ensemble."[10]

This transcription is not meant to be played exclusively by drummers. After listening closely to a recording of this solo, nondrummers are encouraged to practice the transcription by playing the rhythms articulated by the ride cymbal, snare, and tom-toms, using a blues scale or any combination of notes. Try to incorporate these rhythmic concepts when creating your own improvisation. (A key is provided at the end of the transcription.)

[9] Steve Grover, e-mail conversation with author, Gorham, ME, 1999.

[10] Ibid.

1st chorus
(behind tenor)

(solo begins)

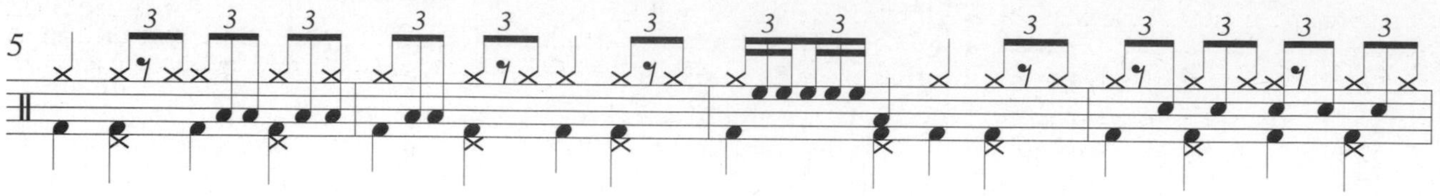

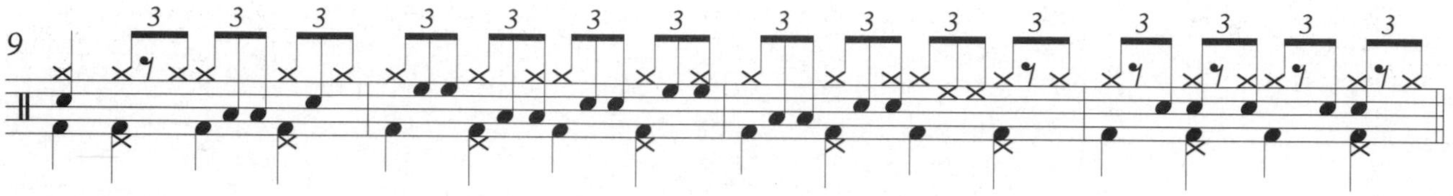

2nd chorus

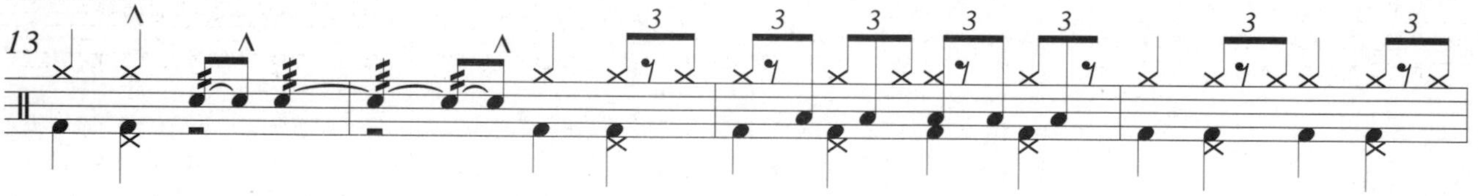

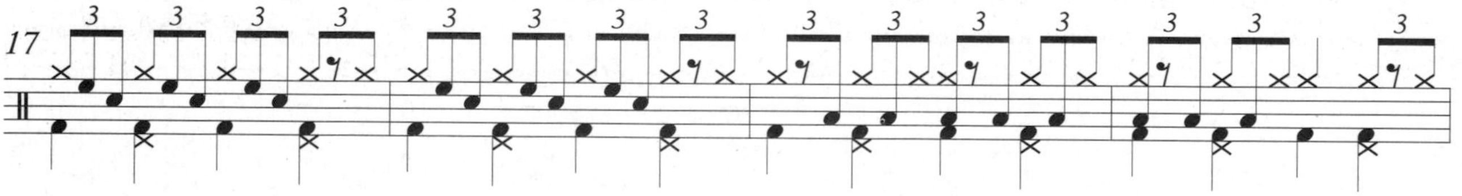

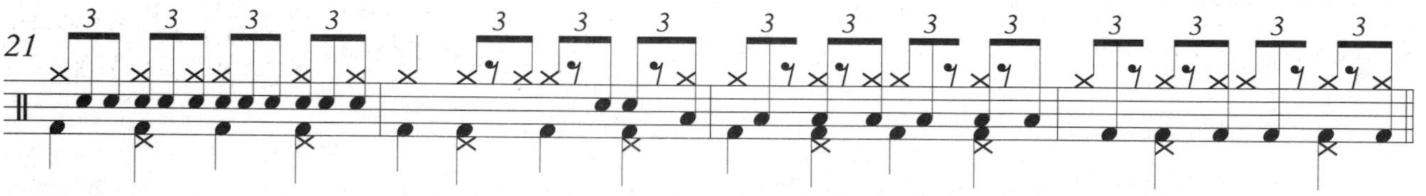

3rd chorus

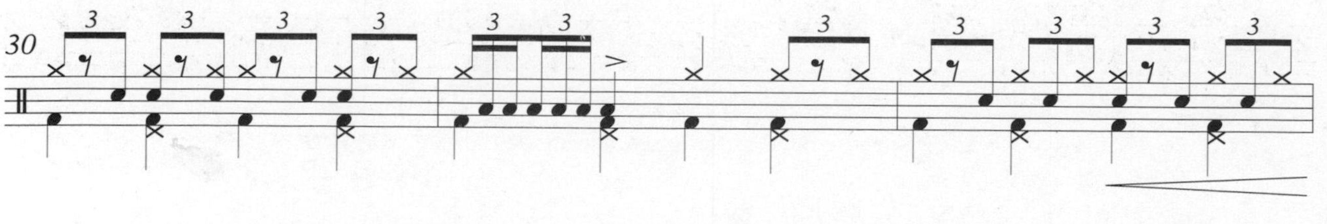

33
4th chorus
37
41
45
5th chorus
49
52
56
6th chorus
61

65
69
7th chorus
73
76
79
82

Key:

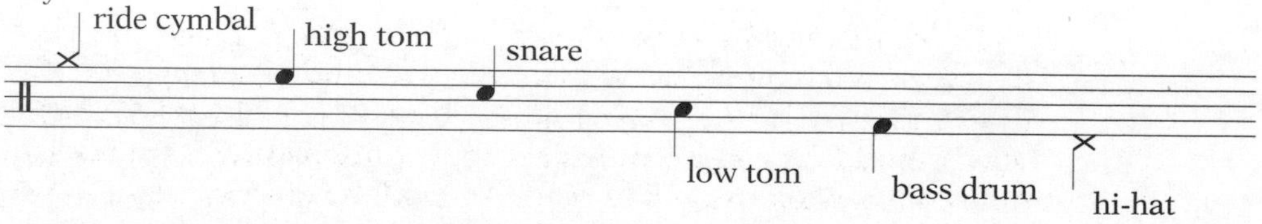
ride cymbal
high tom
snare
low tom
bass drum
hi-hat

PART 2 Diatonic Chords and the Modes in the Major Scale

4

Major Scales and Major 7th Chords

"The joy of playing music,
whether written or improvised,
is not possible when one still has to
struggle with material.
The goal should be complete mastery…
so that one can focus on other issues,
such as inspiration,
and that's where the important music is made.

pianist Kenny Werner[1]

The *major scale*, also known as the *ionian mode*, consists of the ascending pattern: whole step, whole step, half step, whole step, whole step, whole step, half step.

C Major Scale

It is the first scale (or mode) in the family that also includes the dorian, phrygian, lydian, mixolydian (dominant), aeolian (pure or natural minor), and locrian modes. The notes of the major scale may be used when improvising over the following chords: major triads, major 6th chords, major 7th chords, major 9th chords, and major 13th chords. (In jazz, a triangle is sometimes used as an abbreviation for major.)

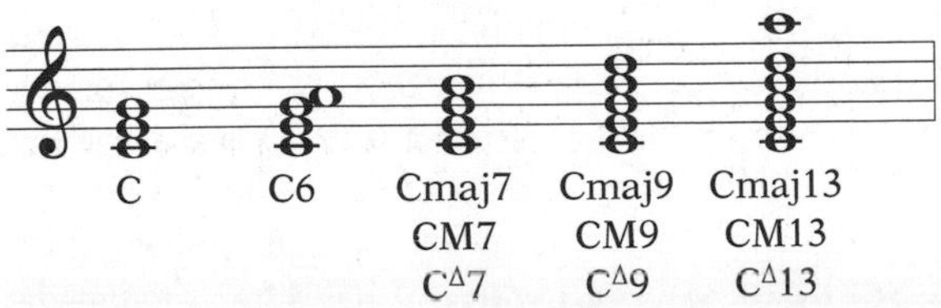

The *major triad* consists of a root, a major 3rd, and a perfect 5th. A *major 6th chord* is a major triad with a major 6th added; a *major 7th chord* is a major triad with a major 7th; and a *major 9th chord* is a major 7th chord with a major 9th. If the 11th is added to the chord, the augmented 11th is used. (This chord tone comes from the lydian mode and will be discussed in Chapter 9.) A major 13th can also be added to the major 9th chord, creating a *major 13th chord*.[2]

In a major key, major chords function as I or tonic chords (chords built on the first note of the scale) and IV or subdominant chords (chords built on the fourth note of the scale). The major scale is the best scale choice when the chord

[1] Scott Reeves, "Two Conversations with Kenny Werner," *Jazz Educators Journal* vol. XXXI, no. 4 (January 1999) 113.
[2] See the Appendix if you are unfamiliar with names of intervals.

is functioning as a I chord, while the lydian mode is the best choice when the chord is functioning as a IV chord. The first note of the major scale lacks tension and color and is not an interesting choice with which to begin or end a phrase. The fourth note of the scale clashes with the third of the chord and usually sounds best as a passing tone.

Theory/Ear Exercises

1. Write major scales in all twelve keys.
2. Write major 9th chords in all twelve keys.
3. *Keyboard skills*: Play major 9th chords on the piano, and listen to the sound or color that characterizes this chord.
4. *Melodic dictation*: Have another musician or teacher play melodies based on major scales. Notate the melodies by identifying the intervals between the notes or by sensing the tendency of the unstable notes in the scale (the second, fourth, sixth, and seventh notes) to resolve to stable notes (the first, third, and fifth notes).
5. *Harmonic dictation*: Have another musician or teacher play chord progressions of major 9th chords on the piano. Write down the chord progression by listening to the intervals in the bass line.
6. *Transcription*: Transcribe a melody, a chord progression, or an improvised solo from a recording.

Gaining Facility with Major Scales and Major 7th Chords

Practice the following exercises over the chord progression below, using either a metronome or the play-along recordings from *Creative Beginnings: An Introduction to Jazz Improvisation* (track 4) or vol. 21, *Gettin' It Together* (disc 1, track 10), of *A New Approach to Jazz Improvisation* by Jamey Aebersold. If you find yourself struggling with an exercise, slow it down, simplify it, or sing it while visualizing yourself playing it. After familiarizing yourself with the exercises, pick one or two to practice repeatedly, until you can play them without any conscious thought.

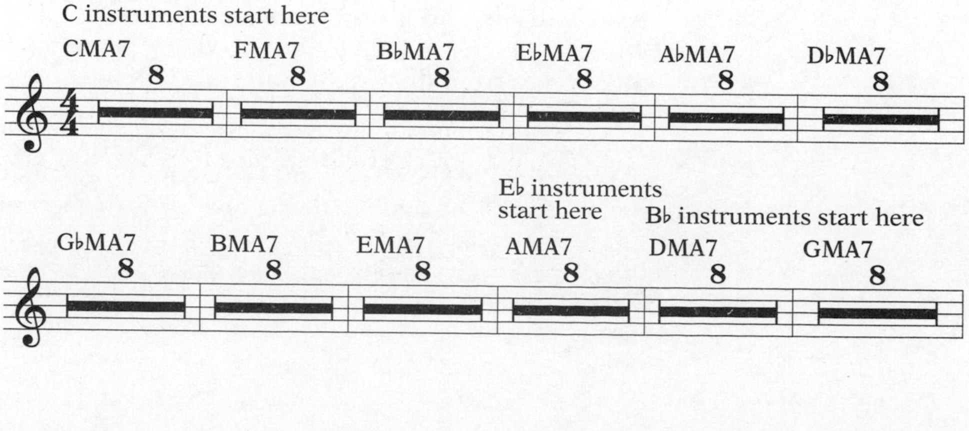

1. *Call and response warmups*: Have another musician or teacher play a phrase that fits over a major 7th chord. Play back the phrase you have just heard.

2. Ascending by the major scale; descending by the major scale with an added ♭6th (also known as the *bebop major* scale).

MM ______________

3. The major 7th arpeggio, ending on the 7th.

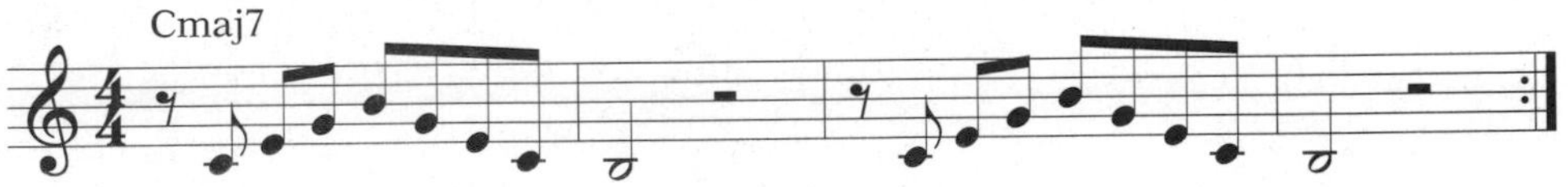

MM ______________

4. A major 9th arpeggio, descending.

MM ______________

5. The major scale in 3rds, ascending. Also practice this exercise in a descending sequence.

MM ______________

6. A Sonny Rollins pattern from his "Tune-Up" solo (Sonny Rollins, *Newk's Time,* Blue Note 4001). This pattern outlines the major triad with the notes a step above and below each chord tone (referred to as *upper and lower neighbor tones*).

MM ______________

7. A Sonny Rollins pattern based on a major 7th arpeggio, also transcribed from his solo on "Tune-Up" (Sonny Rollins, *Newk's Time*, Blue Note 4001). This pattern can be simplified by practicing each measure separately.

MM ______________

8. A John Coltrane pattern from his "Oleo" solo (Miles Davis, *Relaxin'*, Prestige 7129) in which a chromatic leading-tone preceeds each diatonic triad. This pattern can be simplified by omitting the chromatic leading tones.

MM ____________

9. *Creative Jazz Improvisation*: Improvise over the chord progression, without looking at the book or thinking about the notes in the scale. Think only of playing rhythms; let the notes take care of themselves.

10. Make up your own patterns and melodic ideas based on major scales and major 7th chords.

a.

MM ____________

b.

MM ____________

Improvising on Jazz Compositions Based on Major 7th Chords

Following is a partial list of jazz compositions in which major 7th chords are frequently used. These compositions are found in *The New Real Book*, vol. 1 (NRB), *The New Real Book*, vol. 2 (NR2), one of the volumes of Jamey Aebersold's *New Approach to Jazz Improvisation* (JA), or *Creative Beginnings: An Introduction to Jazz Improvisation* (CB). Memorize the most frequently played songs, and practice them in different keys.

Compositions Based Exclusively on Major 7th Chords

"Another Spring"—Scott Reeves (CB)
"Beatitude"—Jamey Aebersold (JA vol. 5)

Compositions in Which Major 7th Chords Occur Frequently

"A Child Is Born"—Thad Jones (NR2)
"After the Rain"—John Coltrane (NR2)
"Dear Lord"—John Coltrane (JA vol. 28, NR2)
"Fantasy in D"—Cedar Walton (JA vol. 35)

"Forest Flower (Sunrise)"—Charles Lloyd (JA vol. 74)
"Friends"—Chick Corea (NR2)
"I Mean You"—Thelonious Monk (JA vol. 56, NRB)
"Little Sunflower"—Freddie Hubbard (NRB)
"My Favorite Things"—Richard Rodgers (JA vol. 25)
"On Green Dolphin Street"—Kaper/Washington (JA vols. 34, 59, and 85)
"St. Thomas"—Sonny Rollins (JA vols. 8 and 74, NRB)
"The Water's Edge"—Tom Harrell (JA vol. 63)
"This I Dig of You"—Hank Mobley (JA vols. 38 and 59)
"Well You Needn't"—Thelonious Monk (JA vol. 56, NRB)

Louis Armstrong's Improvised Solo on "Hotter Than That"

Louis Armstrong's improvised trumpet solo on Lillian Hardin Armstrong's composition "Hotter Than That" demonstrates why he is considered the first great improviser in jazz. The solo was transcribed from the *Smithsonian Collection of Classic Jazz* and was originally recorded in 1927 by Armstrong's Hot Five group. Despite this early date, the phrasing and rhythmic concepts sound strikingly modern. An appreciation of Louis's genius may be obtained by comparing his solos with those of his contemporaries. Unlike the choppy rhythms used by other early jazz practitioners, Louis's feeling for swing anticipates the loose, triplet-based approach of Lester Young and Charlie Parker more than a decade later. Armstrong also popularized a type of vibrato called *terminal vibrato*, which occurs at the end of many of his longer notes.

"Hotter Than That" is a 32-bar binary composition in an ABAC form, with a two-bar break at the end of the B section. The first six bars of each A section stay on the E♭ major tonic chord and demonstrate Louis's lyrical use of the major scale.[3] Note how the ideas in the first chorus, which he plays on trumpet, are very similar to those from the second chorus, which he scat-sings. His trumpet was truly an extension of his voice, and vice-versa.

The first chorus is also characterized by its wide range and large melodic intervals. In bar 19, he implies a chord substitution—a diminished chord not part of the regular progression. In his vocal chorus, he uses the blues scale as well as the major scale over major chords (see bars 37, 64, 65, and 66). We also find many exceptional uses of rhythm. Bars 40–43 are phrased over the barlines, so exact notation becomes difficult. In bars 50–57, Armstrong uses a two-against-three polyrhythm, daring even by modern standards. The other musicians seem to be on the brink of losing their places, but Louis resolves the polyrhythm with great assurance. All of this takes place at a brisk, driving tempo (𝅗𝅥 = 104).

After listening closely to the recording, practice the solo at different tempos with the metronome clicking on beats 2 and 4. Then continue improvising on the chord progression in the same style.

[3] All pitches referred to in the text are concert pitches.

Treble-clef C instruments:

32
2 E♭
vib.
vib.
37
vib.
B♭7
3
3
3
3
hold back
42
vib.
vib.
47
E♭ break
E♭
vib.
52
E♭7
A♭
57
A°7
E♭/B♭
vib.
C7
vib.
F7 vib.
62
B♭7
E♭ break
delay
(×)
3
vib.

B♭ instruments:

32
2
F
vib.
vib.
37
vib.
C7
3
3
3
3
hold back
42
vib.
vib.
47
F
break
F
vib.
52
F7
B♭
57
B°7
F/C
vib.
D7
vib.
G7
vib.
62
C7
F
break
delay
3
vib.

E♭ instruments:

32
2
C
vib.
vib.
37
vib.
G7
3
3
3
3
hold back
42
vib.
vib.
47
C
break
C
vib.
52
C7
F
57
F°7
C/G
vib.
A7
vib.
D7
vib.
62
G7
C
break
delay
(×)
3
vib.

Bass-clef instruments:

32
2
E♭
vib.
vib.
37
vib.
B♭7
3
3
3
3
hold back
42
vib.
vib.
47
E♭
break
E♭
vib.
52
E♭7
A♭
57
A°7
E♭/B♭
vib.
C7
vib.
F7
vib.
62
B♭7
E♭
break
delay
3
vib.

5

Mixolydian and Bebop 7th Scales, and Dominant 7th Chords

"It's a spiritual music,
from the creator—to the artist—to you.
Split second timing,
and you're part of it."

drummer Art Blakey[1]

The *mixolydian scale*, also known as the *dominant scale*, consists of the ascending pattern: whole step, whole step, half step, whole step, whole step, half step, whole step.

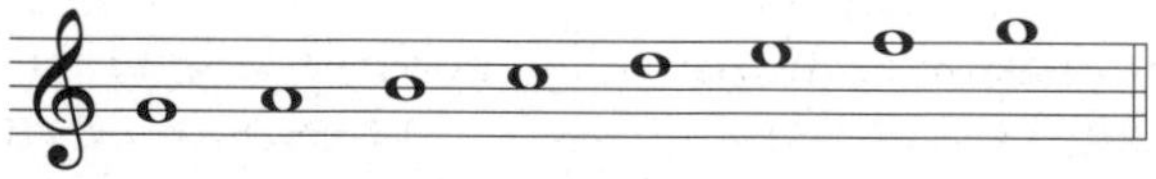

G Mixolydian Mode

The mixolydian scale is the fifth mode in the major scale family and contains the same notes as the major scale a perfect 5th below. You may also think of the mixolydian scale as a major scale with the seventh note lowered a half step.[2] This scale is typically used when improvising over *unaltered dominant chords*, such as dominant 7th, dominant 9th, dominant 13th, and dominant 7th suspended 4th (sus. 4) chords.

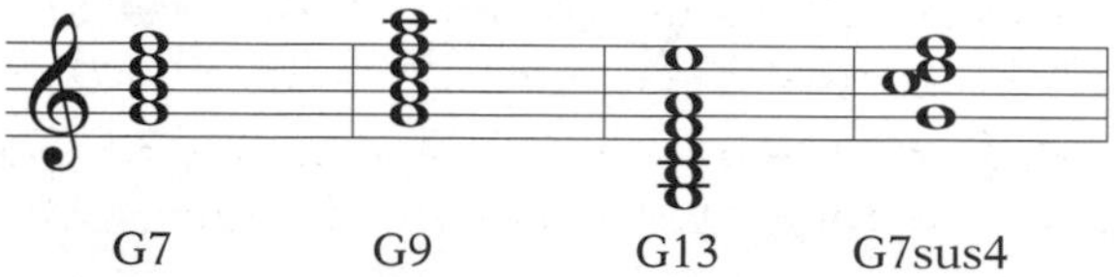

G7 G9 G13 G7sus4

The *dominant 7th chord* consists of a root, a major 3rd, a perfect 5th, and a *minor* 7th. Adding a major 9th and a major 13th to the dominant 7th chord creates *dominant* 9th and *dominant 13th chords*, respectively. When the 11th (or 4th scale degree) is used over a dominant chord, it is suspended in place of the 3rd, creating a *dominant 7th sus. 4 chord*. Sometimes an augmented 11th is added to the dominant 7th chord, but this color is derived from the lydian dominant scale and will be discussed in Chapter 18.

In major and minor keys, the dominant chord usually functions as a V chord, which has a strong tendency to resolve to the I (*tonic*) chord. It may also function as a *secondary dominant* chord, acting as a V chord to a chord other

[1] "Art Blakey—the Jazz Messenger" Public Broadcasting System, 1987.

[2] Comparing a scale to another scale that contains the same notes is called the *relative* approach. Relating a scale to a different scale that starts on the same note is called the *parallel* approach.

than the I chord. In major keys, we find secondary dominants built on the first scale degree of the major scale (V7 of IV), the second degree (V7 of V), the third degree (V7 of vi), the sixth degree (V7 of ii), and the seventh degree (V7 of iii). In minor keys, secondary dominants can be built on the first degree of the natural minor scale (V7 of iv), the second degree (V7 of V), the third degree (V7 of VI), the fourth degree (V7 of VII), and the lowered seventh or *subtonic* degree (V7 of III). Although a dominant chord typically functions as either a V7 chord or a secondary dominant, in jazz it can occasionally act as a tonic chord, as in the case of the blues progression. With the exception of dominant 7th sus. 4 chords, the fourth note in the mixolydian scale is best used as a passing tone over dominant 7th chords. The second, third, sixth, and seventh scale degrees have the richest color.

A common variant of the mixolydian scale is known as the *bebop 7th scale*. It became common practice in the bebop era to insert the major 7th as a passing tone between the ♭7 and the octave.

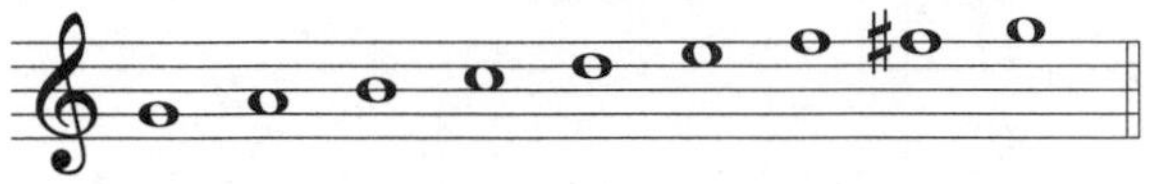

G Bebop 7th Scale

This scale can be used over unaltered dominant chords, as well as the minor 7th chord a perfect 4th below the first note of the scale. Some of the exercises relating to the use of the bebop 7th scale are derived from this author's study with David Baker at Indiana University. For further exercises in the use of this scale, I recommend his book, *Improvisational Patterns: The Bebop Era*.[3]

Theory/Ear Exercises

1. Write the mixolydian scale in all twelve keys.
2. Write the various types of unaltered dominant chords in all twelve keys.
3. *Keyboard skills*: Play dominant 9th chords on the piano, and listen to the sound or color that characterizes this chord.
4. *Melodic and harmonic dictation*: Notate melodies and chord progressions based on mixolydian scales and dominant 7th chords.
5. *Transcription*: Transcribe a melody, a chord progression, or an improvised solo from a recording.

Gaining Facility with Mixolydian and Bebop 7th Scales, and Dominant 7th Chords

Practice the following exercises over the chord progression below, using either a metronome or the play-along recording from *Creative Beginnings: An Introduction to Jazz Improvisation* (track 5) or Vol. 84, *Dominant Seventh Workout* (disc. 1, track 13), of *A New Approach to Jazz Improvisation* by Jamey Aebersold.

[3] David Baker, *Improvisational Patterns: The Bebop Era*, vol. 1 (New York: Charles Colin, 1979).

If you find yourself struggling with an exercise, slow it down, simplify it, or sing it while visualizing yourself playing it. After familiarizing yourself with the exercises, pick one or two to practice repeatedly, until you can play them without any conscious thought.

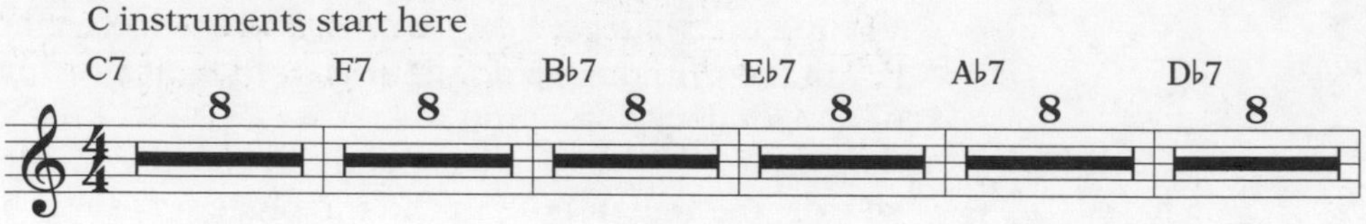

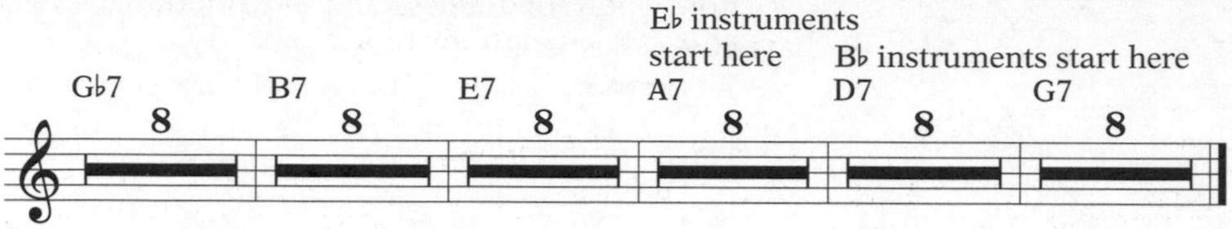

1. *Call and response warmups*: Have another musician or teacher play a phrase that fits over a dominant seventh chord. Play back the phrase you have just heard.
2. The mixolydian scale.

MM ____________________

3. The bebop 7th scale.

MM ____________________

4. The bebop 7th scale, descending from the 3rd.

MM ____________________

5. The bebop 7th scale, descending from the 7th.

MM ____________________

6. Bebop players often surround chord tones with the notes a half-step above and below the chord tones (called *upper and lower chromatic neighbor*

tones). This pattern begins with the bebop 7th scale ascending from the 5th, approaches the 3rd of the chord with upper and lower chromatic neighbor tones, and resolves with a 3–5–7–9 arpeggio.

MM ____________

7. This pattern surrounds the root and 5th of the chord with upper and lower chromatic neighbor tones.

MM ____________

8. *Creative jazz improvisation*: Improvise on the progression without looking at the book or thinking about the notes in the scale. Concentrate on keeping your body relaxed. Let go of any tension or anxiety, physical or mental, that might creep into your playing.

9. Make up your own patterns and melodic ideas based on mixolydian and bebop 7th scales.

a.

MM ____________

b.

MM ____________

Improvising on Jazz Compositions Based on Dominant 7th Chords

Following is a partial list of jazz compositions in which unaltered dominant 7th chords are frequently used. These compositions are found in *The New Real Book*, vol. 1 (NRB), *The New Real Book*, vol. 2 (NR2), one of the volumes of Jamey Aebersold's *New Approach to Jazz Improvisation* (JA), or *Creative Beginnings: An Introduction to Jazz Improvisation* (CB). Memorize the most frequently played songs, and practice them in different keys.

Compositions Based Exclusively on Unaltered Dominant 7th Chords

"Freddie Freeloader"—Miles Davis (JA vol. 50)
"India"—John Coltrane (JA vol. 81)
"Kirsten and Her Puppy Katie"—David Baker (JA vol. 76)

"Sabor"—Joao Donato (JA vol. 64)
"Sister Cynda"—Scott Reeves (CB)
"Sister Sadie"—Horace Silver (JA vol. 17)
"Soul Sister"—Dexter Gordon (JA vol. 82)
"This Here"—Bobby Timmons (JA vol. 13)
"Tunji"—John Coltrane (NR2)
"Watermelon Man"—Herbie Hancock (JA vols. 11, 54, and 85)
"Well You Needn't"—Thelonious Monk (NRB)

Compositions In Which Unaltered Dominant 7th Chords Occur Frequently

"Adam's Apple"—Wayne Shorter (JA vol. 33)
"And What If I Don't"—Herbie Hancock (JA vol. 11)
"Crisis"—Freddie Hubbard (JA vols. 38 and 60)
"Dig"—Miles Davis (JA vol. 7, NRB)
"Doxy"—Sonny Rollins (JA vols. 8 and 54)
"Epistrophy"—Thelonious Monk (JA vol. 56)
"I Mean You"—Thelonious Monk (JA vols. 36 and 56, NRB)
"In a Mellotone"—Duke Ellington (JA vol. 48)
"Killer Joe"—Benny Golson (JA vols. 14 and 70, NR2)
"Maiden Voyage"—Herbie Hancock (JA vols. 11 and 54)
"Manteca"—Gillespie/Fuller (JA vol. 64)
"Sweet Georgia Brown"—Bernie/Pinkard/Casey (JA vols. 67 and 70)
"Thelonious"—Thelonious Monk (JA vol. 56)
"The Preacher"—Horace Silver (JA vol. 17)

Lester Young's Improvised Solo on "Lester Leaps In"

Lester Young's improvised tenor saxophone solo on his composition "Lester Leaps In" illustrates how mixolydian scales were used prior to the advent of the bebop period. The solo was transcribed from the *Smithsonian Collection of Classic Jazz,* and was originally recorded in 1939 by Count Basie's Kansas City Seven, a small group within the Basie big band that included Count on piano, Buck Clayton on trumpet, Dicky Wells on trombone, Freddie Green on guitar, Walter Page on bass, and Jo Jones on drums.

Lester, also known as "Prez," was a key figure in the evolution of jazz in the 1930s. Before his emergence on the scene, the most widely imitated saxophonist was Coleman Hawkins, who was renowned for his large tone and the manner in which he clearly delineated each chord change, typically through the use of chord arpeggios. Coleman also had a very deliberate rhythmic style, often accenting all four beats in the measure. In contrast, Lester played with a light, airy tone, and often he only alluded to the chord changes, preferring to play in a more melodic manner. His style of rhythm was less heavily accented, conveying a loose, relaxed feeling of swing. At first his radically new style was not well received by other members of the Basie band, but gradually his influence became widespread. Saxophonists such as Stan Getz, Alan Eager, Zoot Sims, and Al Cohn were influenced by his sound and phrasing, and his approach to rhythm had a great impact on the bebop style that followed.

"Lester Leaps In" is based on the chord changes to "I Got Rhythm," but with a slightly modified A section (see Chapter 11). After playing the head, Lester takes one chorus with the complete rhythm section 'comping; during the second chorus, he and Count Basie play a duet over the A section with a stop-time accompaniment. The tempo is brisk at 𝅗𝅥 = 120. Throughout his solo, Lester uses space to separate his ideas and plays swinging, rhythmic motives, as seen in bars 33–36 and 57–60. He also quotes the melody in bars 31–32 and 56–61. Although the A section of "Lester Leaps In" contains many different chords, they all function in the key of B♭, allowing Lester to primarily improvise on one scale —typically either a mixolydian scale with chromatic passing tones, as in bars 9–13, 37–40, and 62–64, or the major pentatonic scale (a mixolydian scale with the fourth and seventh scale degrees omitted), as in bars 1–8 and 41–43. The B section is based on a series of dominant chords moving around the cycle of 4ths. Over these chords, Lester generally stays within the corresponding mixolydian scale, as in bars 17–21 and 49–55. In the last bar of the B section (bar 23), he adds a ♯ 5th to the dominant chord, forming a dominant 7th ♯5 arpeggio.

After listening closely to a recording of this solo, practice it at different tempos with the metronome clicking on beats 2 and 4. Then continue improvising on the chord progression in the same style.

Treble-clef C instruments:

35
Bb6/F
C-7
F7
vib.
Bb6
Bb6/D
Eb6
E°7
3
39
Bb6/F
C-7
F7
Bb6
Bb6/D
Eb6
E°7
vib.
Bb6/F
44
C-7
F7
Bb6
Bb6/D
Eb6
E°7
3
Bb6/F
F7
vib.
48
Bb6
vib.
D7
G7
52
C7
F7
56
Bb6
Bb6/D
Eb6
E°7
Bb6/F
C-7
F7
61
Bb6
Bb6/D
Eb6
E°7
Bb6/F
F7
Bb6
vib.
sub-tone

B♭ instruments (Trumpet—8va bassa where indicated):

35
C6/G
D-7
G7
vib.
C6
C6/E
F6
F♯°7
trpt.-8va bassa
3
39
C6/G
D-7
G7
C6
C6/E
F6
F♯°7
vib.
C6/G
(8va)
trpt.-8va bassa
44
D-7
G7
C6
C6/E
F6
F♯°7
C6/G
G7
vib.
(8va)
3
48
C6
vib.
E7
A7
52
D7
G7
56
C6
C6/E
F6
F♯°7
C6/G
D-7
G7
61
C6
C6/E
F6
F♯°7
C6/G
G7
C6
vib.
sub-tone

E♭ instruments:

35
G6/D A-7 D7 G6 G6/B C6 C♯°7
vib.
3
39
G6/D A-7 D7 G6 G6/B C6 C♯°7 G6/D
vib.
44
A-7 D7 G6 G6/B C6 C♯°7 G6/D D7
vib.
3
48
G6 B7 E7
vib.
52
A7 D7
56
G6 G6/B C6 C♯°7 G6/D A-7 D7
61
G6 G6/B C6 C♯°7 G/D D7 G6
vib.
sub-tone

Bass-clef instruments:

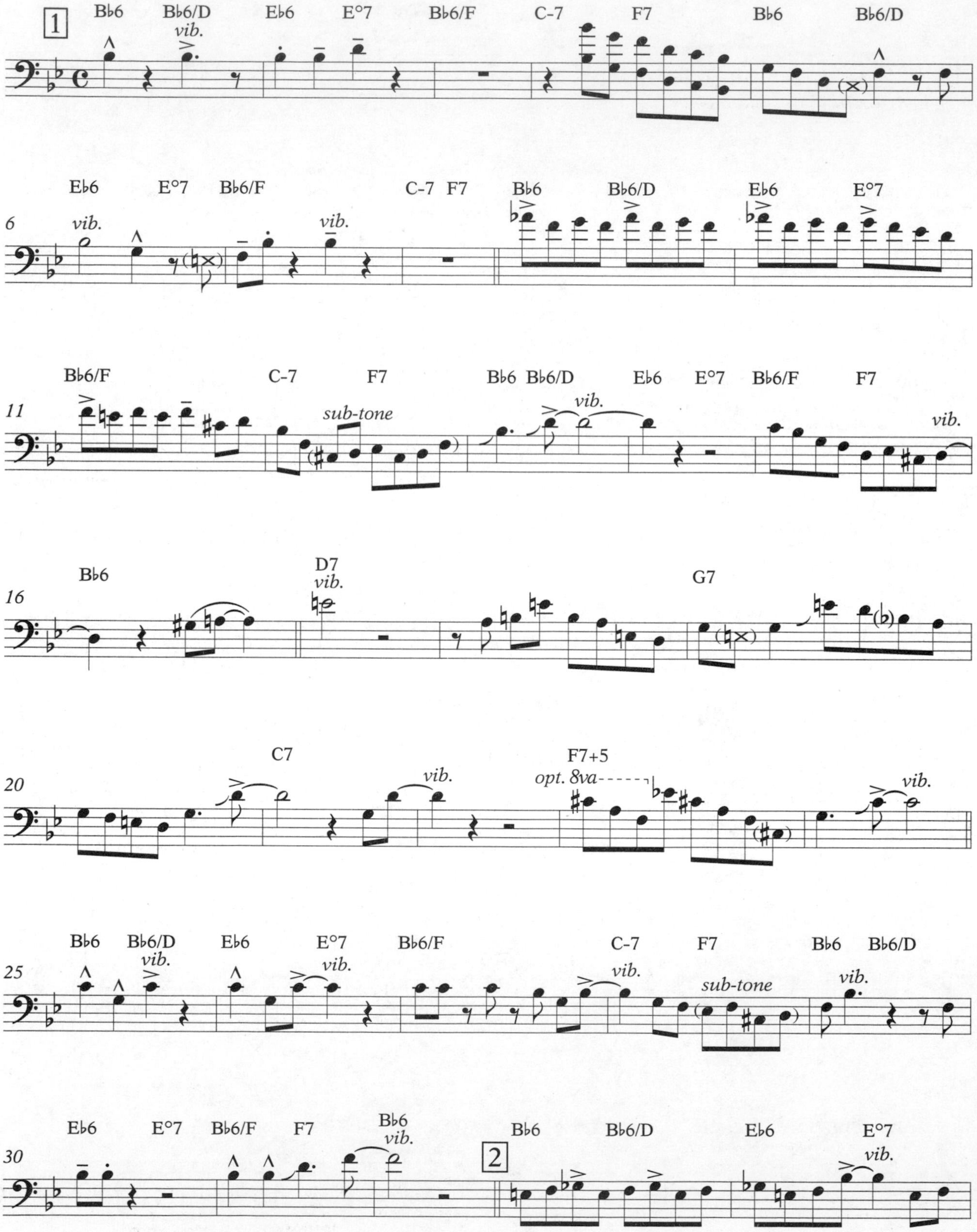

35
Bb6/F C-7 F7 Bb6 Bb6/D Eb6 E°7
vib.
opt. 8va
3
39
Bb/F C-7 F7 Bb6 Bb6/D Eb6 E°7 Bb6F
(8va)
opt. 8va
vib.
44
C-7 F7 Bb6 Bb6/D Eb6 E°7 Bb6/F F7
(8va)
3
vib.
48
Bb6 D7 G7
vib.
52
C7 F7
56
Bb6 Bb6/D Eb6 E°7 Bb6/F C-7 F7
61
Bb6 Bb6/D Eb E°7 Bb6/F F7 Bb6
vib.
opt. 8va
sub-tone

6

Dorian Scales and Minor 7th Chords

"Don't think about how you can
express your virtuosity,
look for what the compositions calls for."

saxophonist Dick Oatts discussing what he learned while playing with the Mel Lewis Orchestra[1]

The *dorian scale* consists of the ascending pattern: whole step, half step, whole step, whole step, whole step, half step, whole step.

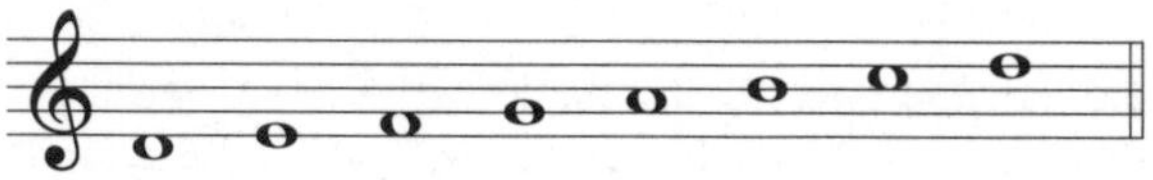

D Dorian Mode

The dorian scale is the second mode in the major scale family and contains the same notes as the major scale a major 2nd below. The dorian scale may also be thought of as a major scale with the 3rd and 7th notes lowered a half step. This scale is typically used when improvising over minor triads, minor 6th, minor 7th, minor 9th, minor 11th, and minor 13th chords. (In jazz, a dash is sometimes used as an abbreviation for minor.)

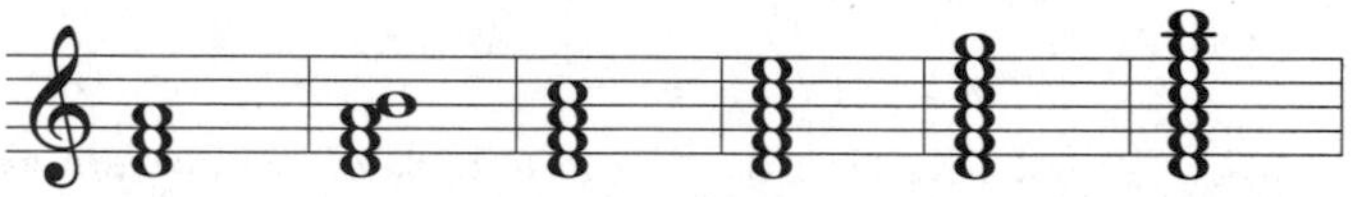

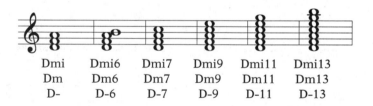

Dmi	Dmi6	Dmi7	Dmi9	Dmi11	Dmi13
Dm	Dm6	Dm7	Dm9	Dm11	Dm13
D-	D-6	D-7	D-9	D-11	D-13

The *minor triad* consists of a root, a minor 3rd, and a perfect 5th. A *minor 6th chord* is a minor triad with a major 6th added; a *minor 7th chord* is a minor triad with a minor 7th; and a *minor 9th chord* consists of a minor 7th chord with a major 9th. Adding the perfect 11th and major 13th creates *minor 11th* and *minor 13th* chords, respectively. Notice that a minor 13th chord contains all of the notes in the dorian scale, stacked in thirds.

In a major key, minor chords function as ii (*supertonic*), iii (*mediant*), and vi (*submediant*) chords. In a minor key, minor chords function as i (*tonic*) and iv (*subdominant*) chords. The dorian scale is the preferred choice when improvising over minor chords functioning as ii chords in a major key, iv chords in a minor key, or where the chord lasts four measures or more (*modal compositions*). Every note in the dorian scale may be used over the minor chord, but the second, fourth, and sixth degrees have the richest color.

[1] Personal conversation, Lake Placid Seminars, 8/24/98.

Theory/Ear Exercises

1. Write the dorian scale in all twelve keys.
2. Write the various types of minor chords in all twelve keys.
3. *Keyboard skills*: Play minor 9th chords on the piano, and listen to the sound or color that characterizes this chord.
4. *Melodic and harmonic dictation*: Notate melodies based on dorian, mixolydian, and major scales and chord progressions based on minor 7th, dominant 7th, and major 7th chords.
5. *Transcription*: Transcribe a melody, chord progression, or an improvised solo from a recording.

Gaining Facility with Dorian Scales and Minor 7th Chords

Practice the following exercises over the chord progression below, using either a metronome or the play-along recording from *Creative Beginnings: An Introduction to Jazz Improvisation* (track 6). By changing the length of each chord to four measures, you can also use vol. 21, *Gettin' It Together* (disc 2, track 6), of *A New Approach to Jazz Improvisation by* Jamey Aebersold. If you find yourself struggling with an exercise, slow it down, simplify it, or sing it while visualizing yourself playing it. After familiarizing yourself with the exercises, pick one or two to practice repeatedly, until you can play them without any conscious thought.

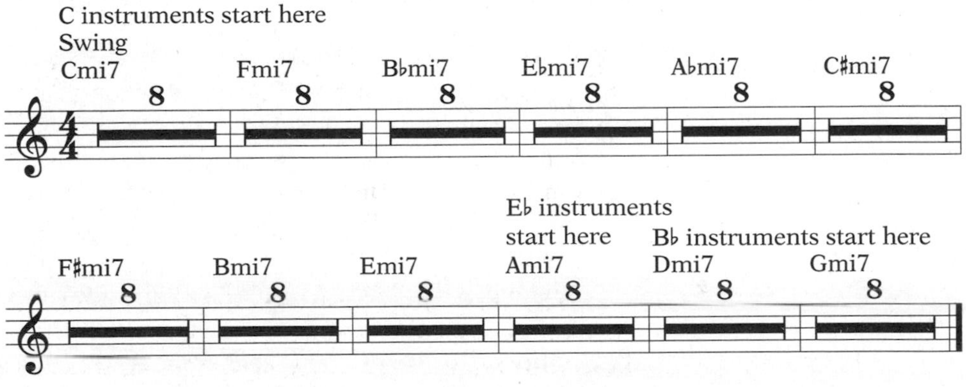

1. *Call and response warmups*: Have another musician or teacher play a phrase that fits over a minor seventh chord. Play back the phrase you have just heard.
2. The basic scale ascending to the 9th.

MM __________________

3. The minor 9th arpeggio, starting on the ♭3rd.

MM ____________________

4. A paraphrase of a motive from Miles Davis's "So What" solo, based on a descending minor 11th arpeggio (Miles Davis, *Kind of Blue*, Columbia KCS 8163, or *Smithsonian Collection of Classic Jazz*).

MM ____________________

5. A variation on a riff used by Joe Farrell in his composition "Village Green" (Elvin Jones, *Puttin' It Together*, Blue Note Records). You may play this pattern starting either on the first or fourth note of the scale.

MM ____________________

6. A variation on a Freddie Hubbard idea from his solo on "The Night Has A Thousand Eyes" (Freddie Hubbard, *Sweet Return*, Blue Note Records). Freddie played the first note with an alternate fingering, creating a color change between the first two notes.

MM ____________________

7. *Creative Jazz Improvisation*: Improvise over the chord progression, without looking at the book or thinking about the notes in the scale. Don't feel you have to play constant eighth notes. Think of the rhythm as a vast expanse of time in which you have the freedom to play anything you can imagine.

8. Make up your own patterns and melodic ideas based on dorian scales and minor 7th chords.

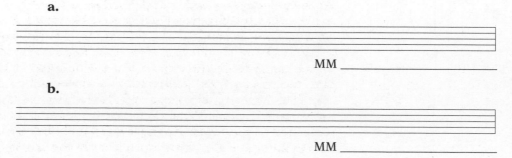

a.

MM ____________________

b.

MM ____________________

Improvising on Jazz Compositions Based on Minor 7th Chords

Following is a partial list of jazz compositions in which minor 7th chords are frequently used, often in a modal context. These compositions are found in *The New Real Book*, vol. 1 (NRB), *The New Real Book*, vol. 2 (NR2), one of the volumes of Jamey Aebersold's *New Approach to Jazz Improvisation* (JA), or *Creative Beginnings: An Introduction to Jazz Improvisation* (CB). Memorize the most frequently played songs, and practice them in different keys.

Compositions Based Exclusively on Minor 7th Chords

"Blues Minor"—John Coltrane (JA vol. 27)
"Impressions"—John Coltrane (JA vols. 28 and 54, NR2)
"Maiden Voyage" (exclusive of bass pedal)—Herbie Hancock (JA vols. 11, 54, 81, and 85)
"So What"—Miles Davis (JA vol. 50)

Compositions In Which Minor 7th Chords Occur Frequently

"Angel"— Wes Montgomery (JA vol. 62)
"Aulil"—David Baker (JA vols. 10 and 76)
"Cantaloupe Island"—Herbie Hancock (JA vols. 11, 54, and 85)
"Gibraltar"—Freddie Hubbard (JA vol. 60)
"Hope Street"—Tom Harrell (JA vol. 63)
"Invitation"—Bronislav Kaper (JA vol. 34)
"Like Sonny"—John Coltrane (JA vol. 27, NR2)
"Jeannine"—Duke Pearson (JA vol. 65)
"Jungle Juice"—Horace Silver (JA vol. 86)
"Little Sunflower"—Freddie Hubbard (NRB)
"Milestones" (new version)—Miles Davis (JA vol. 50)
"Recordame" ("No Me Esqueca")—Joe Henderson (JA vol. 38, NRB)
"Scene"—Tom Harrell (JA vol. 63)
"Silver's Serenade"—Horace Silver (JA vol. 17, NR2)
"Soleil d'Altamira"—David Baker (JA vol. 10)
"Song for My Father"—Horace Silver (JA vols. 17 and 54, NR2)

Miles Davis's Improvised Solo on "So What"

Miles Davis's improvised trumpet solo on his composition "So What" is a masterpiece of melodic restraint and impeccable timing. It was transcribed from his album *Kind of Blue* (Columbia PC 8163) and is also available on the *Smithsonian Collection of Classic Jazz*. This recording also features Cannonball Adderly on alto sax, John Coltrane on tenor sax, Bill Evans on piano, Paul Chambers on bass, and Jimmy Cobb on drums, all masters in their own right.

Like Picasso in the visual arts, Miles is an example of an artist who, having mastered a particular style, moved on to create an entirely new genre. After his formative years learning the bebop vocabulary with Charlie Parker's group, he became one of the prime innovators in the late-1940s movement known as *cool jazz*. He then returned to his bebop roots in the 1950s with a style often referred to as *hard bop*. In 1958 and 1959, with the recordings *Milestones* and *Kind of Blue*, he popularized the concept of modality (songs in which the chords last four bars or move). During this time, he also simplified his melodic content from that of his highly chromatic bebop style. In the mid-1960s, Miles, along with his sidemen Wayne Shorter, Herbie Hancock, Ron Carter, and Tony Williams, experimented with elements of the free jazz style first introduced by Ornette Coleman. In the 1970s he went on to combine elements of jazz with R&B and rock rhythms, creating a genre now referred to as fusion.

"So What" is based on an AABA form, consisting of sixteen bars of Dmi7, eight bars of E♭mi7, and eight bars of Dmi7. This version is played at a relaxed tempo (𝅗𝅥 = 72), but subsequent recordings of the piece are much faster.

It is interesting to contrast the approaches of the different soloists. Cannonball and 'Trane take a harmonic approach, whereas Miles and Bill Evans are lyrical and use more space in their lines. Miles's sense of timing is very subtle, laying behind the beat at times and marking the center of the beat at others. He also anticipates the chord changes as seen in bars 24, 48, and 56. There are several instrumental nuances, including a variety of articulations, ghosted notes, and half-valve effects. Most of the notes in his melodies are derived from the dorian scale, but we also find usage of the harmonic minor scale in bars 13, 24, and 63. He often explores the upper extensions of the chord; in bars 34, 49, 58, and 59 he plays the 11th, 9th, and 7th of the minor chord, which may also be thought of as playing a C major triad over a D minor 7th chord. The blues scale is hinted at in bar 41, where he slips in the ♭5th.

After listening closely to the solo, practice it at different tempos with the metronome clicking on beats 2 and 4. Then continue improvising on the chord progression, trying to capture the same style.

Treble-clef C instruments:

34
(½v)
39
(½v)
(½v)
43
(½v)
48
E♭-7
52
56
D-7
61
(½v)

B♭ instruments:

34
(½v)
39
(½v)
(½v)
43
(½v)
48
F-7
52
56
E-7
61
(½v)

E♭ instruments:

34
39
43
opt. 8va bassa
C-7
48
52
loco
56
B-7
61

Bass-clef instruments:

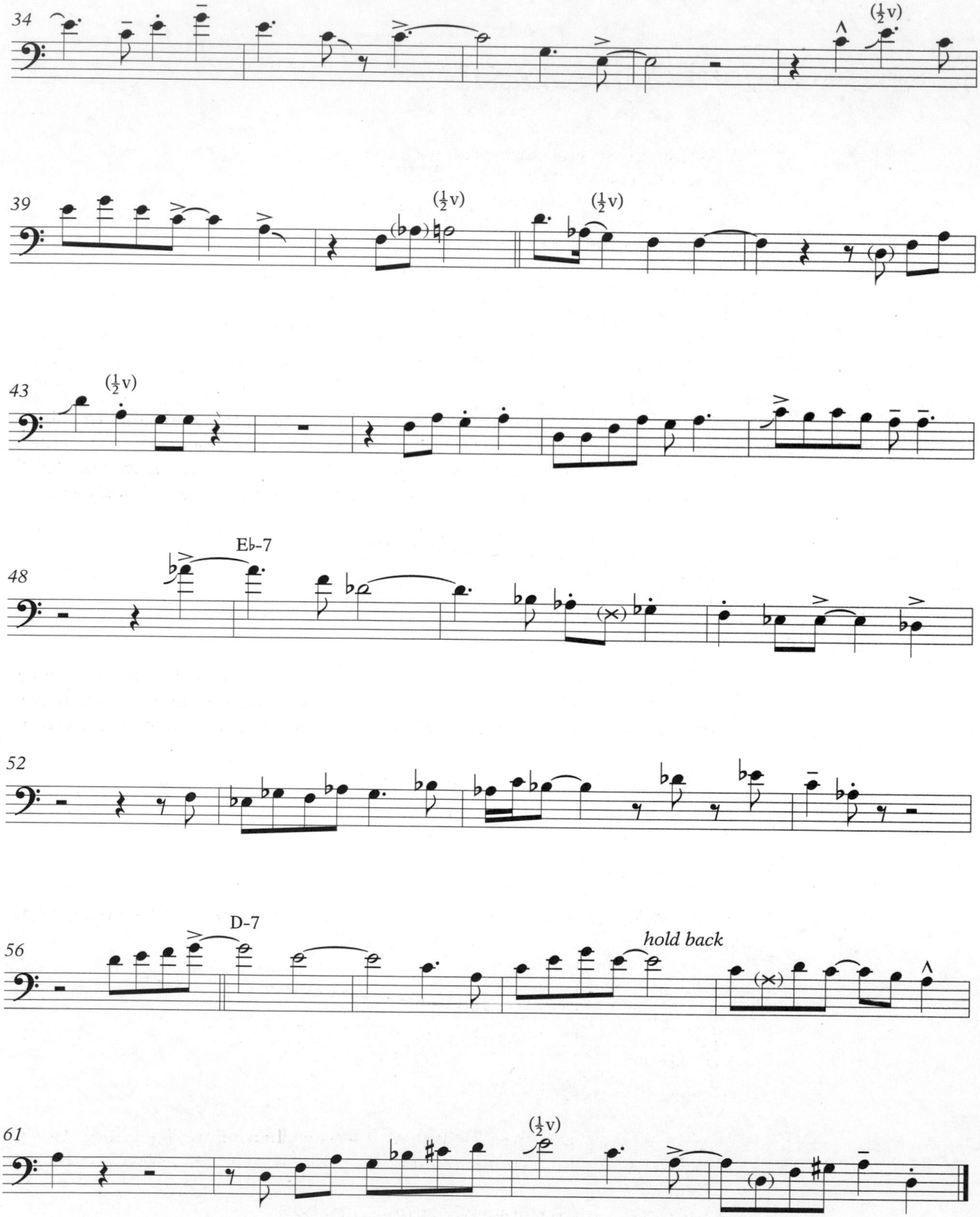
E♭-7
D-7
hold back

7
The ii–V–I Progression

"You always gotta remember what made you
start out in music in the first place.
You got turned on to it somehow
and it was pure when you loved it,
and that's the reason you played.
You must always try to go back to that
because you'll lose sight of that
unless you think about it."

saxophonist David Liebman[1]

Diatonic chords are derived from the same "parent" scale and function within the same key. These chords are built on each note in the scale and are labeled with Roman numerals.[2] For example, in the key of C major, if we start on C and select other notes in the scale, we end up with the C major 7th chord.

C Major 7th Chord

Because this chord is built on the first note in the scale (the *tonic*), it is referred to as the *I chord*. Likewise, if we build a chord on the second note (the *supertonic*), we end up with a D minor 7th chord, which is called the *ii chord*.

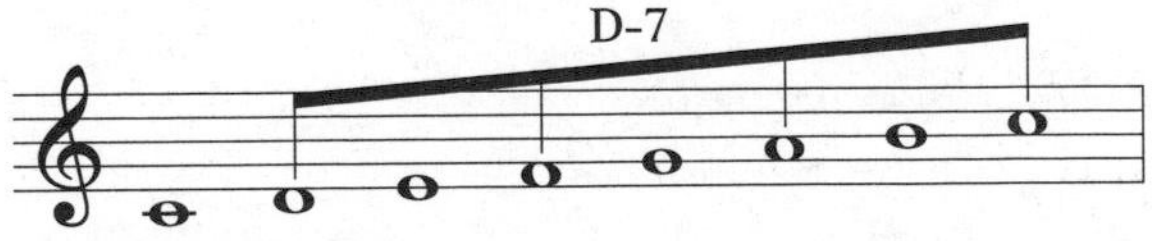

D Minor 7th Chord

Similarly, building a chord on the fifth note (the *dominant*) will yield a G dominant 7th chord, referred to as the *V chord*.

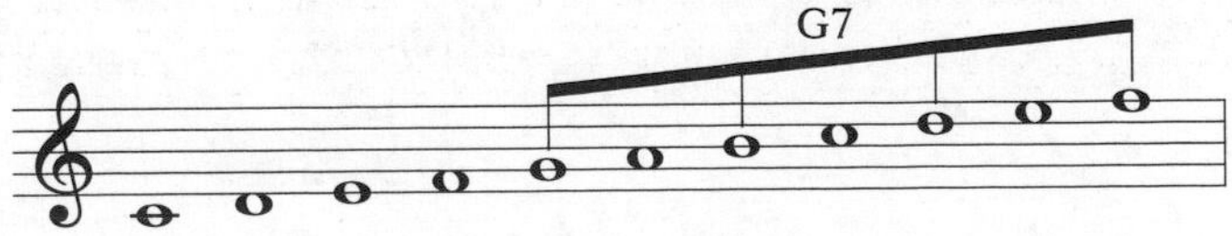

G Dominant 7th Chord

In a major key, the ii7 chord will always be a minor 7th chord, the V7 chord a dominant 7th chord, and the IM7 chord a major 7th chord. (Lowercase

[1] Bill Milkowski, "Paths of Creativity," *Jazz Times* (June 1998) 57.

[2] Refer to the Appendix for a complete list of chords in major and minor scales.

Roman numerals are used to denote minor chords, while uppercase Roman numerals are used to denote major or dominant chords. The inclusion of an uppercase "M" is used to distinguish a major 7th chord from a dominant 7th chord.) In *functional harmony*, the ii chord typically progresses up a perfect 4th (or down a perfect 5th) to the V chord, which in turn progresses up a perfect 4th (or down a perfect 5th) to the I chord. Technically this is called a *ii7–V7–IM7 progression*, but is usually referred to as a *ii–V–I*.

ii–V–I Progression in C Major

Often we find only a portion of this progression, such as a ii–V or V–I.

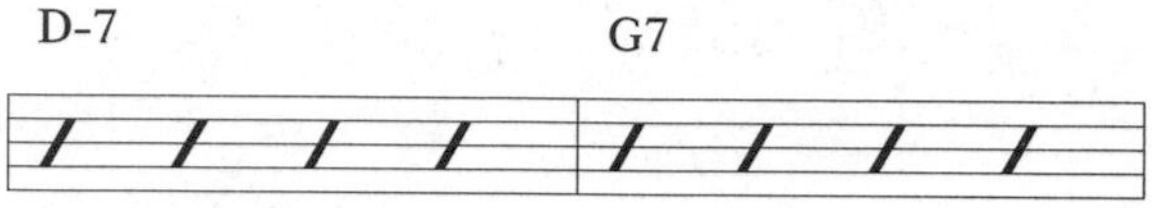

ii–V Progression in C Major

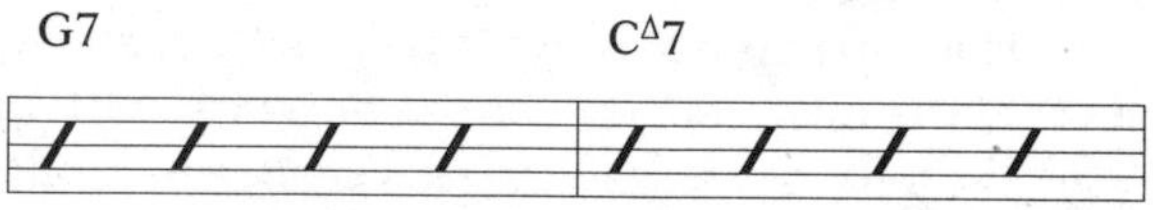

V–I Progression in C Major

Another common variant of this progression adds the minor chord built on the sixth degree of the scale. Usually, this progression occurs in the sequence I–vi–ii–V–I.

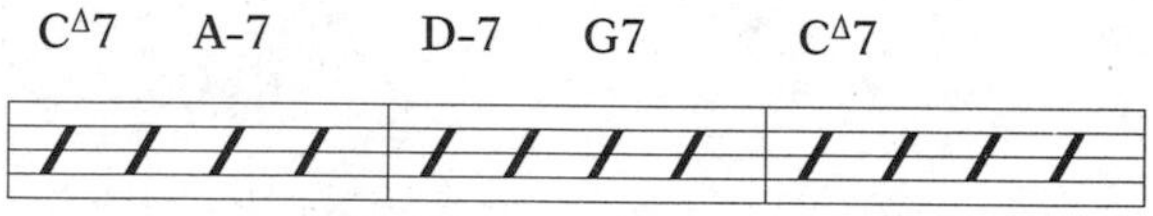

I–vi–ii–V–I Progression in C Major

Sometimes the vi and ii chords are changed to dominant 7th chords and are referred to as *secondary dominants*. Because the dominant chord on the sixth degree has a V–I relationship to the ii chord and the dominant chord built on the second degree has a V–I relationship to the V chord, they are called V/ii (pronounced "V of ii") and V/V ("V of V"), respectively.

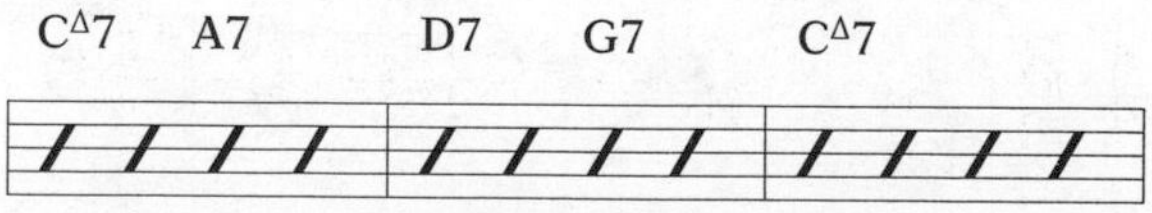

I–V/ii–V/V–V–I Progression in C Major

The vi chord can also be replaced with a half-diminished chord built on a chromatically raised first scale degree, and the V chord replaced by a fully-diminished chord built on the chromatically raised second scale degree. In functional harmony, diminished chords are typically built on the seventh note (or *leading tone*) of the scale. Because these two chords form vii-i relationships to the ii and iii chords, they are called *secondary leading-tone chords* and labeled vii$^{\varnothing}$7/ii and vii°7/iii, respectively.

I–vii$^{\varnothing}$7/ii–ii–vii°7/iii–iii Progression in C Major

Frequently a minor chord built on the third degree of the scale is substituted for the I chord, creating a iii–vi–ii–V–I or iii–V/ii–ii–V–I progression. When one of these progressions occurs at the end of a tune, it is referred to as a "turnaround."

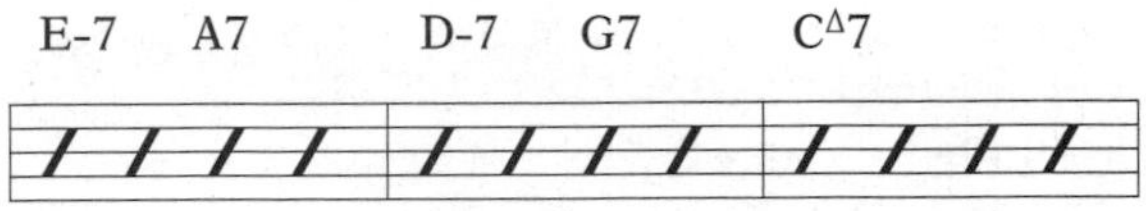

iii–V/ii–ii–V–I Progression in C Major

The ii–V7–I progression is the most common chord progression in jazz. Being able to recognize this progression greatly simplifies the process of improvising on chord changes. For example, in C major, the ii chord would be colored by a D dorian scale, the V chord by a G mixolydian scale, and the I chord by a C major scale. These three scales all contain the same notes; therefore, you can remain in one key when improvising over all three chords in the progression.

Theory/Ear Exercises

1. Examine a variety of jazz compositions found in a fake-book. Circle all ii–V, V–I, ii–V–I, and iii–vi–ii–V–I progressions, and analyze the various harmonic formulas employed by different composers. Reduce the harmony to the basic tonal centers or keys in which the chords function.
2. *Keyboard skills*: Play ii–V–I progressions on the piano, using the two following sets of voicings.[3]
   a. Starting with the 3rd of the chord as the lowest note in the right hand:

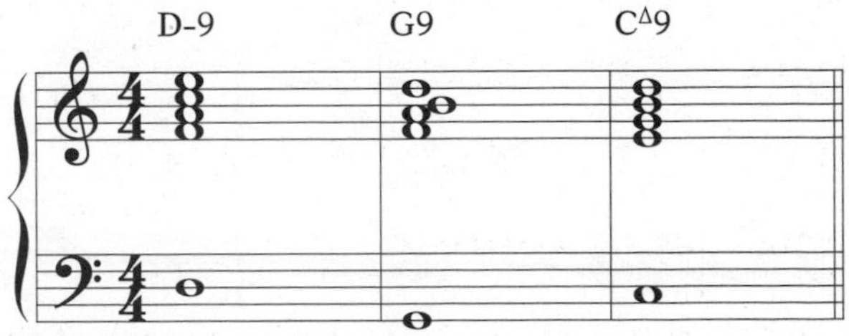

[3] For further detail on ii–V–I voicings, see Dan Haerle, *Jazz/Rock Voicings for Keyboard Players* (Studio P/R-Columbia, 1974).

b. Starting with the 7th of the chord as the lowest note in the right hand:

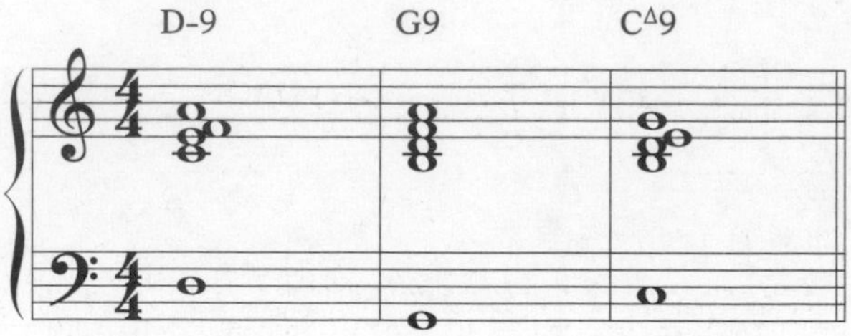

3. *Transcription*: Transcribe a melody, a chord progression, or an improvised solo from a recording.

Gaining Facility with ii–V–I Progressions

Practice the following exercises over the chord progression below, using either a metronome or the play-along recordings from *Creative Beginnings: An Introduction to Jazz Improvisation* (track 7) or volume 3, The ii–V–I Progression (track 2), of *A New Approach to Jazz Improvisation* by Jamey Aebersold. If you find yourself struggling with an exercise, slow it down, simplify it, or sing it while visualizing yourself playing it. After familiarizing yourself with the exercises, pick one or two to practice repeatedly, until you can play them without any conscious thought.

C instruments begin here

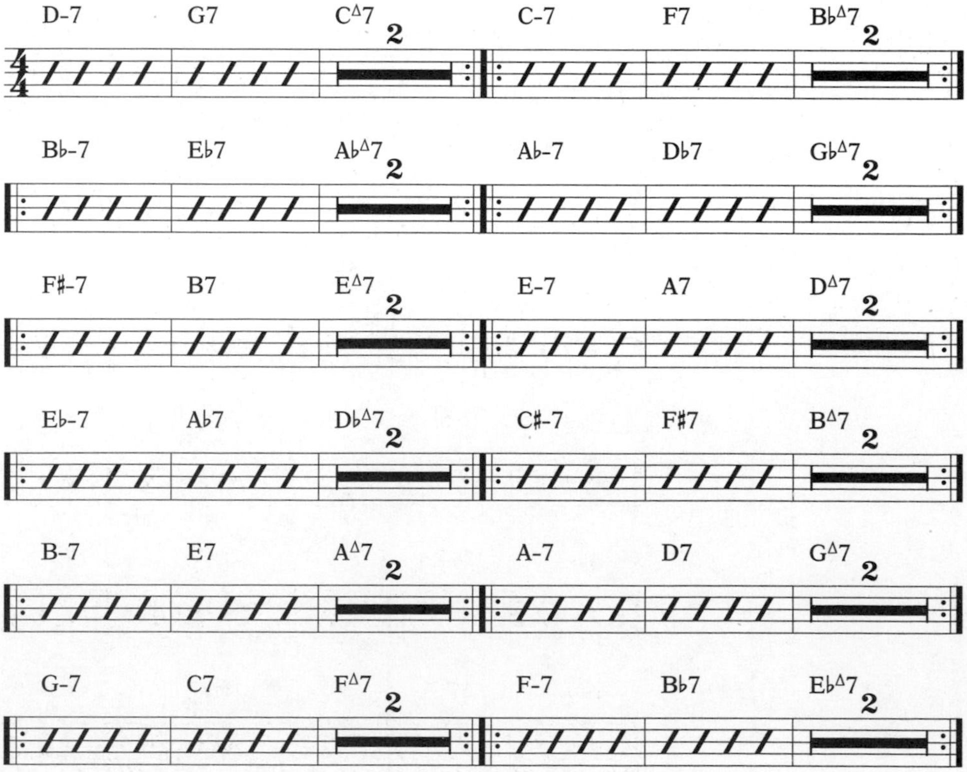

B♭ instruments begin here

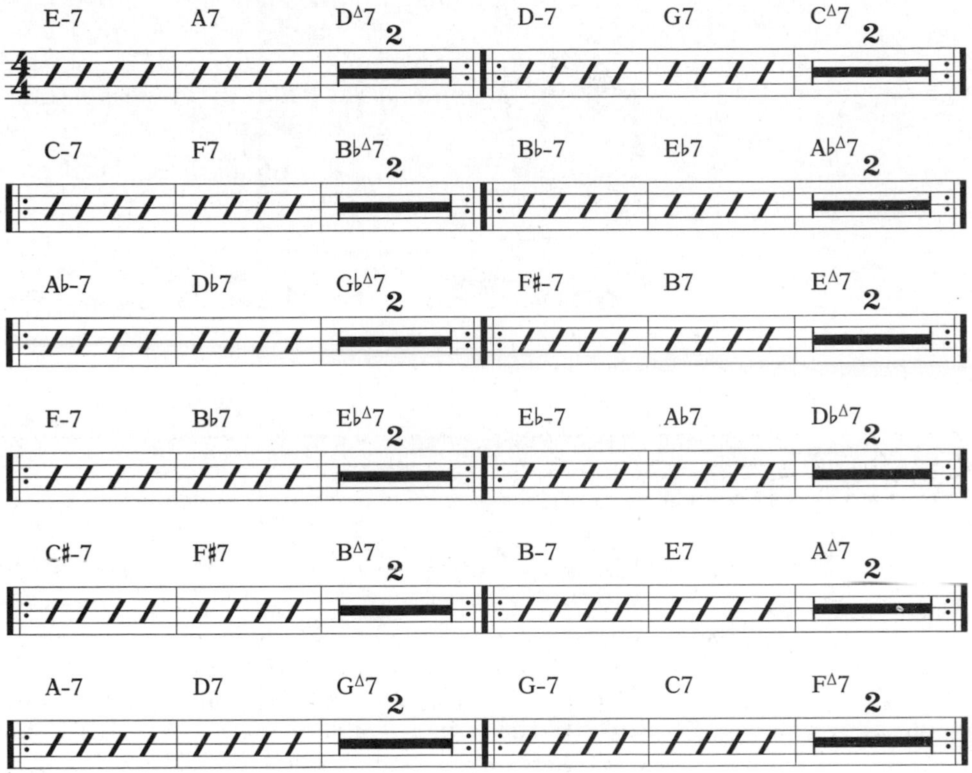

E♭ instruments begin here

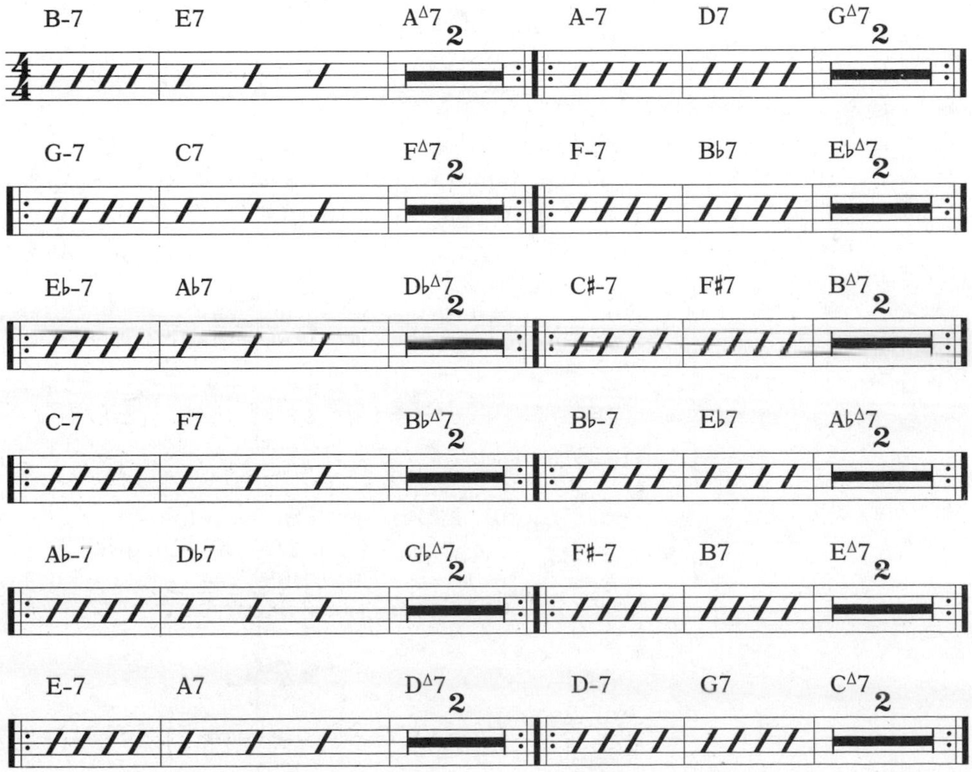

1. *Warmups:*
   a. Have another musician or teacher play a phrase that fits over a ii–V–I progression. Play back the phrase you have just heard.
   b. Have another musician or teacher play random sequences of ii–V and ii–V–I progressions. Play the corresponding scales on your instrument or solo over the chords using your ear to determine the correct key area.
2. Using the major scale over all three chords.

MM ____________________

3. Using the bebop 7th scale over all three chords.

MM ____________________

4. A Woody Shaw pattern from his "Softly As in a Morning Sunrise" solo (Larry Young, *Unity*, Blue Note 4221).

MM ____________________

5. Ascending by minor 7th and dominant 9th arpeggios; descending by the major scale in quarter-note triplets.

MM ____________________

6. A Sonny Rollins pattern from his "Tune-Up" solo that uses an arpeggio over the ii chord and the mixolydian scale over the V7 chord (Sonny Rollins, *Newk's Time*, Blue Note 4001).

MM ____________________

7. A Tom Harrell pattern based on the bebop 7th scale (live taping).

MM ____________________

8. A variation on a Clifford Brown motive from his "Pent-Up House" solo, which introduces a passing major 7th on the ii chord (*Smithsonian Collection of Classic Jazz*).

MM ____________________

9. A Tom Harrell pattern, which uses a lower chromatic neighbor tone in the first bar, and the upper and lower chromatic neighbor tones in the second bar (live taping).

MM ____________________

10. A Charlie "Bird" Parker ii–V7–I pattern from his "Ko-Ko" solo (*Smithsonian Collection of Classic Jazz*). Bird, as well as other players such as Sonny Rollins, used this pattern often.

MM ____________________

11. A Sonny Rollins pattern that uses the major and bebop 7th scales over the ii chord and the ♯ 5th over the V7 chord (Sonny Rollins, *Newk's Time*, Blue Note BLP4001).

MM ____________________

12. *Guide-tone improvisation*: A guide-tone line is a series of notes that outline the chord progression, typically the 3rd and 7ths of the chords. To create a guide-tone line, start on either the 3rd or 7th of the first chord, then move to either the 3rd or 7th of the following chord, whichever is closest. After practicing the two guide-tone lines over the progression, create an improvisation by embellishing the guide-tones with notes of your choice.

Example:

MM ______________________

13. *Creative Jazz Improvisation*: Improvise over the chord progression, without looking at the book or thinking about the notes in the scale. Let your fingers or hands move without consciously controlling them, using your ear find resolutions within the key center.[4]

14. Make up your own patterns and melodic ideas based on ii–V–I progressions.

a.

MM ______________________

b.

MM ______________________

Improvising on Jazz Compositions Based on ii–V or ii–V–I Progressions

Following is a partial list of jazz compositions that contain ii–V or ii–V–I progressions. These compositions are found in *The New Real Book*, vol. 1 (NRB), *The New Real Book*, vol. 2 (NR2), one of the volumes of Jamey Aebersold's *New Approach to Jazz Improvisation* (JA), or *Creative Beginnings: An Introduction to Jazz Improvisation* (CB). Memorize the most frequently played songs, and practice them in different keys.

Compositions Based Exclusively on ii–V–I Progressions

"At Twilight"—David Baker (JA vol. 76)
"Changes"—David Baker (JA vol. 76)
"Countdown"—John Coltrane (JA vol. 28)
"Eclipse"—David Baker (JA vol. 76)
"Everybody's Song"—David Baker (JA vol. 76)
"Giant Steps"—John Coltrane (JA vol. 28)
"Joy Spring"—Clifford Brown (JA vol. 53)
"Lady Bird"—Tadd Dameron (JA vols. 6 and 70, NRB)
"Moment's Notice"—John Coltrane (JA vol. 38, NR2)

[4] Kenny Werner, private lesson, Scotch Plains, NJ, 1992.

"Penny"—Horace Silver (JA vol. 86)
"Pent-Up House"—Sonny Rollins (JA vol. 8, NRB)
"Satin Doll"—Duke Ellington (JA vols. 12 and 54, NRB)
"To The Fore"—David Baker (JA vol. 76)
"Tune-Up"—Vinson/Davis (JA vols. 7, 65, and 67, NRB)

Compositions In Which ii–V–I Progressions Occur Frequently

"Afternoon in Paris"—John Lewis (JA vol. 43 & 70)
"Airegin"—Sonny Rollins (JA vol. 8)
"All the Things You Are"—Hammerstein/Kern (JA vols. 43, 55, and 67, NRB)
"Along Came Betty"—Benny Golson (JA vols. 14 and 65, NR2)
"April In August"—David Baker (JA vol. 76)
"Are You Real"—Benny Golson (JA vol. 14)
"Avalon"—Jolson/Rose (JA vol. 39 79)
"Beyond All Limits"—Woody Shaw (JA vol. 9)
"Billy Boy"—traditional (JA vol. 80)
"Blue Moon"—Hart/Rodgers (JA vols. 34 and 70)
"Blue Room"—Hart/Rodgers (JA vol. 39)
"Body and Soul"—Heyman, Sour, Egton, and Green (JA vols. 41, 74, and 75, NR2)
"Boston Bernie"—Dexter Gordon (JA vol. 82)
"But Not For Me"—George & Ira Gershwin (JA vols. 65 and 75)
"Bye Bye Blackbird"—Dixon/Henderson (NR2)
"Caravan"—Ellington, Mills, Tizol (JA vol. 59)
"Ceora"—Lee Morgan (JA vols. 38 and 59)
"Cherokee"—Ray Noble (JA vols. 15 and 61, NR2)
"Confirmation"—Charlie Parker (JA vols. 6, 65, 67, and 69)
"Day By Day"—Cahn, Stordahl, Weston (JA vol. 59, NR2)
"Dearly Beloved"—Kern/Mercer (JA vol. 55, NRB)
"Del Sasser"—Sam Jones (JA vol. 13)
"Dewey Square"—Charlie Parker (JA vols. 6 and 69)
"Donna Lee"—Charlie Parker (JA vols. 6 and 69)
"Don't Get Around Much Anymore"—Duke Ellington (JA vol. 48)
"Doujie"—Wes Montgomery (JA vol. 62)
"East Of The Sun"—Brooks Bowman (JA vol. 71)
"Exactly Like You"—Field/McHugh (NR2)
"Falling In Love With Love"—Rodgers/Hart (JA vol. 71)
"Flamingo"—Anderson/Grouya (JA, NR2)
"Fly Me to the Moon"—Bart Howard (JA vol. 65, NR2)
"For Regulars Only"—Dexter Gordon (JA vol. 82)
"Four"—Miles Davis (JA vols. 7, 65, and 67, NRB)
"Four Brothers"—Jimmy Guiffre (JA vol. 46, NRB)
"Fried Bananas"—Dexter Gordon (JA vol. 82)
"Get Happy"—Koehler/Arlen (NR2)
"Gone With The Wind"—Wrubel/Magidson (JA vol. 58, NRB)
"Good Bait"—Dameron/Basie (JA vol. 65)
"Groovin' High"—Dizzy Gillespie (JA vol. 43)
"Hallucinations"—Bud Powell (NRB)
"Have You Met Miss Jones?"—Hart/Rodgers (JA vols. 25 and 74)
"Honeysuckle Rose"—Razaf/Waller (JA vol. 71, NR2)
"I Can't Get Started"—Gershwin/Duke (JA vols. 25 and 74)
"If I Were a Bell"—Frank Loesser (JA vol. 46, NRB)
"If You Could See Me Now"—Dameron/Sigman (JA vol. 71)
"I Let a Song Go Out of My Heart"—Duke Ellington (JA vol. 12)

"I Remember You"—Mercer/Schertzinger (JA vol. 22)
"I Want More"—Dexter Gordon (JA vol. 82)
"I Wish I Knew"—Gordon/Warren (JA vol. 71)
"I'll Remember April"—Raye/DePaul (JA vol. 43)
"Illegal Entrance"—David Baker (JA vol. 76)
"I'll Take Romance"—Oakland/Hammerstein (JA vol. 58)
"Imagination"—Burke/Van Heusen (NRB)
"I'm All Smiles"—Martin/Leonard (NRB)
"I'm In The Mood For Love"—McHugh/Fields (JA vol. 71)
"I'm Old Fashioned"—Mercer/Kern (JA vol. 55, NRB)
"In a Mellotone"—Duke Ellington (JA vol. 48)
"Indiana"—MacDonald/Hanley (JA vols. 61 and 80)
"In Your Own Sweet Way"—Dave Brubeck (NR2)
"Invitation"—Kaper/Webster (JA vols. 34 and 59)
"It's You Or No One"—Cahn/Styne—Ray Noble (JA vols. 61 and 67)
"Jeannine"—Duke Pearson (JA vols. 13 and 65)
"Jitterbug Waltz"—Fats Waller (JA vol. 71)
"Juicy Lucy"—Horace Silver (JA vol. 86)
"Just Friends"—Davies/Klenner/Lewis (JA vols. 34 and 59)
"Just Squeeze Me"—Ellington/Gaines (JA vols. 48 and 71)
"Just The Way You Look Tonight"—Kern/Fields (JA vol. 55)
"Just You, Just Me"—Klages/Greer (JA vol. 71)
"Let's Fall In Love"—Arlen/Koehler (JA vol. 58, NRB)
"Like Someone In Love"—Burke/Van Heusen (JA vol. 58, NRB)
"Long Ago (And Far Away)"—Kern/Gershwin (JA vol. 55, NRB)
"Lover"—Rodgers/Hart (JA vol. 61)
"Lover Man"—Davis, Ramirez, and Sherman (JA vol. 32)
"Mambo Inn"—Bauza/Sampson/Woodlen (JA vol. 64)
"Manteca"—Gillespie/Fuller (JA vol. 64)
"Marmaduke"—Charlie Parker (JA vol. 69)
"Mean To You"—Ahlert/Turk (JA vol. 65)
"Meditation"—Antonio Carlos Jobim (JA vol. 31)
"Milestones" (older version)—Miles Davis (JA vol. 7)
"Misty"—Earl Garner (JA vols. 41, 49, and 70)
"Moment's Notice"—John Coltrane (JA vols. 38 and 65, NR2)
"Mood Indigo"—Duke Ellington (JA vol. 12)
"Moon Rays"—Horace Silver (JA vol. 86)
"My Little Suede Shoes"—Charlie Parker (JA vols. 6 and 69)
"My Secret Love"—Parish/Sherwood (JA vol. 34)
"Once I Loved"—Antonio Carlos Jobim (JA vol. 31)
"On Green Dolphin Street"—Bronislav Kaper (JA vols. 34 and 59)
"Ornithology"—Charlie Parker (JA vols. 6 and 69)
"Out of Nowhere"—Heyman/Green (JA vols. 22 and 59)
"Peace"—Horace Silver (JA vol. 17, NR2)
"Perdido"—Juan Tizol (JA vols. 12, 65, and 67, NR2)
"Peri's Scope"—Bill Evans (JA vol. 45)
"Pick Yourself Up"—Kern/Fields (JA vol. 55)
"Polka Dots and Moonbeams"—Van Heusen/Burke (JA vol. 58, NRB)
"Quicksilver"—Horace Silver (JA vol. 18, NR2)
"Recordame" ("No Me Esqueca")—Joe Henderson (JA vol. 38, NRB)
"Rain Check"—Billy Strayhorn (JA vol. 66)
"Rose Room"—Williams/Hickman (JA vol. 79)
"Ruby My Dear"—Thelonious Monk (JA vol. 56, NRB)
"Saint Thomas"—Sonny Rollins (JA vols. 8 and 74, NRB)

"Satin Doll"—Ellington/Strayhorn/Mercer (JA vols. 12, 54, and 66, NRB)
"Scrapple from the Apple"—Charlie Parker (JA vols. 6 and 69)
"Secret Love"—Parish/Sherwood (JA vols. 34 and 61)
"Seven Steps to Heaven"—Victor Feldman (JA vol. 50, NR2)
"Shoutin' Out"—Horace Silver (JA vol. 86)
"Skylark"—Mercer/Carmichael (JA vol. 32)
"Solar"—Davis/Evans (JA vol. 7, NRB)
"Sophisticated Lady"—Duke Ellington (JA vol. 12)
"Speak Low"—Nash/Weill (JA vols. 25 and 65)
"Stablemates"—Benny Golson (JA vols. 14 and 65, NR2)
"Star Eyes"—Raye/DePaul (JA vols. 34 and 59)
"Stella by Starlight"—Victor Young (JA vol. 22)
"Street Of Dreams"—Lewis/Young (JA vol. 71)
"Strollin'"—Horace Silver (JA vol. 18)
"Sweet and Lovely"—Arnheim/Tobias/Lemare (JA vol. 59, NR2)
"Take the 'A' Train"—Billy Strayhorn (JA vols. 12, 65, and 66, NR2)
"Tangerine"—Mercer/Schertzinger (JA vol. 22)
"10/21/17"—David Baker (JA vol. 76)
"That's All"—Brandt/Haymes (NR2)
"The Countess"—Scott Reeves (CB)
"The Hardbop Grandpop"—Horace Silver (JA vol. 86)
"The Lamp Is Low"—DeRose/Shefter/Parish (JA vol. 71)
"The Nearness Of You"—Washington/Carmichael (JA vol. 59)
"The Second Time Around"—Cahn/Van Heusen (JA vol. 71)
"There Is No Greater Love"—Symes/Jones (JA vol. 34)
"The Song Is You"—Hammerstein/Kern (JA vols. 15 and 55, NRB)
"The Way You Look Tonight"—Kern/Fields (JA vol. 61)
"Three Little Words"—Kalmar/Ruby (JA vol. 51, NR2)
"Up Jumped Spring"—Freddie Hubbard (JA vol. 60, NRB)
"Valse Hot"—Sonny Rollins (JA vol. 8)
"Velvet Rose"—David Baker (JA vol. 76)
"Waltz for Debbie"—Bill Evans (JA vol. 45, NRB)
"Why Do I Love You"—Kern/Hammerstein (JA vol. 55)
"Weaver of Dreams"—Elliot/Young (JA vol. 46, NRB)
"What's New"—Burke/Haggard (JA vol. 41, NRB)
"Without a Song"—Rose/Youmans (JA vol. 34)
"Yardbird Suite"—Charlie Parker (JA vols. 6 and 69)
"You Made Me Love You"—McCarthy/Monaco (JA 79)
"You're My Everything"—Dixon, Young & Warren (JA vol. 41, NR2)
"You Stepped Out of a Dream"—Kahn/Brown (JA vols. 34, 59, and 70)

Clifford Brown's Improvised Solo on "Pent-Up House"

Clifford Brown's improvised trumpet solo on the Sonny Rollins composition "Pent-Up House" demonstrates "Brownie's" gift for melody and mastery of the ii–V–I vocabulary. It was transcribed from the *Smithsonian Collection* and is also available on Prestige PR 7821. The recording was made in 1956 by the Clifford Brown/Max Roach Quintet, which included Sonny Rollins on tenor sax, Richie Powell on piano, George Morrow on bass, and Max Roach on drums.

Although Dizzy Gillespie, Fats Navarro, Miles Davis, and Kenny Dorham were the first bebop trumpet stylists, Clifford was one of the most influential players of the next generation. He completely assimilated and extended the language of bebop during his tragically short career. He had the innate ability to pick out colorful chord alterations, and played magnificently long lines with great rhythmic vitality and personal warmth.

The melody of "Pent-Up House" is based on a syncopated motive which is developed through repetition and sequence. The chord progression is comprised entirely of ii–V and ii–V–I progressions, and the form is a 16-bar AABA structure. Clifford begins his solo with a quote from the melody (bars 1–3), and follows with a series of eighth notes. This approach of playing a simple melodic idea in the first part of each chorus and complex eighth-note lines in the second half can be seen frequently during the solo. This allows him to develop his ideas by sequencing them through the chord changes, as in bars 9–12, 16–19, 31–32, 33–38, 55–56, 61–62, 71–73, and 81–84.

Dominant chords are often colored by alterations derived from the diminished/whole-tone and diminished scales (see Chapters 14 and 17). Clifford uses the ♯ 5th over the dominant chord in bar 2, the ♯ 9th in bar 6, the ♭9th in bars 78 and 84, the ♯ 9th and the ♭9th in bars 22, 70, 82, 86, and 94, and the ♯9th, ♭9th, and ♯ 5th in bar 14. He also brings out the ♯ 11th of the major 7th chord in bar 95, implying the lydian scale. Throughout, there is a great deal of chromaticism, and he frequently preceeds a chord tone with upper and lower chromatic neighbor tones (as in bars 5, 6, 12, 20, 22, 23, 29–31, 74, 77, 85, and 89). Other scales used in this solo include the bebop 7th 9 scale (bars 25 and 60) and the blues scale (bars 46–47).

This solo contains several wonderful lines worth extracting and practicing in all keys, particularly those in bars 5–8, 13–15, 20–23, 27–28, 43–44, 69–71, and 75–76. Other interesting points include a corrected "mistake" in bar 91 (a major 3rd on a minor chord), and the use of lipped ghosted notes in bars 32, 36, and 38. When listening to the recording, notice how Sonny Rollins begins his solo with the same idea with which Clifford ended his solo.

The eighth notes are swung and the tempo is approximately 𝅗𝅥 = 96. After listening closely to a recording of this solo, practice it at different tempos with the metronome clicking on beats 2 and 4. Then continue improvising in the same style.[5]

[5] A slightly different transcription of this solo is available in *Clifford Brown Trumpet Solos*, by Ken Slone (Louisville, KY, Ducknob Music, 1982).

Treble-clef C instruments:

36
A-7
D7
GΔ7
41
D-7
G7
C-7
F7
45
A-7
D7
(½v)
GΔ7
4
A-7
D7
51
GΔ7
A-7
D7
55
GΔ7
D-7
G7
59
C-7
F7
A-7
62
D7
GΔ7
5
A-7
66
D7
GΔ7
A-7

70
D7
G∆7
D-7
74
G7
C-7
F7
77
A-7
D7
G∆7
81
6
A-7
D7
G∆7
84
B-7
E7
A-7
D7
87
G∆7
D-7
G7
91
C-7
F7
A-7
D7
95
G∆7
7
A-7
D7
G∆7

B♭ instruments (Saxophone—8va where indicated):

36
B-7
E7
A^Δ7
41
E-7
A7
D-7
sax. 8va
G7
45
B-7
E7
(½ v)
A^Δ7
4
B-7
E7
trpt. 8va bassa
51
A^Δ7
(8va)
B-7
E7
55
A^Δ7
E-7
A7
59
D-7
G7
B-7
62
E7
A^Δ7
5
B-7
66
E7
A^Δ7
B-7

70
E7
A∆7
E-7
74
A7
D-7
sax. 8va
G7
77
B-7
(8va)
E7
A∆7
6
81
B-7
E7
A∆7
84
C-7
F7
B-7
E7
87
A∆7
E-7
A7
91
D-7
G7
B-7
E7
95
A∆7
7
B-7
E7
A∆7

E♭ instruments:

36
F♯-7
B7
EΔ7
41
B-7
E7
A-7
D7
45
F♯-7
B7
(½v)
EΔ7
4
F♯-7
B7
51
EΔ7
F♯-7
B7
55
EΔ7
B-7
E7
59
A-7
D7
F♯-7
62
B7
EΔ7
5
F♯-7
66
B7
EΔ7
F♯-7

70 B7 EΔ7 B-7
74 E7 A-7 D7
77 F♯-7 B7 EΔ7
6 81 F♯-7 B7 EΔ7
84 G♯-7 C♯7 F♯-7 B7
87 EΔ7 B-7 E7
91 A-7 D7 F♯-7 B7
95 EΔ7 7 F♯-7 B7 EΔ7

Bass-clef instruments:

36
A-7
D7
G^Δ7
41
D-7
G7
C-7
F7
45
A-7
D7
(½v) G^Δ7
A-7
opt. 8va
4
D7
51
G^Δ7
(8va)
A-7
D7
55
G^Δ7
(8va)
D-7
G7
59
C-7
F7
A-7
62
D7
G^Δ7
5
A-7
66
D7
G^Δ7
A-7

70 D7 G∆7 D-7
74 G7 C-7 F7
77 A-7 D7 G∆7
6 81 A-7 D7 G∆7
84 B-7 E7 A-7 D7
87 G∆7 D-7 G7
91 C-7 F7 A-7 D7
95 G∆7 7 A-7 D7 G∆7

8

Locrian and Aeolian Scales, and Minor $ii^{\varnothing}7$–V7–i Progressions

"Don't let what you've practiced
dictate the way you play.
Play what you hear,
not what you've memorized."

saxophonist Joe Lovano[1]

The *aeolian scale*, also known as the *pure minor* or *natural minor scale*, consists of the ascending pattern: whole step, half step, whole step, whole step, half step, whole step, whole step.

A Aeolian Mode

The aeolian scale is the sixth mode in the major scale family and contains the same notes as the major scale down a major 6th (or up a minor 3rd). The aeolian scale may also be thought of as a dorian scale with the 6th note lowered a half-step. Like the dorian scale, this scale may be used to improvise over minor triads, minor 7th chords, minor 9th chords, or minor 11th chords. Since the aeolian mode contains a minor 6th degree, it is not typically used to color a minor 6th chord (which contains a major 6th).

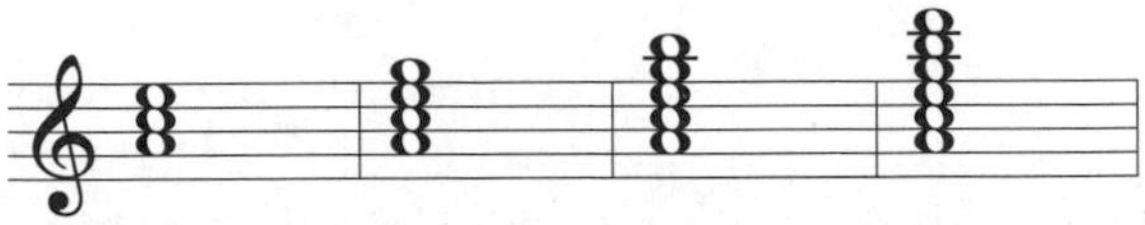

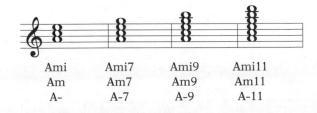

Ami	Ami7	Ami9	Ami11
Am	Am7	Am9	Am11
A-	A-7	A-9	A-11

The aeolian scale sounds best when used over a minor chord functioning as a *tonic chord* (i in a minor key), or as a *submediant chord* (vi in a major key). The dorian mode is usually the preferred choice when the minor chord is functioning as a *supertonic chord* (ii in a major key), or when used in a *modal compositions* such as John Coltrane's *Impressions* or Miles Davis' *So What*. The aeolian mode may also be used in a modal context, such as the bridge of the Miles Davis' *Milestones* (the modal version), but it occurs less frequently in this context than the dorian mode. Every note in the aeolian scale works well over

[1] Personal conversation, Lake Placid Seminars, 8/17/98.

the minor 7th chord with the exception of the ♭6th, which has a tendency to resolve down a half step to the 5th. The 2nd and 4th scale degrees possess the richest color in relationship to the minor chord.

The *locrian scale* consists of the ascending pattern: half step, whole step, whole step, half step, whole step, whole step, whole step.

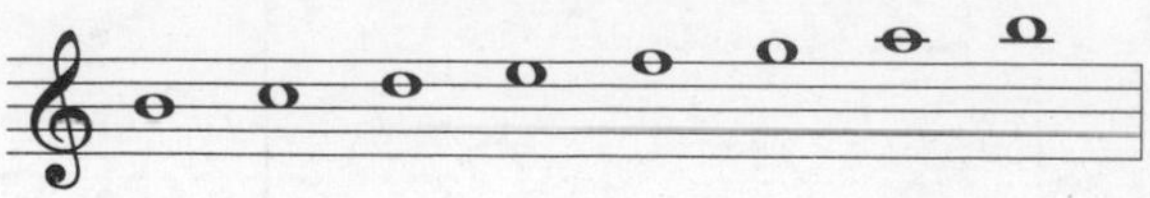

B Locrian Mode

The locrian scale is the seventh mode in the major scale family and contains the same notes as the major scale a minor 2nd above. The locrian scale is the least stable mode in the major scale modal family because of the interval of a diminished 5th between the first and fifth notes in the scale. The locrian scale is used when improvising over the half-diminished chord, which may be thought of as a minor 7th chord with a flatted 5th.

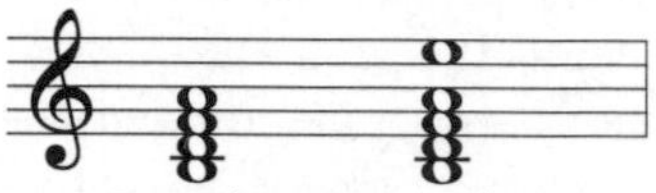

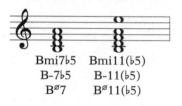

Bmi7♭5	Bmi11(♭5)
B-7♭5	B-11(♭5)
Bø7	Bø11(♭5)

The *half-diminished 7th chord* consists of a root, a minor 3rd, a diminished 5th, and a minor 7th. The lowered 2nd of the locrian scale (or ♭9th) is not typically considered to be a usable chord extension, but the 11th is frequently added. Occasionally a major 9th is added to the half-diminished chord, but this note is derived from a mode of the melodic minor family called the *locrian ♯2 scale* (see Chapter 17).

The half-diminished chord is usually used as a supertonic (iiø7) chord in a minor ii–V–i progression, although it may also occur as a *leading-tone* (viiø7) chord in a major key or a *secondary leading-tone* chord (see Chapter 7). In a minor iiø7–V–i progression, the V chord is altered by adding a ♯ 9th or a ♭9th, and often a ♯ 5th or a ♭5th as well. The preferred scale choice for improvising over an altered V7 chord is a mode of the melodic minor family called the *diminished/whole-tone scale*, which will be discussed in Chapter 17.

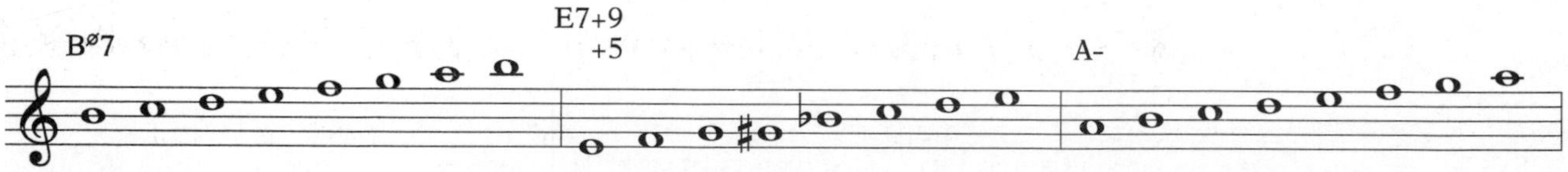

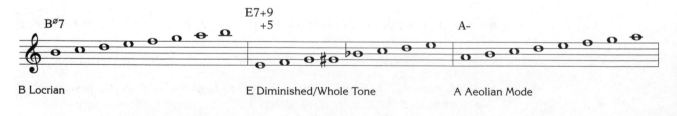

B Locrian — E Diminished/Whole Tone — A Aeolian Mode

Theory/Ear Exercises

1. Write the aeolian and locrian scales in all twelve keys.
2. Write half-diminished chords in all twelve keys.

3. *Keyboard skills*: Play minor ii$^{\varnothing}$7–V7♭9–i progressions in twelve keys as follows:

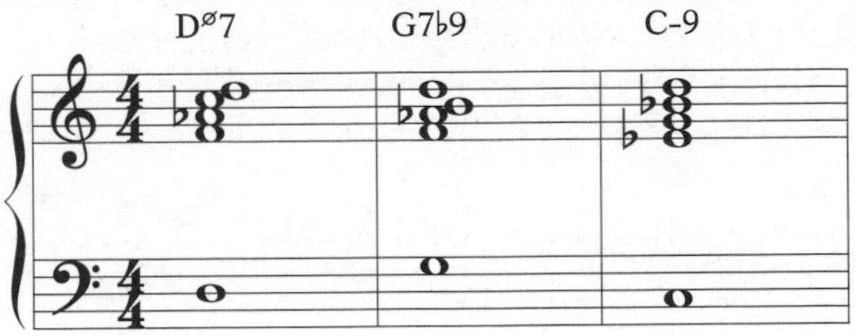

4. *Melodic and harmonic dictation*: Notate melodies based on all scales and chords previously studied.
5. *Transcription*: Transcribe a melody, a chord progression, or an improvised solo from a recording.

Gaining Facility with Minor ii$^{\varnothing}$7–V7–i Progressions

Practice the following exercises over the chord progression below, using either a metronome or the play-along recordings from *Creative Beginnings: An Introduction to Jazz Improvisation* (track 9) or volume 3, *The ii–V–I Progression* (track 5), of *A New Approach to Jazz Improvisation* by Jamey Aebersold. If you find yourself struggling with an exercise, slow it down, simplify it, or sing it while visualizing yourself playing it. After familiarizing yourself with the exercises, pick one or two to practice repeatedly, until you can play them without any conscious thought.

C instruments begin here

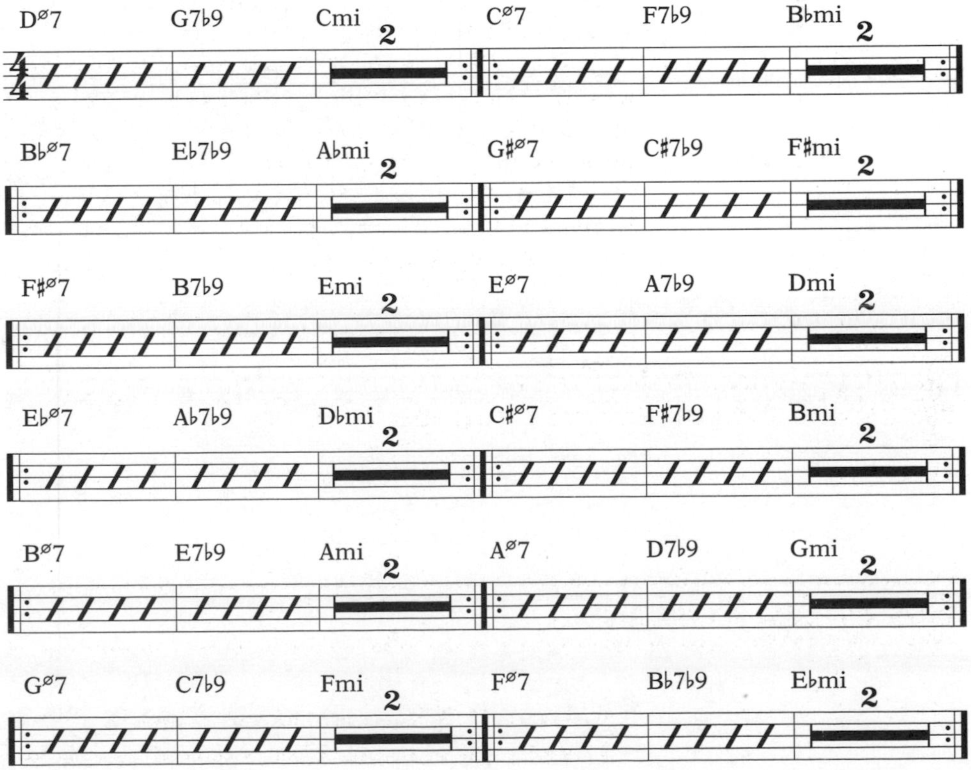

B♭ instruments begin here

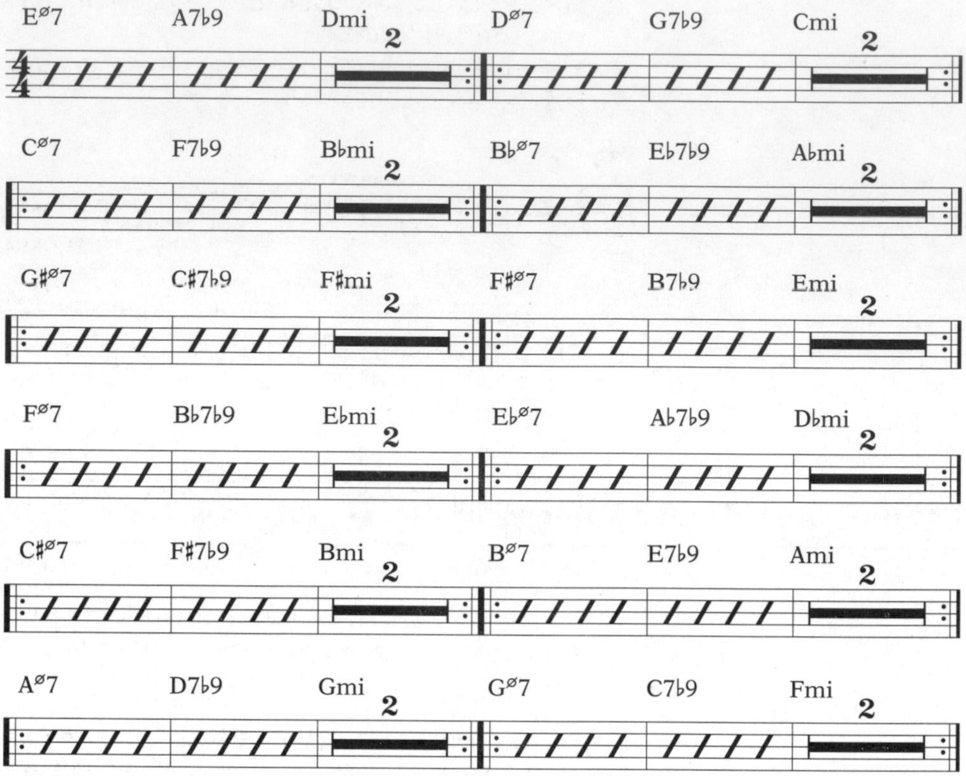

E♭ instruments begin here

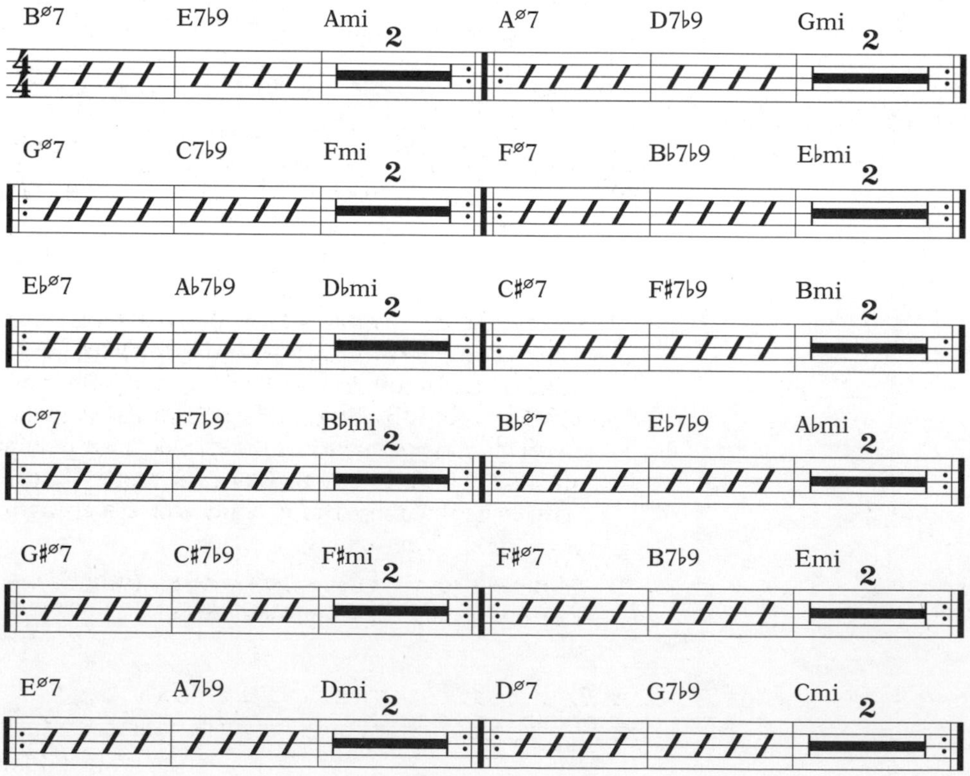

1. *Call and response warmups*: Have another musician or teacher play a phrase that fits over a minor iiø7–V7♭9–i progression. Play back the phrase you have just heard.
2. The locrian scale: Try thinking of the major scale a half-step above the starting note.

MM ____________________

3. The half-diminished 7th and dominant 7th ♭9 arpeggios.

MM ____________________

4. A variation on a Charlie Parker motive from his "The Bird" solo (*Charlie Parker—The Verve Years*, Verve 2501).

MM ____________________

5. A variation on a J. J. Johnson motive from his "Flatback" solo (J. J. Johnson, A *Touch of Satin*, Columbia CS 8537).

MM ____________________

6. *Creative Jazz Improvisation*: Tape record yourself improvising over the chord progression. Listen to the tape and critique your rhythm. Is your tempo steady, or do you rush or drag certain passages? Is your time as solid in the difficult keys as it is in the easy keys? If not, devote yourself to resolving any technical issues that may be hindering your rhythm. Make sure to pay attention to what the rhythm section is doing; don't get absorbed in thinking about what you are going to play. *The rhythm is more important than notes.*
7. Make up your own patterns and melodic ideas based on locrian and aeolian scales and iiø7–i progressions.

   a.

MM ____________________

b.

MM ______________

Improvising on Jazz Compositions Based on ii$^{\varnothing}$7–V7♭9–i Progressions

Following is a partial list of jazz compositions that contain minor ii$^{\varnothing}$7–V7 ♭9–i progressions. These compositions are found in *The New Real Book*, vol. 1 (NRB), *The New Real Book*, vol. 2 (NR2), one of the volumes of Jamey Aebersold's *New Approach to Jazz Improvisation* (JA), or *Creative Beginnings: An Introduction to Jazz Improvisation* (CB). Memorize the most frequently played songs, and practice them in different keys.

Compositions Based Exclusively on ii$^{\varnothing}$7–V7 ♭9–i Progressions

"Airegin"—Sonny Rollins (JA vol. 8)
"Algo Bueno" ("Woody 'n You")—Dizzy Gillespie (JA vol. 65, NR2)
"Autumn Leaves"—Mercer/Kosma (JA vols. 44 and 67, NRB)
"Blue Autumn"—Scott Reeves (CB)
"Blue Bossa"—Kenny Dorham (JA vols. 38 and 54, NR2)
"Catalonian Nights"—Dexter Gordon (JA vol. 82)
"Come Candela"—Mongo Santamaria (JA vol. 64)
"Crescent"—John Coltrane (JA vol. 27)
"Curacao"—Cal Tjader (JA vol. 64)
"Django"—John Lewis (NR2)
"Five Hundred Miles High"—Potter/Corea (NRB)
"Four on Six"—Wes Montgomery (JA vol. 62, NRB)
"If I Should Lose You"—Robin/Ranger (JA vol. 22)
"I Hear A Rhapsody"—Frajos/Baker/Gasparre (JA vol. 80)
"In Walked Bud"—Thelonious Monk (NRB)
"I Remember Clifford"—Benny Golson (JA vol. 14)
"It Don't Mean a Thing"—Duke Ellington (JA vol. 48, NR2)
"Linda Chicana"—Mark Levine (JA vol. 64)
"Milestones" (modal version)—Miles Davis (JA vol. 50)
"Mister P.C."—John Coltrane (JA vol. 27)
"Mo' Joe"—Joe Henderson (NR2)
"Montmartre"—Dexter Gordon (JA vol. 82)
"Morning of the Carnival"—Sigmund/Bonfa (NR2)
"Nature Boy"—Eden Ahbez (NRB)
"Night and Day"—Cole Porter (JA vol. 51)
"Peace"—Horace Silver (JA vol. 17)
"Pretty Eyes"—Horace Silver (JA vol. 86)
"Road Song"—Wes Montgomery (JA vol. 62)
"Round Midnight"—Thelonious Monk (JA vol. 56)
"Softly As in a Morning Sunrise"—Richard Rodgers (JA vol. 40)
"Song for My Father"—Horace Silver (JA vols. 17 and 54, NR2)
"Sugar"—Stanley Turrentine (JA vols. 49 and 70)
"Summertime"—George Gershwin (JA vols. 25 and 54)

"There Is No Greater Love"—Symes/Jones (JA vol. 34, NR2)
"What Is This Thing Called Love?"—Cole Porter (JA vols. 15, 41, and 74)
"Woody 'n You" ("Algo Buena")—Dizzy Gillespie (JA vol. 32, NR2)
"Work Song"—Nat Adderly" (JA vol. 13)
"Yesterdays"—Kern/Harbach (JA vols. 55 and 85, NRB)
"You and the Night and the Music"—Dietz/Schwartz (JA vol. 41)
"You Don't Know What Love Is"—Raye/DePaul (JA vol. 32)

Milt Jackson's Improvised Solo on "Django"

Milt Jackson's improvised vibraphone solo on the John Lewis composition "Django" was transcribed from the *Smithsonian Collection* and is also available on *The European Concert*, Atlantic 2-603. It was recorded in 1960 by the Modern Jazz Quartet, which also included John Lewis on piano, Percy Heath on bass, and Connie Kay on drums.

Milt Jackson was the first vibraphonist to adapt the bebop language to that instrument. At the beginning of his career, he played with Charlie Parker, Miles Davis, Thelonious Monk, and the other important figures in the bebop movement. The nucleus of the Modern Jazz Quartet began as the rhythm section of Dizzy Gillespie's big band; with some personnel changes, it became one of the longest-lived combos in the history of jazz. Their unique approach to group interplay, counterpoint, and compositional structure, combined with restrained, yet bluesy improvisations, captured a large general audience. Milt's virtuosic solos and strong affinity for the blues provided a good foil to John Lewis's more understated, developmental approach.

"Django" consists of one motive that sequences upward for twelve bars, and downward for eight bars in a truncated form. The melody is so well constructed that no notes could be added or taken away from it. The solos are not based on the twenty-bar melody but instead use an AABC form. The A section is a six-bar progression in F minor, the B section an eight-bar ii$^{\varnothing}$7–i progression in B♭ minor over a dominant pedal point, and the C section a twelve-bar phrase consisting of four bars in B♭ minor and eight bars of a bluesy progression in D♭. An interlude derived from the primary motive of the composition occurs between each solo in a shortened two-bar form.

Milt Jackson's solo consists primarily of a continuous melodic line; the only examples of motivic development are in bars 45–48 and 62–65. (This contrasts with John Lewis's solo, which is primarily motivic.) Subtleties of his approach are apparent in the dynamic changes in bars 7, 11, 13, 19, 21, 24, 34, 42, 44, 46, and 52, and in his varied attacks and ghosted notes. His penchant for the blues is evident in his use of the blues scale in bars 3–4, 11–12, 31, 37, and 53, and the minor pentatonic scale in bars 26–27 and 57–64. We also find the use of the locrian and aeolian scales in bars 7–8, 13–19, and 45-51. Chord alterations include the use of the ♯9th and ♭9th in bar 42, and the 3–5–♭7–♭9 arpeggio over the dominant chords in bars 40 and 54. His rhythm is swinging throughout, with prominent use of triplet figures. The tempo is approximately 𝅗𝅥 = 88.

After listening closely to a recording of this solo, practice it at different tempos with the metronome clicking on beats 2 and 4. Then continue improvising in the same style. (The third chorus has been omitted.)

Treble-clef C instruments:

34
Gø7 C7♭9 F7 B♭-7 E♭7 A♭7 D♭7
38
C7ø9 F- Gø7 C7♭9
41
F7 B♭-7 E♭7 A♭7 D♭7 C7♭9 F- Cø7
F ped.
46
B♭- Cø7 B♭- Cø7
50
B♭- Cø7 F7♭9 B♭-
end ped.
54
Cø7 F7♭9 B♭7 E♭7 A♭7 D♭7
57
G♭7 D♭7 G♭7
62
D♭7 Gø7 C7♭9 F-

B♭ instruments (Trumpet—8va bassa where indicated):

34
Aø7 D7♭9 G7 C-7 F7 B♭7 E♭7
3
3
38
D7ø9 G- Aø7 D7♭9
3
3
41
G7 C-7 F7 B♭7 E♭7 D7♭9 G- Dø7
G ped.
f
p
46
C- Dø7 C- Dø7
3
3
f
50
C- Dø7 G7♭9 C-
end ped.
3
ff
3
trpt. 8va bassa
54
Dø7 G7♭9 C7 F7 B♭7 E♭7
3
3
(8va)
57
A♭7 E♭7 A♭7
(8va)
62
E♭7 Aø7 D7♭9 G-

E♭ instruments:

34
E∅7 A7♭9 D7 G-7 C7 F7 B♭7
38
A7∅9 D- E∅7 A7♭9
41
D7 G-7 C7 F7 B♭7 A7♭9 D- A∅7
D ped.
f p
46
G- A∅7 G- A∅7
f
50
G- A∅7 D7♭9 end ped. G-
ff
54
A∅7 D7♭9 G7 C7 F7 B♭7
57
E♭7 B♭7 E♭7
62
B♭7 E∅7 A7♭9 D-

Bass-clef instruments:

34
Gø7 C7♭9 F7 B♭-7 E♭7 A♭7 D♭7
38
C7ø9 opt. 8va F- Gø7 C7♭9
41
F7 B♭-7 E♭7 A♭7 D♭7 C7♭9 F- Cø7
F ped.
46
B♭- Cø7 B♭- Cø7
50
B♭- Cø7 F7♭9 end ped. B♭-
54
Cø7 F7♭9 B♭7 E♭7 A♭7 D♭7
57
G♭7 D♭7 G♭7
62
D♭7 Gø7 C7♭9 F-

9

Lydian and Phrygian Scales, Major 7th ♭5 Chords

"Improvisation is the courage to move
from one note to the next. It's that simple.
Once you conquer that basic fear,
when you are able to make that leap
from one note to the next without thinking
or preparing for it, then you are improvising."

vocalist Bobby McFerrin[1]

The *lydian mode* consists of the ascending pattern: whole step, whole step, whole step, half step, whole step, whole step, half step.

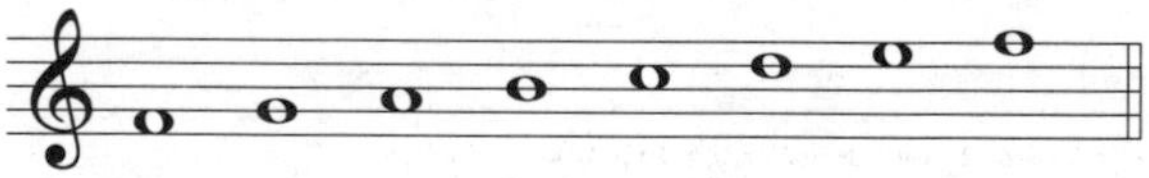

F Lydian Mode

The lydian mode is the fourth mode in the major scale family and contains the same notes as the major scale a perfect 4th below. The lydian mode may also be thought of as a major scale with the fourth note raised a half step. Like the major scale, the lydian mode may be used in improvising over major triads, major 7th chords, and major 9th chords. Because of its raised fourth degree, the lydian mode may also be used over the following chords: major 7th ♭5, major 7th ♯11, and major 13th ♯11 (which may also be written as a bitonal chord: G/F M7).

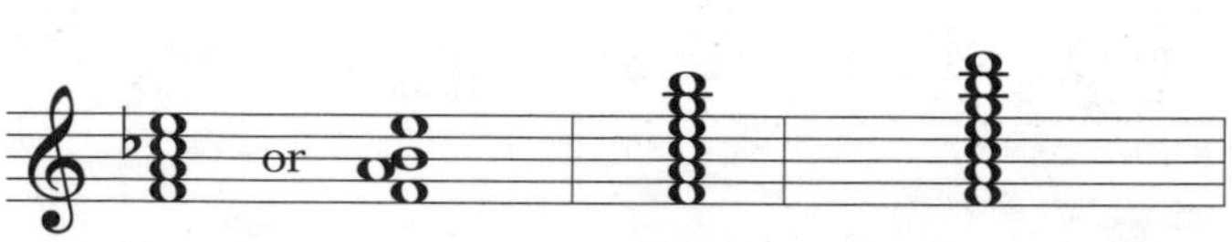

FM7♭5 F△7♭5 | FM7♯11 F△7♯11 | FM13♯11(G/FM7) F△13♯11(G/F△7)

The major 7th ♭5 chord consists of a root, a major 3rd, a diminished 5th, and a major 7th. The major 7th ♯11 chord consists of a root, a major 3rd, a perfect 5th, a major 7th, a major 9th, and an augmented 11th. A major 13th may be added to this chord, resulting in the lydian scale stacked in 3rds.

In a major key, major 7th chords function as either I (tonic) or IV (subdominant) chords. The lydian scale is generally the best scale choice when the major chord is functioning as a IV chord or is altered, while the major scale works best over the I chord in a ii–V–I progression.

[1] Bill Milkowski, "Swing, Soul, Sincerity—A Bobby McFerrin Workshop," *Downbeat*, 60, no. 11 (November 1993), 58.

The major 7th g5 chord may occur as a gII chord in a progression in which the i chord is colored by the phrygian scale and the gII chord by the lydian scale.

When this relationship occurs, both scales will be comprised of the same notes.

The *phrygian scale* consists of the ascending pattern: half step, whole step, whole step, whole step, half step, whole step, whole step.

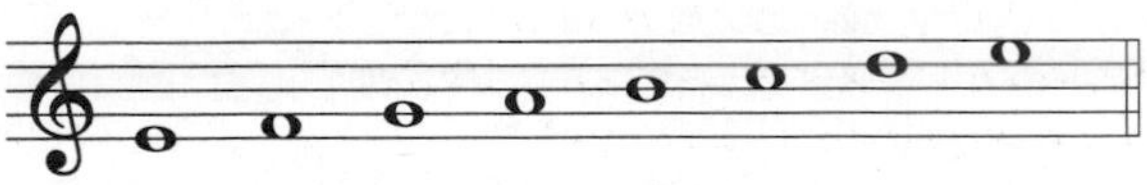

E Phrygian Mode

The phrygian scale is the third mode in the major scale family and contains the same notes as the major scale a major 3rd below. The phrygian scale may also be thought of as an aeolian scale with the second note lowered one half step. Although the phrygian scale is a type of minor scale, it is often used independently from a specific chord. When a phrygian color is desired, the word "phrygian" usually appears in place of a chord symbol:

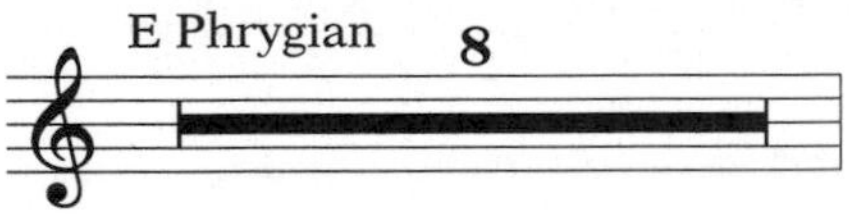

To comp, harmonic instruments generally play a cluster derived from the phrygian scale. Two common phrygian voicings are ♭2–4–5–8 (equivalent to the major 7th ♭5 chord a half step above the tonic of the phrygian mode) and 1–♭2–4–5.

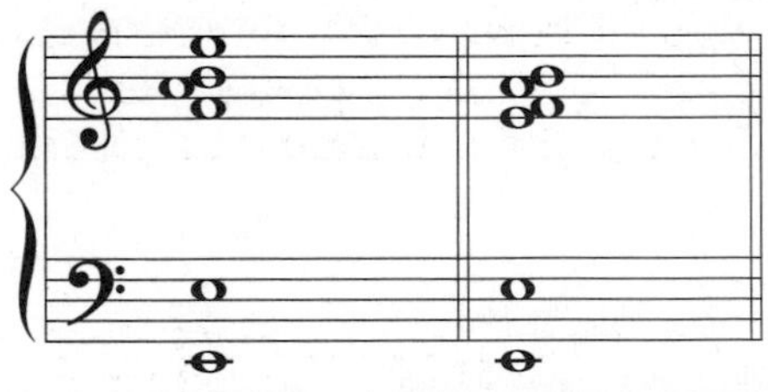

A variation of the phrygian scale, known as the *Spanish phrygian*, replaces the minor 3rd with a major 3rd. It is the fifth mode in the *harmonic minor* scale family,

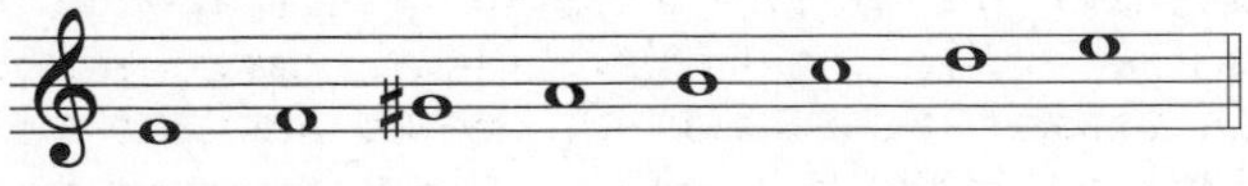

E Spanish Phrygian

and can be used to color all the chords in a I–♭II–♭III progression.

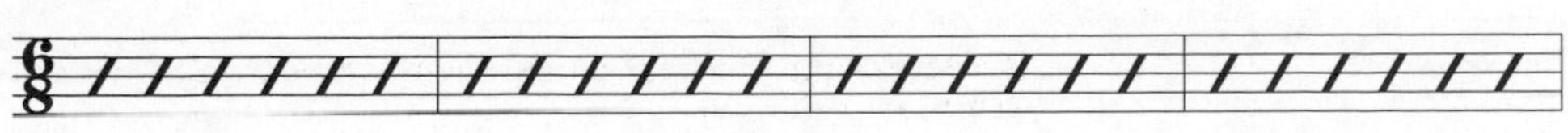

Theory/Ear Exercises

1. Write the lydian and phrygian scales in all twelve keys.
2. *Melodic and harmonic dictation*: Notate melodies based on all scales and chords previously studied.
3. *Transcription*: Transcribe a melody, a chord progression, or an improvised solo from a recording.

Gaining Facility with Lydian and Phrygian Scales

Practice the following exercises over the chord progression below, using a metronome. If you find yourself struggling with an exercise, slow it down, simplify it, or sing it while visualizing yourself playing it. After familiarizing yourself with the exercises, pick one or two to practice repeatedly, until you can play them without any conscious thought.

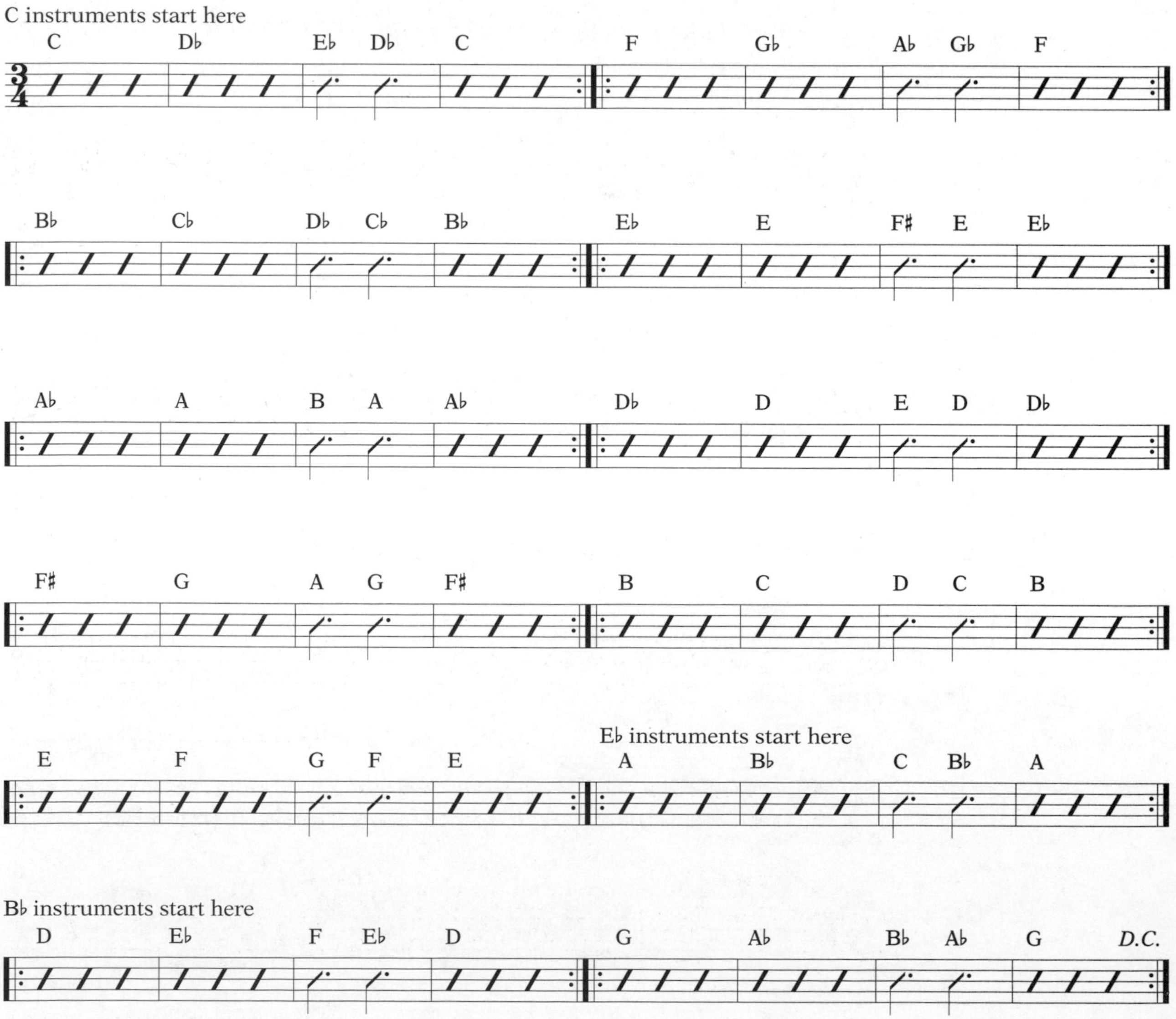

1. *Call and response warmups*: Have another musician or teacher play a phrase that fits over a ♭II–i progression. Play back the phrase you have just heard.
2. The lydian and phrygian scales.

MM ____________________

3. The Spanish phrygian scale.

MM ____________________

4. A variation on a Michael Brecker idea (Chick Corea, *Three Quartets*, Warner Brothers BSK 3552).

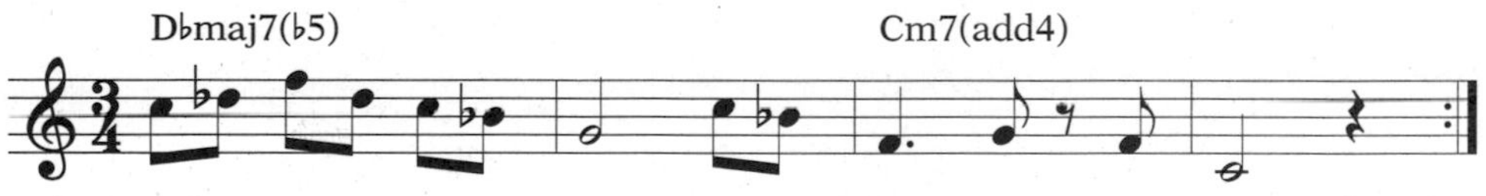

MM ____________________

5. The major 7 ♭5 arpeggio, ascending stepwise.

MM ____________________

6. The major 7 ♭5 arpeggio, descending stepwise.

MM ____________________

7. A variation on a Chick Corea motive from his *Captain Senor Mouse* solo (Chick Corea, *Hymn of the Seventh Galaxy*, Warner Brothers BSK 3552).

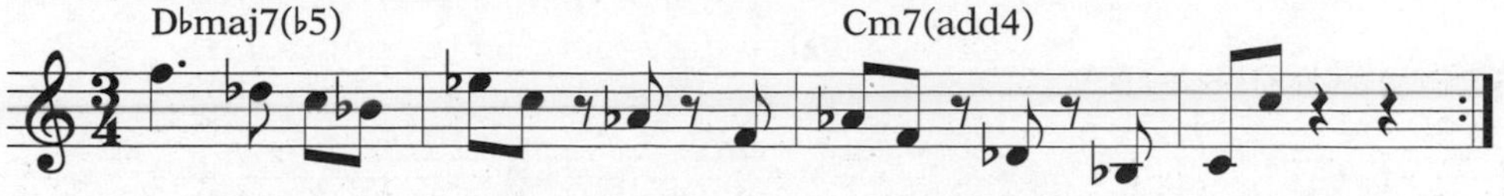

MM ____________________

8. A variation on a Chick Corea motive from his *Cosmic Rain* solo (Chick Corea, *Hymn of the Seventh Galaxy*, Warner Brothers BSK 3552).

MM ______________________

9. *Creative Jazz Improvisation*

a. Sing, clap, or play polyrhythms of two-against-three (dotted quarters in 3/4 meter). Then improvise over the chord progression without looking at the chord symbols, using polyrhythms in your improvisation.

b. When improvising over the chord progression, don't feel that you have to play continually. Maintain a calm center, and listen to the silence between your phrases.

10. Make up your own exercises and melodic ideas based on phrygian and lydian scales.

a.

MM ______________________

b.

MM ______________________

Improvising on Jazz Compositions Based on Major 7 ♭5 Chords and Lydian Scales, or i–♭ii Progressions and Phrygian Scales

Following is a partial list of jazz compositions that contain major 7 ♭5 chords or i–♭ii progressions and phrygian scales. These compositions are found in *The New Real Book*, vol. 1 (NRB), *The New Real Book*, vol. 2 (NR2), one of the volumes of Jamey Aebersold's *New Approach to Jazz Improvisation* (JA), or *Creative Beginnings: An Introduction to Jazz Improvisation* (CB). Memorize the most frequently played songs, and practice them in different keys.

Compositions In Which Major 7th ♭5 Chords and Lydian Scales Occur Frequently

"Afro-Centric"—Joe Henderson (NR2)
"Black Narcissus"—Joe Henderson (NRB)
"Brite Piece"—David Liebman (JA vol. 19)
"Dream" — Andy LaVerne (JA vol. 85)
"E.S.P."—Wayne Shorter (JA vol. 33)
"Gloria's Step"—Scott La Faro (NRB)

"In Case You Haven't Heard"—Woody Shaw (JA vol. 9)
"Infant Eyes"—Wayne Shorter (JA vol. 33)
"Inner Urge"—Joe Henderson (JA vol. 38)
"Katrina Ballerina"—Woody Shaw (JA vol. 9)
"Loft Dance"—David Liebman (JA vol. 19)
"Moon Alley"—Tom Harrell (JA vol. 63)
"Nefertiti"—Wayne Shorter (JA, NRB)
"Scene"—Tom Harrell (JA vol. 63)
"Sky Dive"—Freddie Hubbard (JA vol. 60)
"Time Remembered"—Bill Evans (JA vol. 45, NR2)
"Tomorrow's Destiny"—Woody Shaw (JA vol. 9)
"Wildflower"—Wayne Shorter (JA vol. 33)

Compositions In Which i–♭II Progressions or Phrygian Scales Occur Frequently

"Ana Maria"—Wayne Shorter (NRB)
"A Night in Tunisia"—Dizzy Gillespie (JA vol. 43)
"Buffalo Wings"—Tom Harrell (JA vol. 63)
"Caravan"—Ellington, Mills, Tizol (JA vol. 59)
"El Toro"—Wayne Shorter (JA vol. 38)
"Olè"—John Coltrane (NR2)
"Serenade To A Soul Sister" — Horace Silver (JA vol. 86)
"Spain"—Chick Corea (NR2)
"Speak No Evil"—Wayne Shorter (JA vol. 33, NRB)
"The Sun King"—David Liebman (JA vol. 81)
"Windows"—Chick Corea (NR2)

Miles Davis's Improvised Solo on "Solea"

Miles Davis's improvised trumpet solo on the Gil Evans composition "Solea" was transcribed from the 1960 Miles Davis album *Sketches of Spain* (Columbia Records CS 8721), and may also be found on *Miles Davis & Gil Evans: The Complete Columbia Studio Recordings* (Columbia 67397). This classic recording frames Miles's trumpet with Gil Evans's lush orchestrations for large ensemble, backed by a rhythm section consisting of bassist Paul Chambers and drummer Jimmy Cobb, along with Elvin Jones on percussion.

"Solea" is based on an Andalusian folk song with a flamenco rhythm. Evans stated, "I chose this rhythm because it kind of (swung) and was conducive to development."[2] The title is derived from *soledad*, the Spanish word for *loneliness*, and Miles responds with what critic Nat Hentoff describes as a "great depth of emotion and strength of rhythm that represents a compelling blend of the 'deep song' of flamenco and the cry of the blues."[3]

After a plaintive rubato introduction, Miles improvises over a series of orchestral interludes based on a phrygian vamp. The following transcription begins 9:28 into the 12:15 track and showcases Miles's last two statements. The first episode is accompanied by a continually building orchestral vamp, which winds down at bar 45. Miles then continues with rhythm section alone to close out the piece.

[2] Nat Hentoff, booklet accompanying *Miles Davis & Gil Evans: The Complete Columbia Studio Recordings*, Columbia 67397, Sony Music Entertainment (1996), 130.
[3] Ibid.

Like Ravel's "Bolero," the static harmony of the vamp serves to focus attention on the melodic tension, colorful orchestration, and variations in dynamics. Throughout, Miles develops short rhythmic figures which build to a climax. His use of the range of the trumpet is extraordinary, ranging from the lowest note on the horn (concert E3 in measure 44) to D6 in bar 25, nearly three octaves above. Most of his melodic ideas are based on the phrygian scale or the Spanish phrygian scale, although the blues scale is hinted at in bar 15. Bars 35–39 feature an extensive use of a 3 against 2 polyrhythm. Miles's use of space, strong melodic contours, and half-valve effects are also noteworthy.

The march-like tempo is approximately ♩ = 130 m.m. and is notated with a simple-meter 6/4 time signature. To capture the flavor of the solo, practice it along with the recording, or with other musicians performing the phrygian vamp.

Treble-clef C instruments:

28
p
fz
mf
32
36
freely
39
bend
44
pp
mf
49
52
hold back
f
55
hold back
58
p
hold back
62
hold back
pp

B♭ instruments:

Miles's solo—last two episodes

freely
bend
hold back
hold back
hold back
hold back
p
fz
mf
pp
f

E♭ instruments:

freely
bend
hold back
hold back
hold back
hold back

Bass-clef instruments:

freely
bend
hold back
hold back
hold back
hold back

PART 3 Chord Substitutions, Harmonic Structures, and Forms

10

The Blues Scale, the Blues Form, and Chord Substitutions

"First you find the logical way,
and when you find it, avoid it,
and let your inner self break through
and guide you."

composer Will Marion Cook's advice to the young Duke Ellington[1]

Jazz has its origin in the *blues*, an uniquely African-American contribution to the world's music. The word "blues" means many things—it can denote a feeling of sadness or frustration, or it can refer to a style of music called "The Blues." For most jazz musicians, however, the word "blues" is used to describe a particular form, which may or may not have a "bluesy" feeling.

The Blues Form

The blues form has evolved and changed over the course of the twentieth century. The earliest style of blues, *rural blues*, relied on basic I–V–V chord progressions in three phrases, typically in this format: 1) statement, 2) reiteration of statement, and 3) response. Although the blues form later became standardized to consist of three phrases of four bars each (for a total of twelve bars), rural blues songs were often not so symmetrical, with extra bars or beats often added to the phrases. "Hellhound on My Trail," by Robert Johnson (*Smithsonian Collection, 1st ed.*), demonstrates this personalized approach to the blues form.

The *classic* or *urban blues* style refined and codified the blues form into the 12-bar format, and composers like W. C. Handy began presenting it as notated composition. Most of the blues from this period were variations on this basic progression:

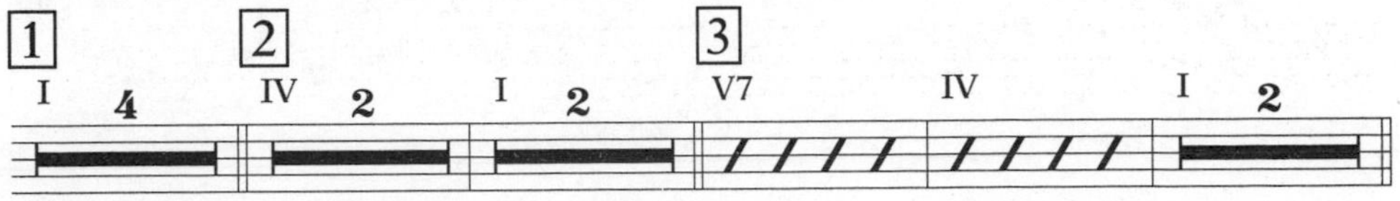

The Basic Blues Progression

[1] John Edward Hasse, *Beyond Catagory: The Life and Genius of Duke Ellington*, Da Capo Press, 1995, p. 78.

A common variation used the IV or V chord in the second bar, omitted the IV chord from the tenth bar, and added a V7 chord in the last bar (referred to as the "turnaround"):

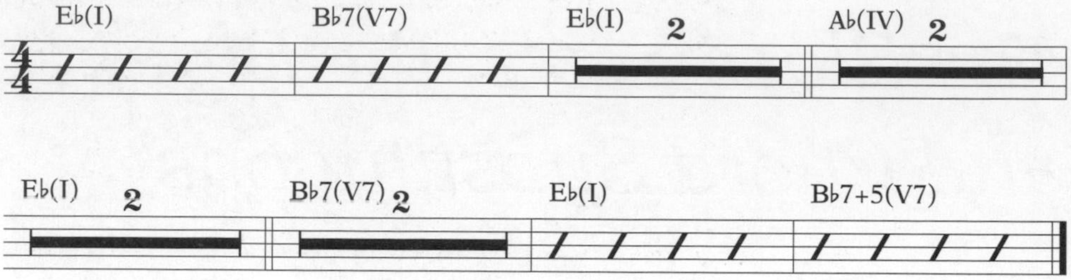

Bessie Smith, "Lost Your Head Blues" (*Smithsonian Collection*)

These same basic progressions are still commonly used and can be found in the music of urban blues performers such as B. B. King and Muddy Waters and early rock'n' roll musicians such as Elvis Presley and Jerry Lee Lewis.

Many of the classic blues compositions also employed verses that were not in the 12-bar format:

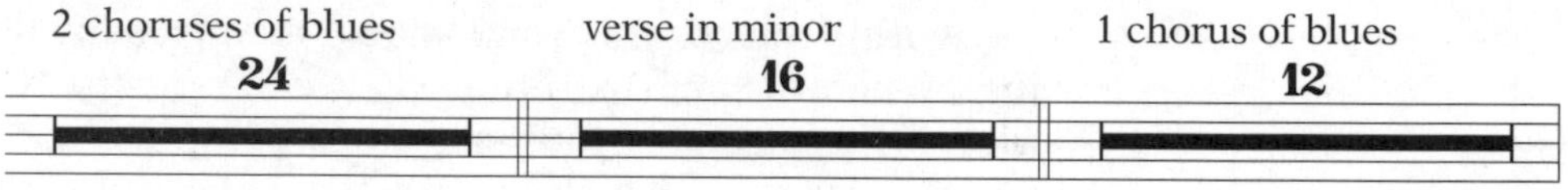

W. C. Handy, "St. Louis Blues" (*Smithsonian Collection*)

Early jazz composers in New Orleans and Chicago began adding some passing chords and chord substitutions to the basic blues progression. Although diatonic chords comprised the majority of the chords, secondary dominant chords began to be employed, such as a V/IV in the fourth bar (a dominant chord built on the tonic), a V/ii in the eighth bar (a dominant chord built on the sixth scale degree), and a V/V in the ninth bar (a dominant chord built on the second scale degree).[2] Passing diminished chords and chord inversions also were used, particularly in the second or sixth bar, to create smooth bass lines.

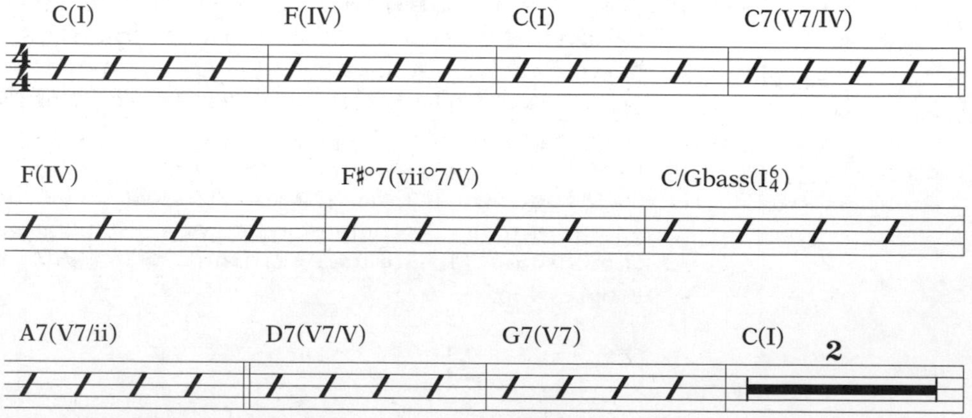

King Oliver, "Dippermouth Blues" (*Smithsonian Collection*)

Some of the compositions from this period called "blues" were not blues at all, but 32-bar binary (ABAB) or song-and-trio forms. Jelly Roll Morton's

[2] For more information on secondary dominants and secondary leading-tone chords, refer to Chapters 5 and 7.

"Wolverine Blues" (*Music of Jelly Roll Morton for Solo Piano, Trio, Quartet and Septet*, Smithsonian 1006) and Louis Armstrong's "Potato Head Blues" (*Smithsonian Collection*) are examples of titled blues that are not in the blues form.

The swing era did not add an abundance of new chord substitutions to the blues form, but 6ths, 7ths, and 9ths were frequently added to the chords. Occasionally, some experimentation was done with the blues form, as in the case of this 18-bar blues written for Andy Kirk's band by Mary Lou Williams and Harry Lawson:

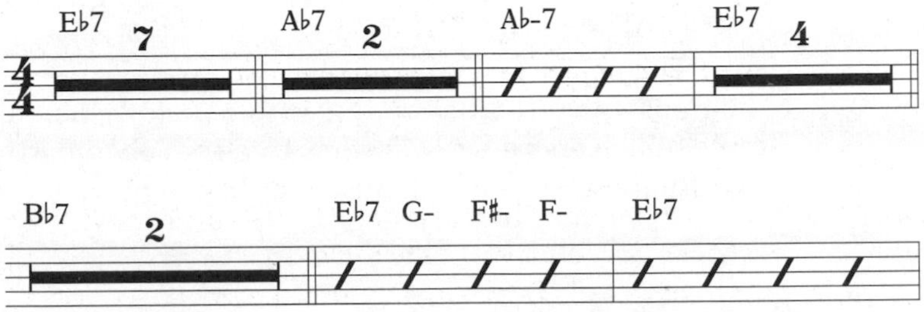

"Big Jim Blues" (head) *(Smithsonian Collection of Big Band Jazz)*

Duke Ellington's "C Jam Blues" added a 4-bar solo break to the beginning of each chorus:

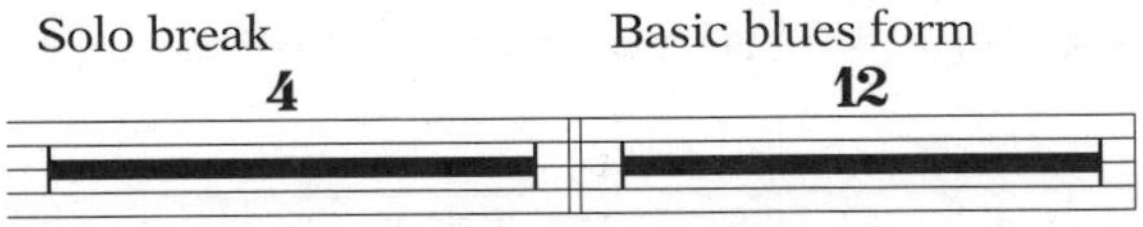

"C Jam Blues" (solos) (*Smithsonian Collection of Big Band Jazz*)

The bebop era brought a significant amount of harmonic variation and chord substitutions to the blues form. The IV chord in the second bar and the V/ii chord in the eighth bar both became commonplace. Bars 9 and 10, as well as the final bar (the "turnaround"), were typically based on ii–V progressions.

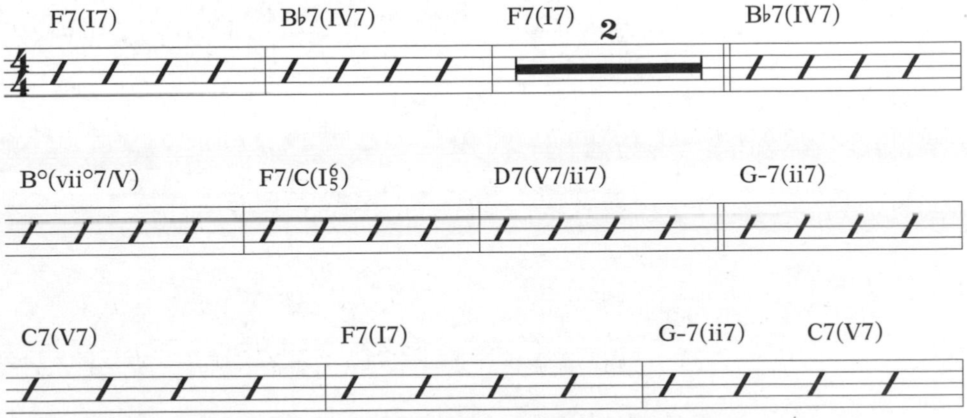

Charlie Parker, "Now's the Time" *(Bird/The Savoy Recordings*, SJL 2201*)*

Sometimes the blues was presented in a major tonality, in lieu of the usual dominant 7th key center. Chord substitutions based on ii–V relationships were added between the I, IV, and V chords.

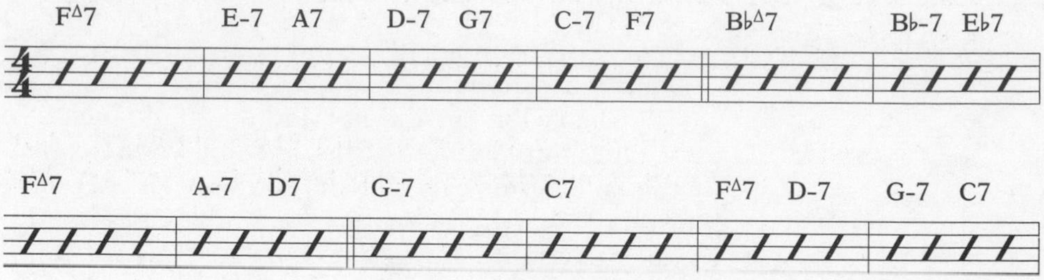

Charlie Parker, "Blues for Alice" (Verve 8010/2515)

The soloist and rhythm section would often use sets of substitutions in their solos that did not appear in the melody, listening to each other to determine which chord substitutions to use in each particular chorus.

In the post-bop era, musicians began playing the blues in different meters:

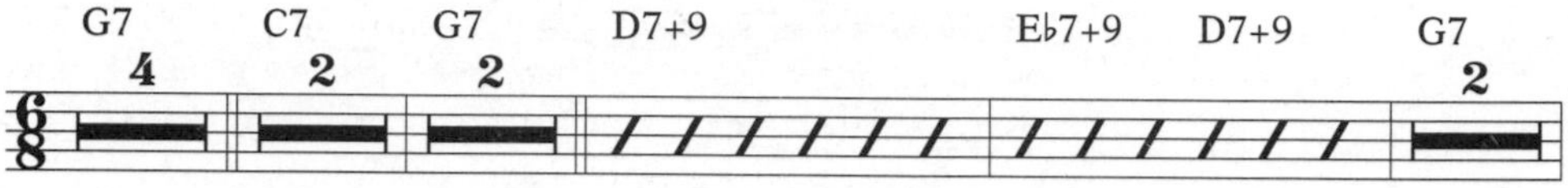

Miles Davis, "All Blues" (*Kind of Blue*, Columbia PC 8163)

Blues in minor keys and experiments in form became more commonplace, as in this 20-bar minor blues:

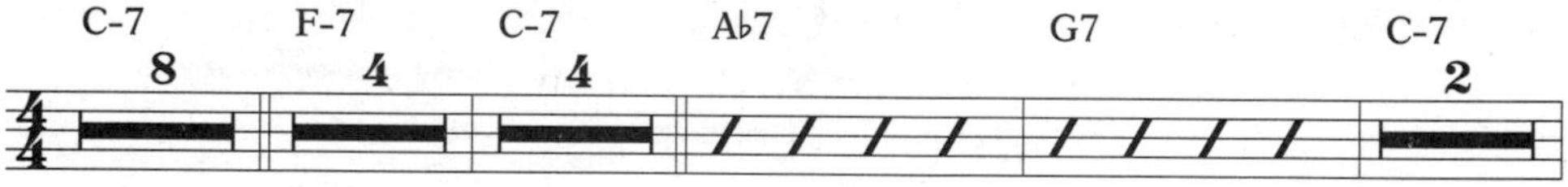

J. J. Johnson, "Shutterbug" (*J. J. Inc.*, Columbia PC 36808)

or this 44-bar blues cast in an AABA form:

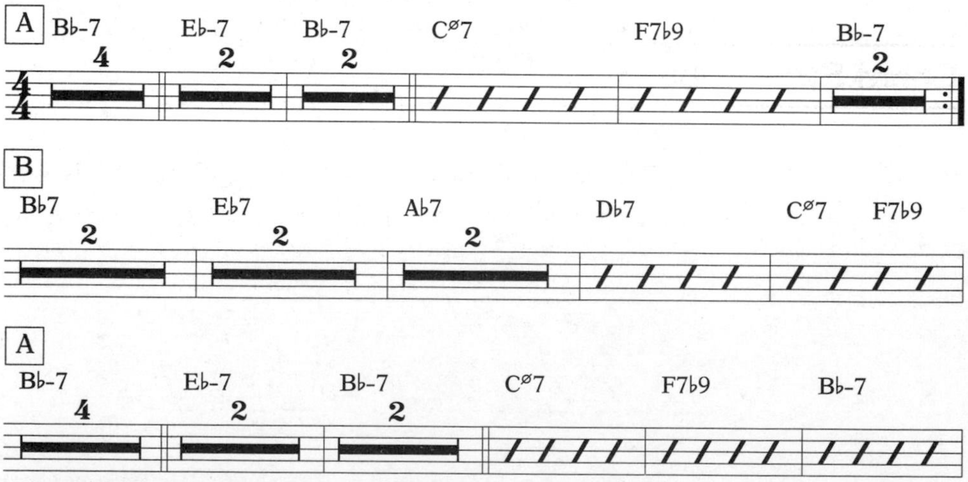

Dexter Gordon, "Bikini" (*Smithsonian Collection*)

In the free jazz period, often only the essential three-phrase structure of the blues was kept intact; the length of the form and the harmonic structure (or lack of one) radically departed from the blues of earlier periods. Yet the basic blues feeling was still at the heart of the music.

The Blues Scale

The *blues scale* is a six-note scale consisting of the ascending pattern: minor 3rd, whole step, half step, half step, minor 3rd, whole step.

C Blues Scale

The pitches a minor 3rd and an augmented 4th (or diminished 5th) above the tonic are often referred to as "blue notes." These are actually an approximation of true "blue notes," which are bent pitches that lie in between the minor and major 3rd and the diminished and perfect 5th. The blues scale may be used in any type of composition to color minor 7th or dominant 7th chords. (In rare instances, it has even been used over major 7th chords.) When it is used over a dominant 7th chord, the minor 3rd of the scale adds an augmented 9th (usually written as a minor 10th) to the chord.

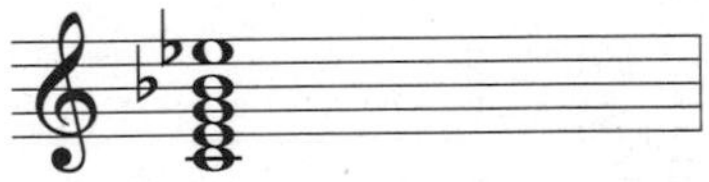

C7♯9 (written enharmonically)

The blues scale built on the root of the I chord can be used to color all the chords in the basic blues progression. This greatly simplifies improvising on the blues, because the player need be concerned with only one scale. Because of its lack of flexibility to imply chord substitutions, the blues scale is best used in combination with other scale choices.

Chord Substitutions

Most chord substitutions are based on the following possibilities:

1. For most dominant 7th chords, you can substitute or add the minor 7th chord a perfect 4th below (and vice versa). Notice that their respective scales have exactly the same notes:

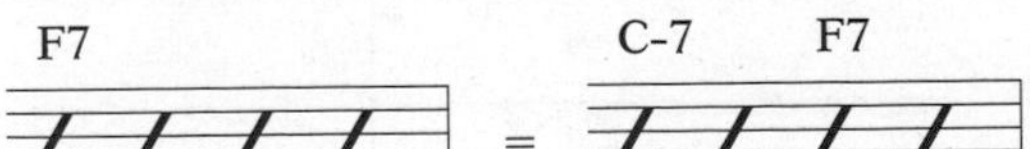

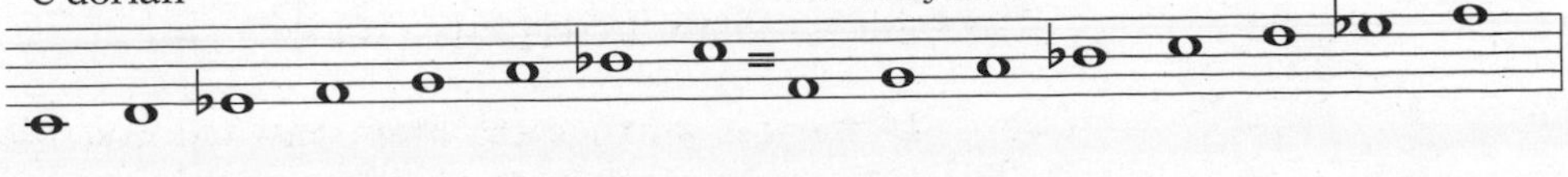

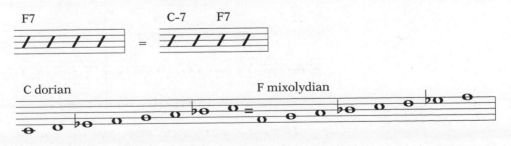

2. For most dominant 7th chords, you can substitute the dominant 7th chord a tritone away. This is commonly referred to as the *tritone substitution*.

Notice that their 3rds and 7ths (the essential members of the chord) are interchangeable:

3. Passing chords may be inserted between the normally occurring chords. This is usually done by means of a stepwise bass line:

or through the use of chord cycles, typically in a ii–V relationship. These chord cycles may move chromatically, by whole steps, 3rds, or 4ths, as long as they resolve logically to the IV chord in the fifth bar and the ii or V chord in the ninth:

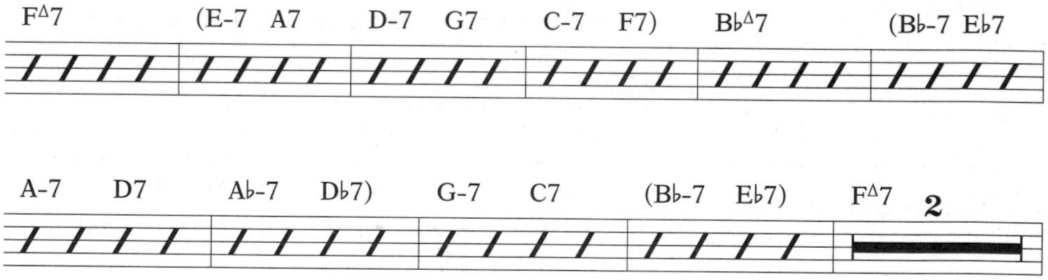

4. Melody permitting, you can change the tonality from a dominant key to a major key (or vice versa):

Blues in F

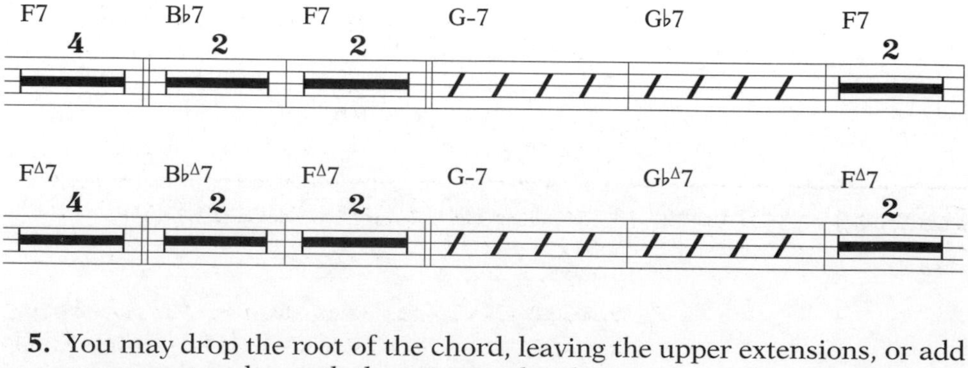

5. You may drop the root of the chord, leaving the upper extensions, or add a new root underneath the existing chord:

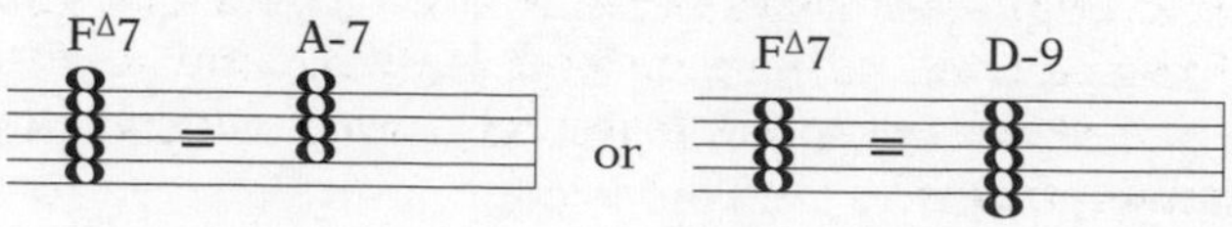

6. Melody permitting, you may substitute any of the dominant 7th chords whose roots belong to the same fully diminished seventh chord:

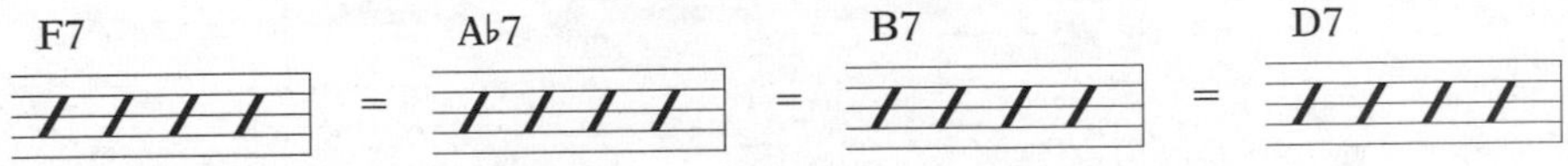

This is due to the fact that all four chords share the same notes in their respective diminished (half-step) scales:

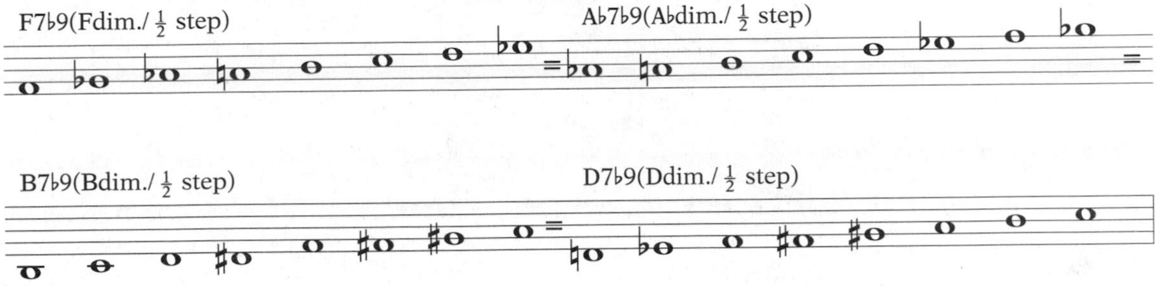

7. In the modern blues form, you may leave the key center or superimpose any tonality, as long as the integrity of the three-phrase structure is maintained.

Theory/Ear Exercises

1. Go through a fake-book and determine which tunes are based on the blues form.
2. Reharmonize a standard tune using the principles of chord substitution discussed in this chapter.
3. *Keyboard skills*: Play the chord progressions from this chapter on the piano.
4. *Transcription*: Transcribe a blues melody or an improvised solo from a recording.

Gaining Facility with the Basic Blues Progression

Practice the following exercises over the chord progression below, using either a metronome or Aebersold play-along volume 42, *Blues in All Keys*. (*Note*: Each track of the play-along starts with the basic blues progression in a different key. Chord substitutions begin after a bell rings on the recording.) If you find yourself struggling with an exercise, slow it down, simplify it, or sing it while visualizing yourself playing it. After familiarizing yourself with the exercises, pick one or two to practice repeatedly, until you can play them without any conscious thought.

C instruments begin here

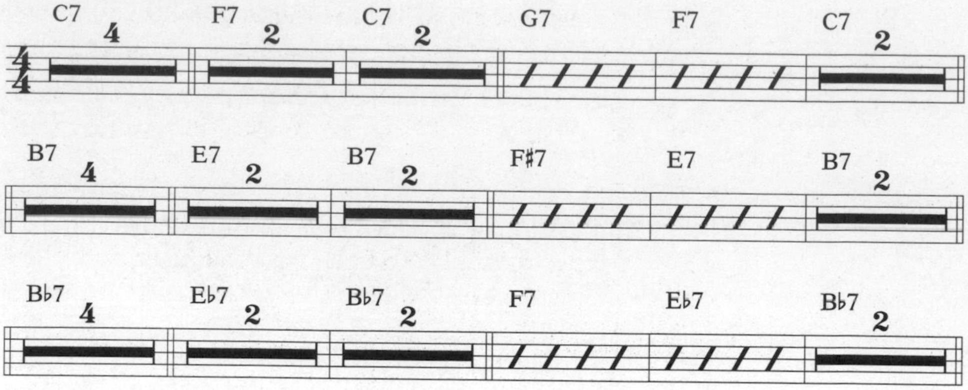

E♭ instruments begin here

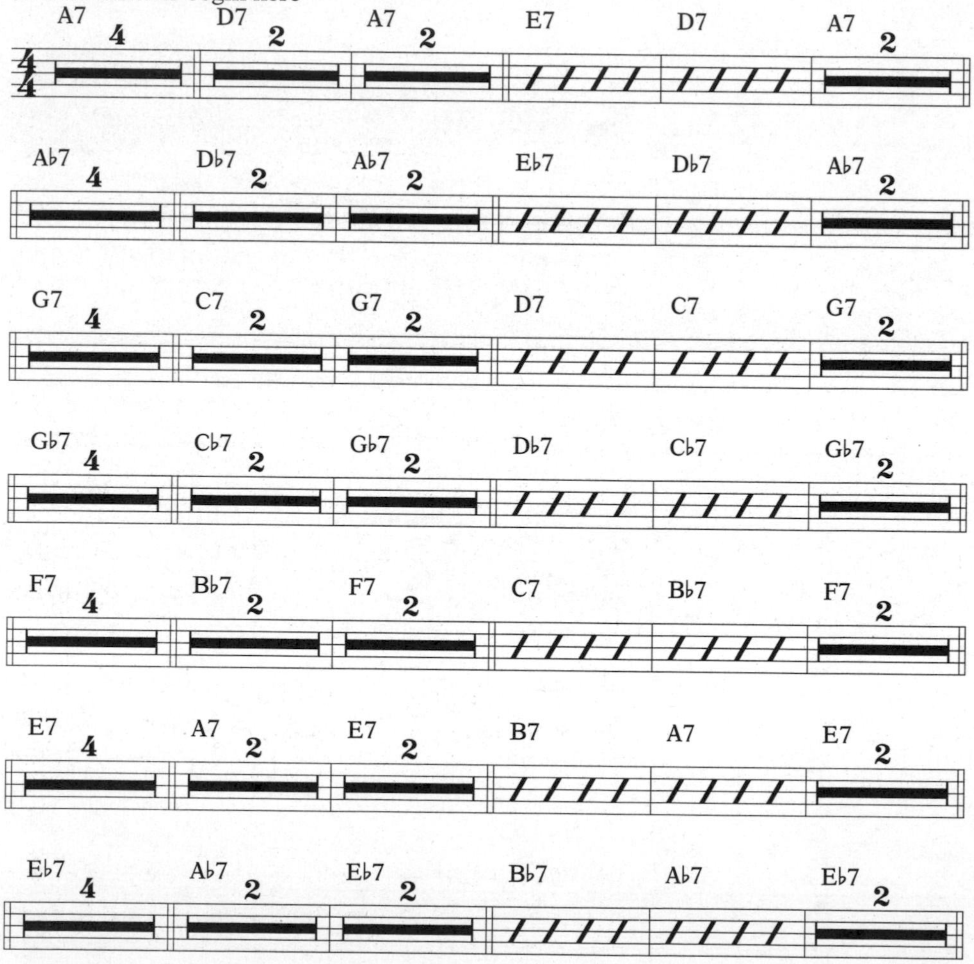

B♭ instruments begin here

1. *Call and response warmups*: Have another musician or teacher play a phrase that fits over the first 4-bar phrase of the blues progression. Play back the phrase you have just heard over the second and third phrase.
2. Outline the blues progression in twelve keys using the blues scale. Use only one blues scale over all the chords in each key.

MM ____________

3. Outline the blues progression in twelve keys using the bebop 7th scale.

MM ____________

4. Many blues tunes are built on a basic idea called a *riff*, which is transposed to fit the chords in the progression. Play the exercise below over the blues progression in twelve keys, then outline the chords with your own riffs.

(continued)

MM ______________________

5. *Creative jazz improvisation*: Trade "fours" with a drummer over the blues progression in all keys, without looking at the chord changes. Don't wait for the drummer to define the first beat of the next "four." Try anticipating the beginning of the phrase by starting with pickup notes.
6. Make up your own exercises and melodic ideas based on blues scales and the blues form.

MM ______________________

Gaining Facility with Blues Substitutions

Note: There is no single play-along recording for all four sets of substitutions used in the progression. Volume 42, *Blues in All Keys*, contains some of these substitutions (after the bell sounds). Volume 6, *All Bird* (track 2), contains progression 1, without the substitution in the fourth bar. Volume 2, *Nothin' But Blues* (track 12), contains progression 2.

C instruments start here

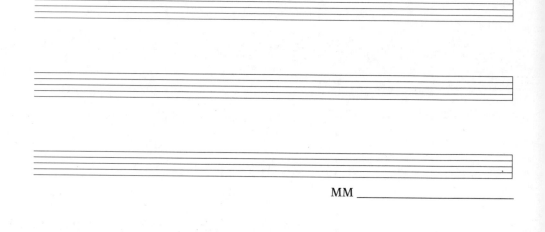

1.

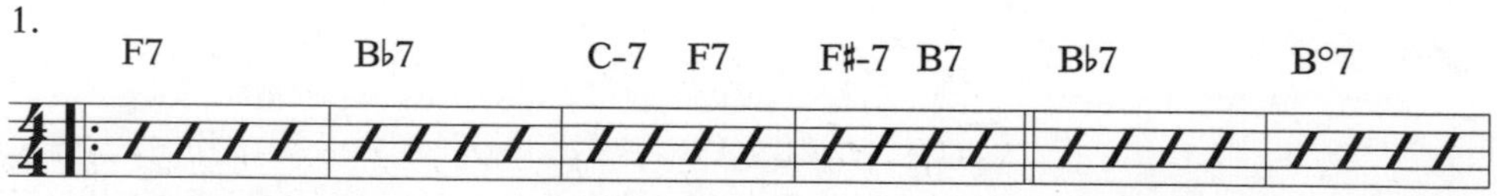

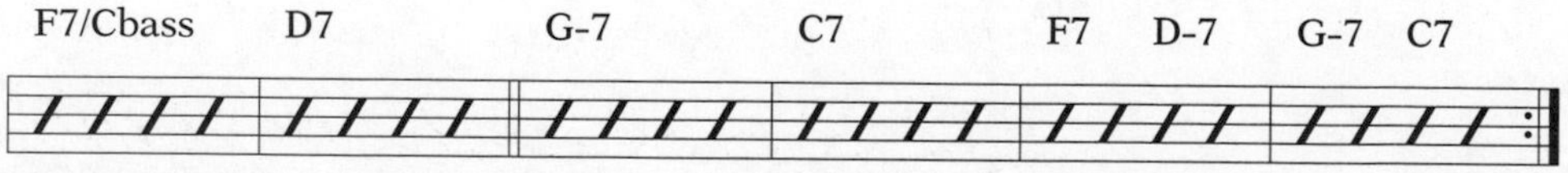

2.

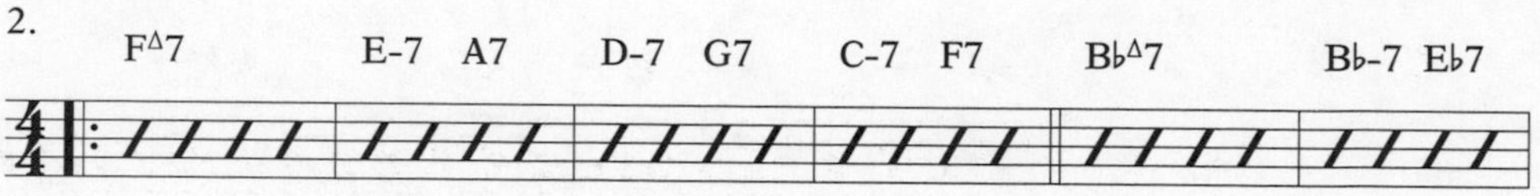

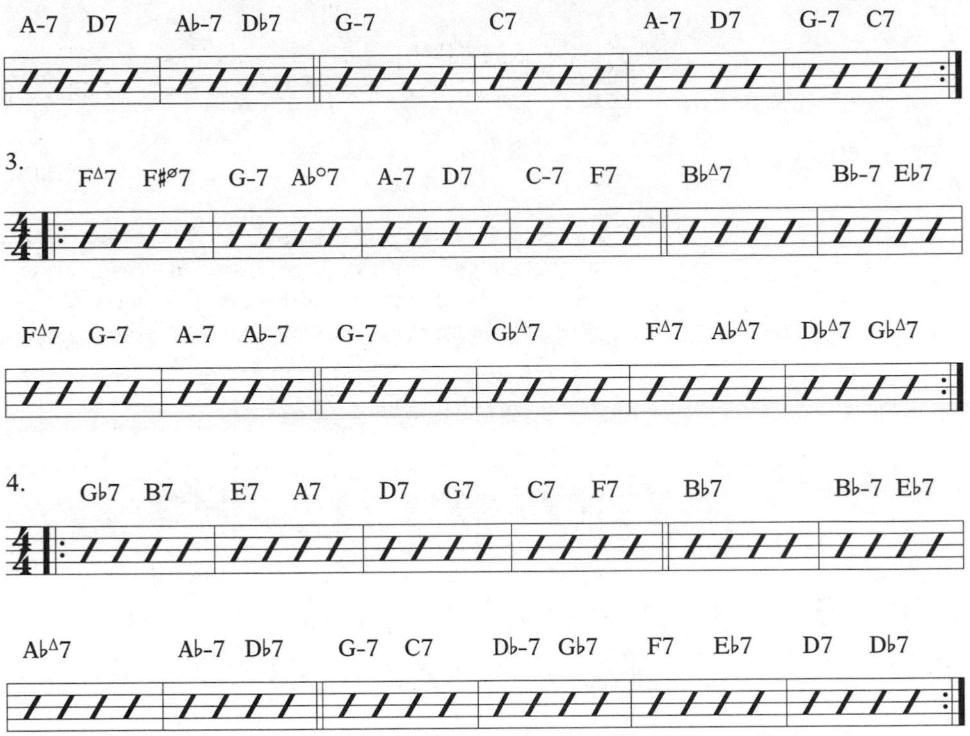

B♭ instruments begin here

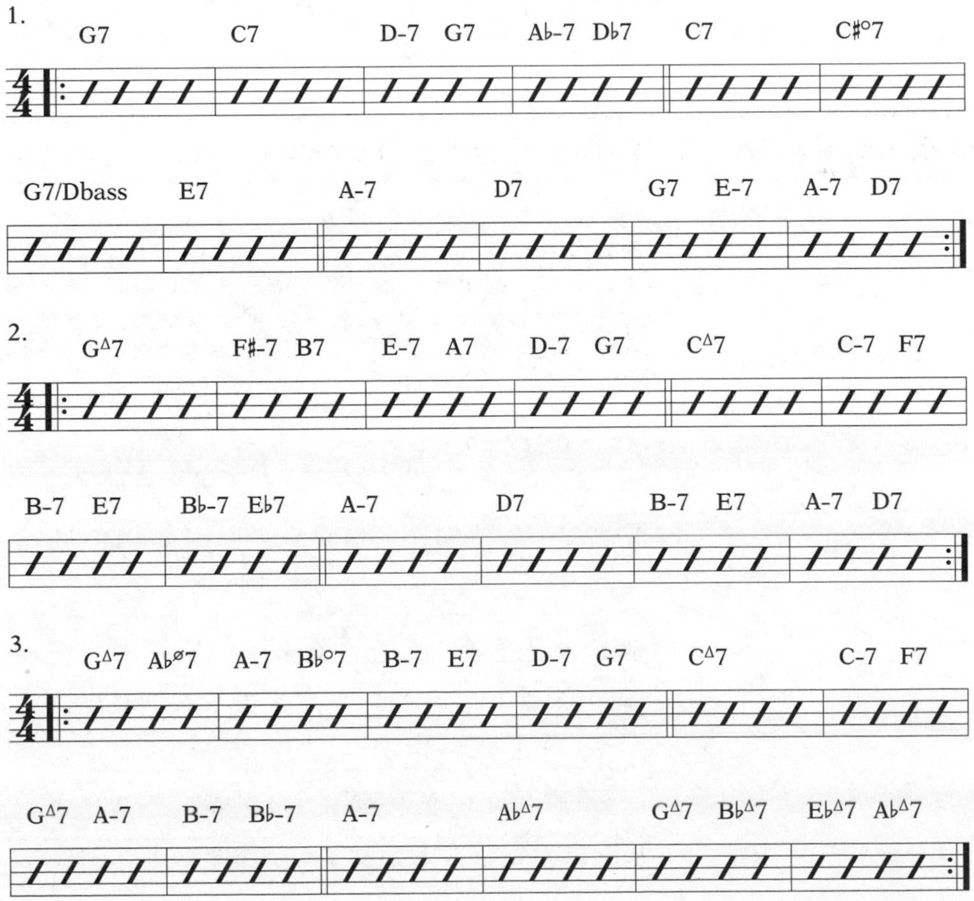

(continued)

4.

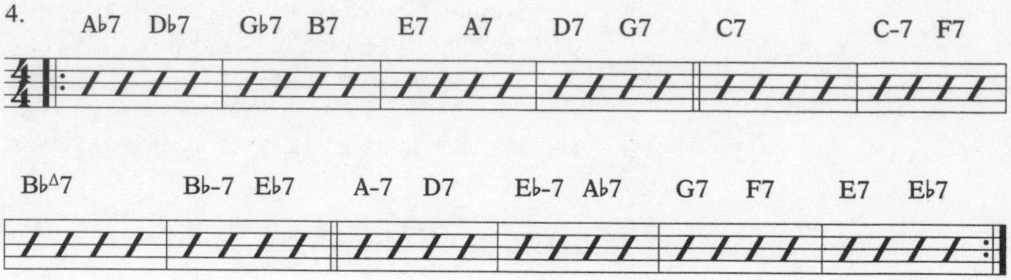

E♭ instruments begin here

1.

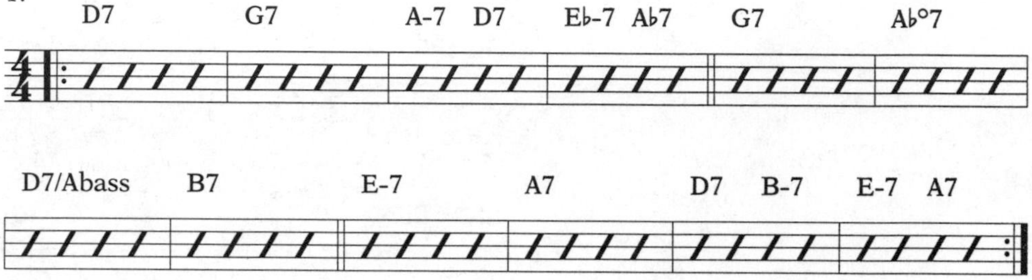

2.

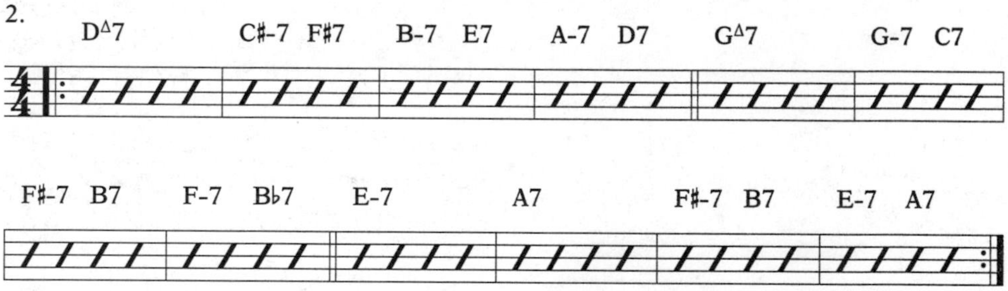

3.

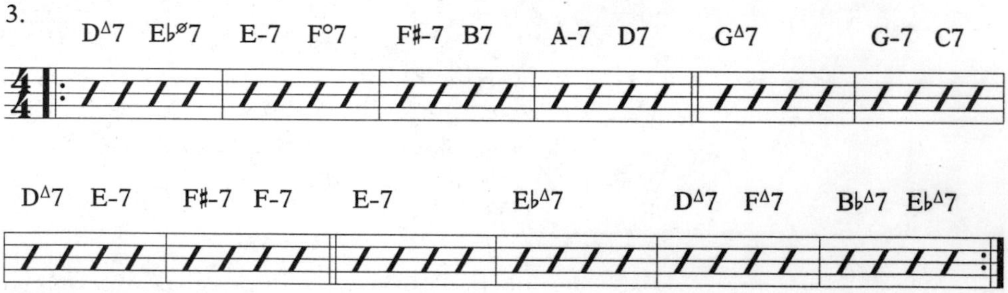

4.

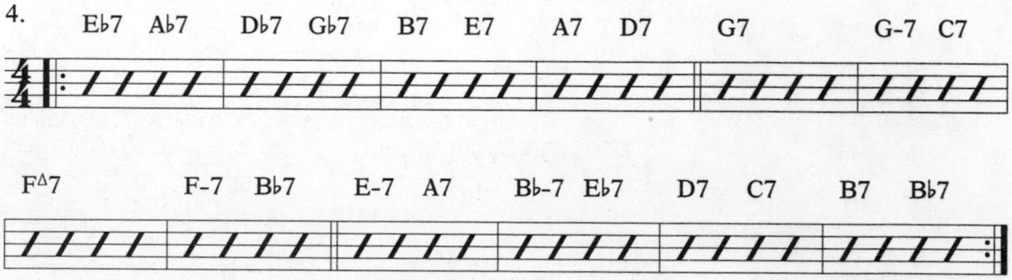

1. Create guide-tone lines, starting on the 7th or the 3rd of the first chord. Move to either the 7th or the 3rd of each successive chord, whichever is closer.

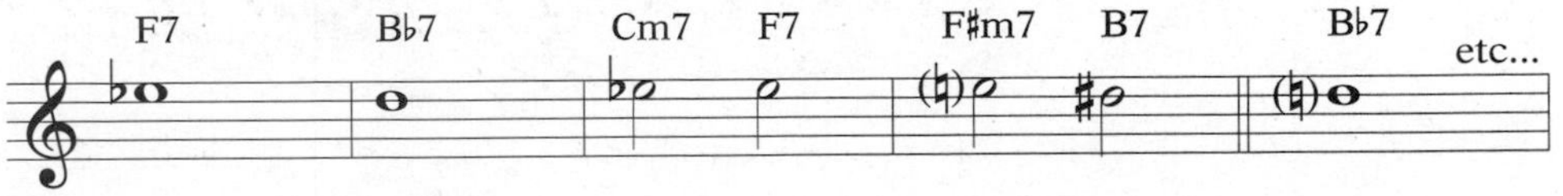

MM ______________________

1a. Improvise freely around the guide-tone lines you have created, embellishing the basic pitches.

2. Outline each progression by playing the chord arpeggio to the 7th. For chords lasting one bar, play the arpeggio up and down; for chords lasting two beats, play the arpeggio up only.

MM ______________________

2a. Improvise freely, using arpeggios as a departure point.

3. Outline each progression by playing, in eighth notes, the scales that fit each chord. For chords lasting one bar, play the scale one octave; for chords lasting two beats, play the first, second, third, and fifth notes of the scale.

MM ______________________

3a. Improvise freely, using scales as a basic for your solo.

4. *Tritone substitutions*: Improvise on progression 1, incorporating the following melodic phrases in the fourth bar. Once the sound becomes familiar, try playing then in all twelve keys.

a.

MM ______________________

b. A J. J. Johnson phrase, from his "Now's the Time" solo (*J. J. in Person*, Columbia 8009):

MM ______________________

c. A Wynton Marsalis phrase (live taping):

MM ______________

d. A variation on a Randy Brecker idea, from his "Footprints" solo (Dave Liebman, *Pendulum*, Artists House 8):

MM ______________

5. *Creative jazz improvisation*: Improvise on blues substitutions, without looking at the changes. Try to play an entire chorus of eighth notes without stopping. Don't worry about what notes you play, just keep the phrase going, making sure that each note is in rhythm.

6. Make up your own chord substitutions on the blues form.

MM ______________

Improvising on Jazz Compositions Based on the Blues Form

Following is a partial list of jazz compositions based on the blues form. These compositions are found in *The New Real Book*, vol. 1 (NRB), *The New Real Book*, vol. 2 (NR2), one of the volumes of Jamey Aebersold's *New Approach to Jazz Improvisation* (JA), or *Creative Beginnings: An Introduction to Jazz Improvisation* (CB). Memorize the most frequently played songs, and practice them in different keys.

Basic Blues in 4/4 with a Major or Dominant Tonality

"Barbados"—Charlie Parker (JA vol. 69)
"Bass Blues"—John Coltrane (NR2)
"Bessie's Blues"—John Coltrane (NR2)
"Billie's Bounce"—Charlie Parker (JA vol. 6)
"Birdlike"—Freddie Hubbard (JA vol. 60)
"Blue Seven"—Sonny Rollins (JA vol. 8)
"Blues March"—Benny Golson (JA vol. 14)

"Blue Train"—John Coltrane (JA vol. 38)
"Buzzy"—Charlie Parker (JA vol. 69)
"C Jam Blues"—Duke Ellington (JA vol. 48)
"D Natural Blues"—Wes Montgomery (JA vol. 62)
"Doodlin'"—Horace Silver (JA vol. 86)
"Eighty-One"—Miles Davis (JA vol. 50, NRB)
"Eta Carina Blue"—Scott Reeves (CB)
"Filthy McNasty"—Horace Silver (NR2)
"Freddie Freeloader"—Miles Davis (JA vol. 50)
"Long Tall Dexter"—Dexter Gordon (JA vol. 82)
"Mr. Day"—John Coltrane (JA vol. 28)
"Now's the Time"—Charlie Parker (JA vol. 6)
"One O'Clock Jump"—Count Basie (JA vol. 71)
"Opus De Funk"—Horace Silver (JA vol. 74)
"Sack 'O Woe"—Cannonball Adderly (JA vol. 13)
"Sandu"—Clifford Brown (JA vol. 53, NRB)
"Solid"—Sonny Rollins (JA vol. 8)
"Sticky Wicket"—Dexter Gordon (JA vol. 82)
"Stop Time Blues"—Jamey Aebersold (JA vol. 70)
"Tenor Madness"—Sonny Rollins (JA vol. 8)
"The Blues Walk"—Chris Woods (attributed to Sonny Stitt) (JA vol.53)
"Twisted"—Ross/Gray (NRB)
"Up Against the Wall"—John Coltrane (JA vol. 28)
"Vierd Blues"—Miles Davis (JA vol. 7)

Basic Blues in 4/4 with a Minor Tonality

Selections from "Minor Blues In All Keys"—Jamey Aebersold (JA vol. 57)
"Antabus"—Dexter Gordon (JA vol. 82)
"Cariba"—Wes Montgomery (JA vol. 62)
"Equinox"—John Coltrane (NR2)
"Mr. P.C."—John Coltrane (JA vols. 27 and 70, NR2)

Blues Substitutions in 4/4 with a Major or Dominant Tonality

"Blues for Alice"—Charlie Parker (JA vols. 2 and 65, NR2)
"Blues on the Corner"—McCoy Tyner (NRB)
"Bonnie's Blue"—David Liebman (JA vol. 19)
"Cedar's Blues"—Cedar Walton (JA vol. 35)
"Freight Trane"—Tommy Flanagan (JA vol. 36)
"Inside Out"—Randy Brecker (JA vol. 83)
"Isotope"—Joe Henderson (JA vol. 38)
"Laird Baird"—Charlie Parker (JA vol. 69)
"Le Miroir Noir"—David Baker (JA vol. 10)
"Some Other Blues"—John Coltrane (JA vol. 27, NR2)

Blues Substitutions in 4/4 with a Minor Tonality

"Blues for Wood"—Woody Shaw (JA vol. 9)
"Blues to Woody"—Scott Reeves (UNC)
"The Jody Grind"—Horace Silver (JA vol. 17)
"The Natives Are Restless Tonight"—Horace Silver (NR2)

Blues in 3/4 or 6/8 with a Major or Dominant Tonality

"All Blues"—Miles Davis (JA vol. 50)
"Kentucky Oysters"—David Baker (JA vol. 10)
"West Coast Blues"—Wes Montgomery (JA vols. 43, 62, and 74, NRB)

Blues Compositions in 3/4 or 6/8 with a Minor Tonality

"Selections from "Minor Blues In All Keys"—Jamey Aebersold (JA vol. 57)
"Afro Blue" (solo changes only)—Mongo Santamaria (JA vol. 64)
"El Corazon"—Scott Reeves (CB)
"Footprints"—Wayne Shorter (JA vol. 33)
"Señor Blues"—Horace Silver (JA vol. 86, NR2)

Blues in an Extended Form with a Major or Dominant Tonality

"Locomotion" (blues with a bridge)—John Coltrane (JA vol. 38)
"St. Louis Blues" (has a verse)—W.C. Handy (JA vol. 79)
"Scotch and Water" (blues with a bridge)—Joe Zawinul (JA vol. 13)
"Unit Seven" (blues with a bridge)—Sam Jones (JA vol. 13, NRB)
"Watermelon Man" (16-bar blues)—Herbie Hancock (JA vols. 11 and 54)

Blues in an Extended Form with a Minor Tonality

"Blues Minor" (24-bar blues)—John Coltrane (JA vol. 27)
"Le Roi" (28-bar blues)—David Baker (JA vol. 10)
"Mahjong" (28-bar blues)—Wayne Shorter (NR2)
"Nutville" (24-bar blues)—Horace Silver (JA vol. 17)
"Stolen Moments"—Oliver Nelson (JA vol. 73)

Tonal-Area or Free-Form Blues

"Blues Connotation"—Ornette Coleman (NRB)
"Matrix"—Chick Corea
"Pursuance" (from A *Love Supreme*)—John Coltrane
"Round Trip"—Ornette Coleman
"Stratusphunk"—George Russell
"Turnaround"—Ornette Coleman

Charlie Parker's Improvised Solo on "Now's the Time"

Charlie Parker's improvised alto saxophone solo on his composition "Now's the Time" was transcribed from *Charlie Parker: The Verve Years* (1952–54) (Verve VE-2-2523). It was recorded August 4, 1953, with a group that included Al Haig on piano, Percy Heath on bass, and Max Roach on drums.

Charlie "Bird" Parker was one of a select group of jazz artists who created a new harmonic-melodic-rhythmic vocabulary, which subsequently became part of the mainstream of jazz. Bird's music, which came to be called *bebop*, was characterized by flowing rhythms consisting primarily of eighth notes, chromatic approaches to chord tones, chords with altered 5ths and 9ths, and a variety of harmonic substitutions. Parker played long, lyrical melodies which also implied complex harmonies and chord alterations. (In this respect, it may be said that his contribution to jazz parallels J. S. Bach's contribution to European art music.) Melodies seemed to flow out of him effortlessly, giving the impression that every note was the perfect choice for that specific context.

"Now's the Time" is a 12-bar blues based primarily on a riff from an older tune called "Do the Hucklebuck." During his solo, Parker implies chord substitutions in the eighth bar of the fourth chorus (bar 44), where he plays A♭mi7 and D♭7 arpeggios; in the fourth bar of the fifth chorus (bar 52), where he implies a B7 chord; and in the last two bars of the fifth chorus (bars 59–60), where he outlines an F7–Gmi7–A♭°7 progression, in lieu of the standard turnaround.

Despite the harmonic complexity, Parker's Kansas City blues heritage is very evident in this solo. He uses the blues scale in bars 16–17, 34–35, and 48–50; the beginning of his second and third choruses are based on bluesy motives in triplet rhythms; and the beginning of his fourth chorus develops a simple blues riff. Parker also incorporates a fair amount of chromaticism, particularly in bars 1, 10, 43, 45, 47 (where he approaches the 5th of chord with upper and lower chromatic neighbor tones), 51, and 54. He frequently uses chord alterations over dominant chords, especially the ♭9th (bars 20, 22, 32, and 58) and the ♯5th (bar 8). The tempo is approximately 𝅗𝅥 = 98.

After listening closely to a recording of this solo, practice it at different tempos with the metronome clicking on beats 2 and 4. Then continue improvising on the chord progression in the same style.[3]

[3] A slightly different transcription of this solo appeared in *The Charlie Parker Omnibook* (Lynbrook, NY: Atlantic Music Corp., 1978).

Treble-clef C instruments:

33 G-7 C7 F7 G-7 C7
37 4 F7 B♭7 F7
40 B♭7
43 A-7 A♭-7 D♭7 G-7
46 C7 F7 G-7 C7
49 5 F7 B♭7 F7
52 (B7) B♭7 A-7
56 D7 G-7 C7
59 F7 G-7 A♭°7 F7

B♭ instruments (Saxophone—8va where indicated):

33 A-7 (8va) D7 G7 A-7 D7
37 4 G7 C7 G7
40 C7
43 B-7 E7 B♭-7 E♭7 A-7
46 D7 G7 A-7 D7
49 5 G7 C7 G7
52 (D♭7) C7 B-7
56 E7 A-7 D7
59 G7 A-7 B♭°7 G7

E♭ instruments:

33 E-7 A7 D7 E-7 A7
4 37 D7 G7 D7
40 G7
43 F♯-7 B7 F-7 B♭7 E-7
46 A7 D7 E-7 A7
5 49 D7 G7 D7
52 (A♭7) G7 F♯-7
56 B7 E-7 A7
59 D7 E-7 F°7 D7

Bass-clef instruments:

33 G-7 C7 F7 G-7 C7
37 4 F7 B♭7 F7
40 B♭7
43 A-7 D7 A♭-7 D♭7 G-7
46 C7 F7 G-7 C7
49 5 F7 B♭7 F7
52 (B7) B♭7 A-7
56 D7 G-7 C7
59 F7 G-7 A♭°7 F7

11
Sectional Forms and Rhythm Changes

"Every musician in the world has some
limitations...
but the wise players are those
who play what they can master."

composer, pianist, band leader Duke Ellington[1]

Most jazz compositions are based on either the blues form or *sectional forms*. Tunes based on sectional forms typically have four, eight, or sixteen bar sections that repeat in a given sequence. The most common sequences are ABAB, ABAC, and AABA, with each letter representing a melodic phrase.

Sectional forms derive from eighteenth- and nineteenth-century European musical forms. A form frequently used in European art music is called the *song-and-trio* (sometimes referred to as a scherzo-and-trio or march-and-trio). This form utilizes an A(*song*)–B(*trio*)–A(*song*) format. Each of these large sections may also contain smaller sections, creating a complex, multisectional structure such as A(aba)–B(abab)–A(aba). John Philip Sousa, as well as other composers of band music in the late nineteenth and early twentieth centuries, used the march-and-trio form extensively. Black brass bands subsequently adopted it in their reinterpretations of band literature, and early New Orleans jazz composers based many of their compositions on similar forms. Jelly Roll Morton's "Wolverine Blues," "Frog-i-More Rag," "Milenburg Joys," "New Orleans Stomp," and "Black Bottom Stomp" are all examples of sectional forms. "Maple Leaf Rag," by Scott Joplin (*Smithsonian Collection*), is cast in an AA–BB–A–CC–DD multisectional form, while the forms of Morton's "Frog-i-More" and "Grandpa's Spells" (*Smithsonian Collection*) are intro–A–B–interlude–trio(abac) and A A1–B B1–A2–C C1 C2 C3, respectively.[2]

The popularity of long sectional forms such as the march-and-trio began to wane at the close of the early jazz period. Simpler structures based on eight-bar phrases became the norm, especially binary or ternary forms. *Binary forms* are typically made up of four- or eight-bar phrases in the sequence ABAB′, ABAC, or AABB. They are called binary forms because the overall form can be divided in half: AB/AB′ or AA/BB. Early jazz compositions with a 32-bar binary form include Lillian Hardin Armstrong's "Struttin' with Some Barbecue," which has an ABAB′ form (*Smithsonian Collection*), King Oliver's "Shake It and Break It," which is based on an AABB form, and Louis Armstrong's "Swing That Music," which has an ABAC form.

[1] "A Duke Named Ellington," *American Masters,* Public Broadcasting System, 1987.
[2] Gene Rush, personal conversation, Memphis State University, 1983.

In *ternary form*, the phrases occur in the sequence AABA. It is called ternary because it divides into three parts: AA/B/A. The A sections are virtually identical, except that the first A section usually ends on a V chord, while the second and third A sections end on the tonic chord. The B section typically consists of a contrasting theme in a new key, which ends up modulating back to the original key. The B section is often referred to as the *bridge* or *release*.

Nineteenth-century American song-writers, such as Stephen Foster, often used a shortened, sixteen-bar version of ternary form, in which each section lasts four measures. Foster's "Old Folks at Home," "Oh Susannah," and "I Dream of Jeannie" are all based on sixteen-bar AABA forms. In the twentieth century, however, composers of Tin Pan Alley popular songs and Broadway musicals gravitated toward the use of eight-bar phrases, resulting in the 32-bar AABA form we typically find in *jazz standards*. Many of the songs from this period also contained an eight- or sixteen-bar introductory verse, which would establish the mood of the song or introduce the story line. However, jazz musicians using these songs as frameworks for improvisation typically tend to omit the verses. Notable exceptions to this practice include Billy Strayhorn's "Lush Life" and Hoagy Carmichael's "Stardust," whose introductory verses are still commonly performed.

Although binary and ternary structures comprise the vast majority of sectional forms, occasionally we find compositions in which no section repeats. These are called *through-composed forms*. The form of Bill Evans's "Time Remembered" consists of an eight-bar A section, a twelve-bar B section, and a six-bar C section, while the form of Steve Swallow's "Falling Grace" consists of a fourteen-bar A section and a ten-bar B section.[3]

During the bebop era of the 1940s, it became common practice to write new melodies based on the chord progressions of existing popular songs. These songs are sometimes referred to as *contrafacts*.[4] Bebop musicians desired melodies that reflected the angularity, speed, and harmonic alterations so prominent in their improvisations. Given the lack of rehearsal time and financial backing for recording sessions, improvising on well-known standard chord progressions also yielded quick results, and since chord progressions alone cannot be copyrighted, the beboppers were also able to secure composer's royalties for their new melodies. Certain standards were repeatedly favored as blueprints for these new compositions. "Back Home Again in Indiana" inspired many new tunes, including Charlie Parker's "Donna Lee"; "Sweet Georgia Brown" produced Miles Davis's "Dig"; and "What Is This Thing Called Love" served as the template for dozens of songs, including Tadd Dameron's "Hot House." An incalculable number of tunes were based on the chord progression to the George Gershwin song "I Got Rhythm."[5] *Rhythm changes*, as they are referred to, are based a 32-bar AABA form. (Gershwin's original added a two-bar tag to the 32-bar form, but the extra two bars are typically omitted in most contrafacts.) The A section consists of a simple progression that stays in the tonic key, while the B section modulates up a major 3rd to a dominant chord and returns to the tonic key by means of the cycle of 4ths:[6]

[3] "Time Expired" is from the reconding *Bill Evans Trio with Symphony Orchestra*, Verve V-8640; "Falling Grace" is from the recording *Gary Burton and Chick Corea, Crystal Silence*, ECM 1-1024.

[4] David Baker, personal conversation, Indiana University, 1981.

[5] The New Expanded Bibliography of Jazz Compositions Based on the Chord Progressions of Standard Tunes, Reese Markewich, 39 Gramercy Park, NY, NY 10010.

[6] See Chapters 5 and 7 for an explanation of secondary dominants; br. iv indicates a iv chord borrowed from the parallel minor of B♭ minor.

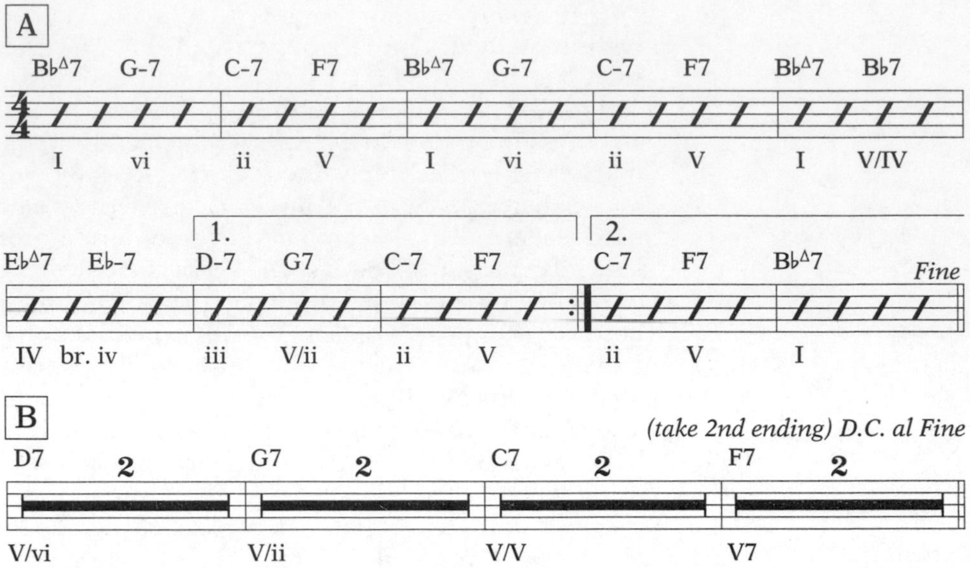

As is the case with the blues form, numerous substitutions are often imposed on this basic formula. In the first four bars of the A section, a bass line moving from the tonic up to the iii chord creates diminished and diatonic passing chords:

Miles Davis, "Serpent's Tooth" (Prestige Records)

An unusual substitution in the first four bars, used by Don Byas in his "I Got Rhythm" solo (*Smithsonian Collection of Classic Jazz*), is based on dominant 7th chords moving around the cycle of 4ths. By working backwards from the I chord in bar 5, we end up starting the progression with the dominant chord built on the lowered sixth degree (a tritone substitute for V/V):

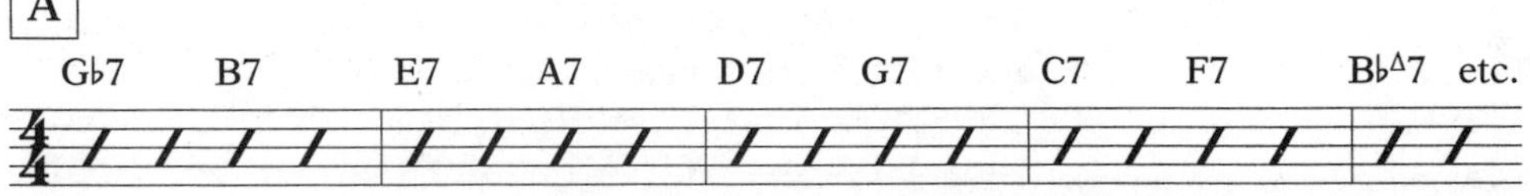

In bar 5, we occasionally find the minor chord built on the fifth degree. In the sixth bar, a diminished passing chord built on the raised fourth degree is often used:

Charlie Parker, "Thriving on a Riff" (Savoy SJL 2201)

In the first ending, a chromatic bass line yields these substitutions:

Charlie Parker, "Dexterity"

In the bridge, the minor 7th chords a perfect 4th below each dominant chord (except for the third bar) are often added, creating ii–V relationships:

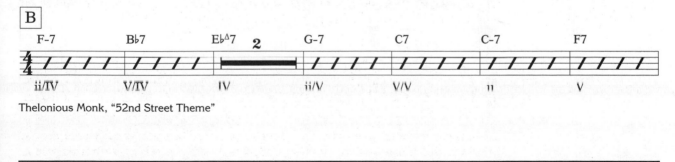

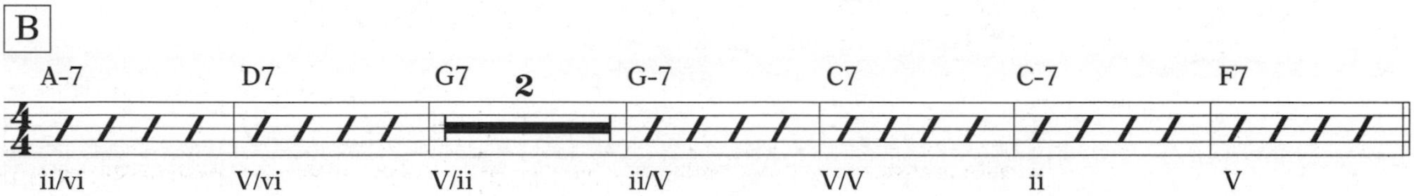

Charlie Parker, "Dexterity"

It is also possible to use tritone substitutions in lieu of the second and fourth dominant chords in the bridge:

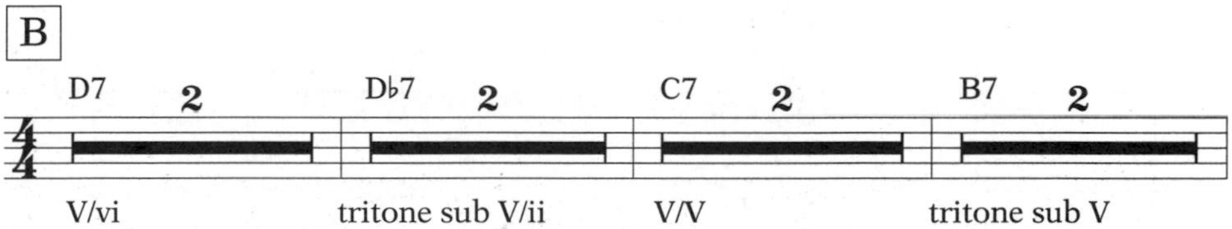

Fats Navarro, "Eb-Pob"

Sometimes an entirely different harmonic formula is used in the first four bars of the bridge. Instead of moving to the V/vi chord and progressing by the cycle of 4ths, this formula temporarily modulates to the IV chord in the first four bars. Bars 5–8 remain the same:

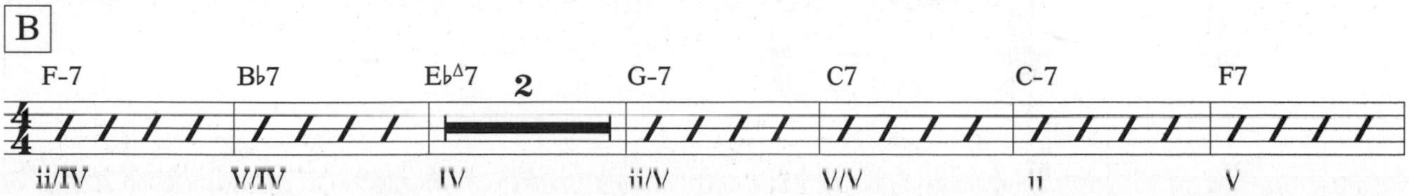

Thelonious Monk, "52nd Street Theme"

Theory/Ear Exercises

1. Go through a fake-book and determine the forms of the tunes. Categorize them as blues, binary, ternary, or through-composed forms. Make special note of the ternary forms that are based on the "rhythm changes."
2. *Keyboard skills*: Play the chord progressions from this chapter on the piano.
3. *Composition*: Compose a melody based on the chord progression to "I Got Rhythm."

Gaining Facility with Rhythm Changes

Practice the following exercises over the chord progression below, using either a metronome or Aebersold play-along volume 47, *I Got Rhythm*. If you find yourself struggling with an exercise, slow it down, simplify it, or sing it while visualizing yourself playing it. After familiarizing yourself with the exercises, pick one or two to practice repeatedly, until you can play them without any conscious thought.

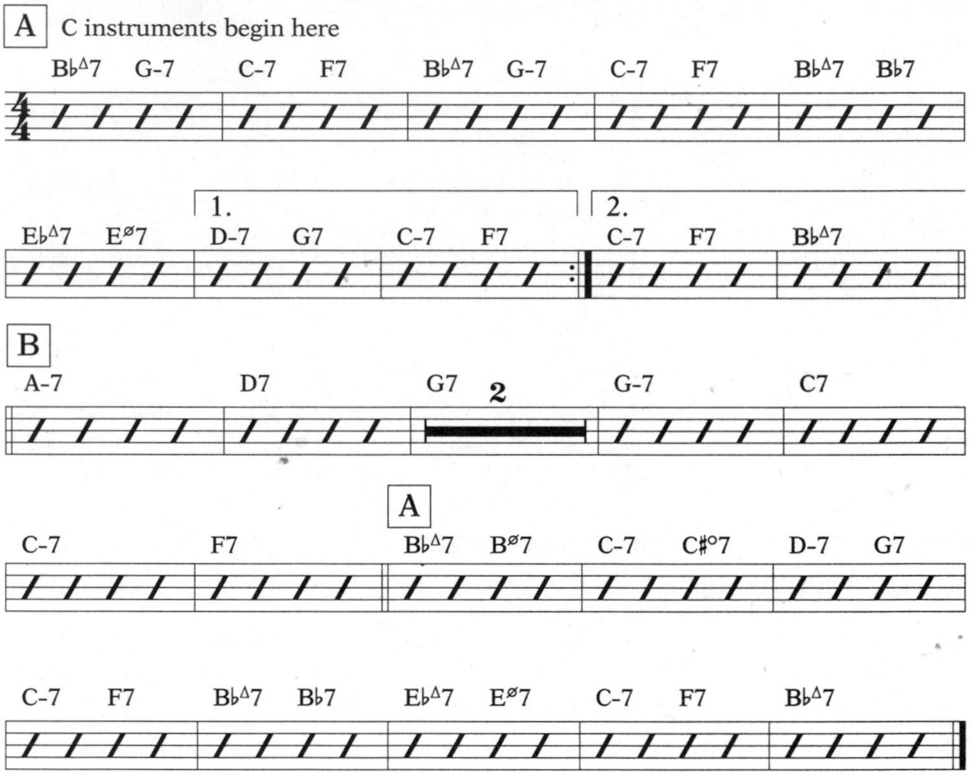

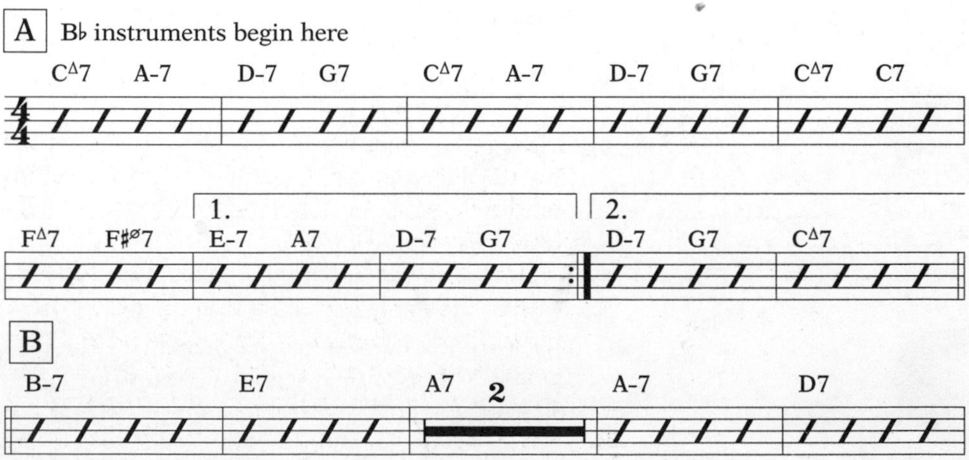

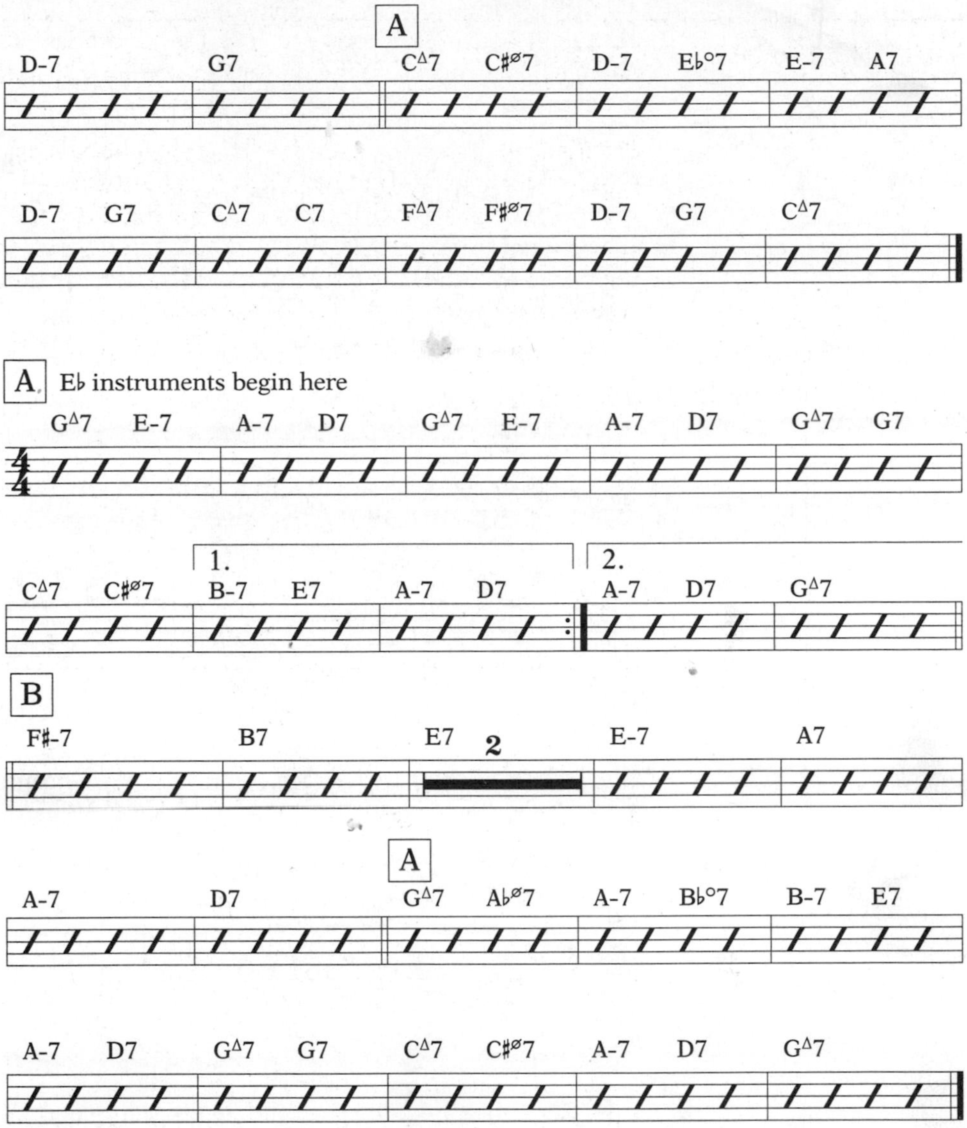

1. Create guide-tone lines, starting on the 7th or the 3rd of the first chord. Move to either the 7th or the 3rd of each successive chord, whichever is closest.

1a. Improvise freely around the guide-tone lines you have created, embellishing the basic pitches.

2. Outline the progression by playing the chord arpeggio in eighth notes. Play the arpeggio up and down twice over chords lasting two measures, up and down once over chords lasting one measure; and ascending only over chords lasting two beats.

2a. Improvise freely, using arpeggios as a departure point.

3. Outline the progression by playing in eighth notes, the scales that fit each chord. Over chords lasting two bars, play the scale up and down; over chords lasting one bar, play the scale ascending; over chords lasting two beats, play the first, second, third, and fifth notes of the scale.

3a. Improvise freely, using scales as a basis for your solo.

The following melodic phrases may be used over the A section of rhythm changes. Learn each pattern in all twelve keys. Then improvise on rhythm changes, incorporating the pattern into your solo at the appropriate place in the progression.

4. A Tom Harrell line that uses the diminished scale over the V chord (live taping). Use this idea over the first three bars of the first two A sections.

MM ____________________

5. A pattern based on a 3–5–7–9 arpeggio over the I and ii chords, a ♯9 and ♭9 over the V/ii chord, and a ♯5th over the V chord. Use this idea over the first three bars of the first two A sections.

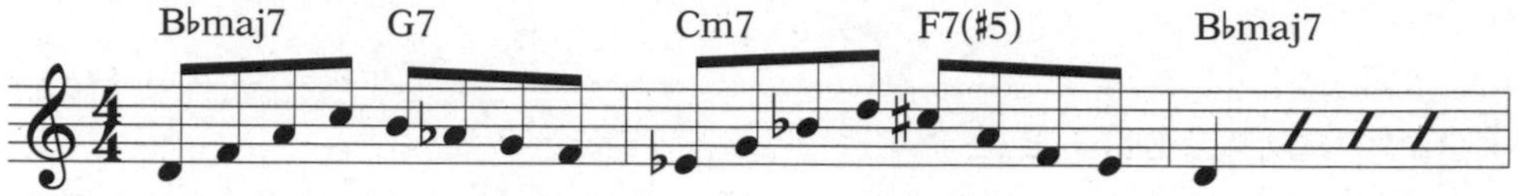

MM ____________________

6. A common bebop pattern that uses descending arpeggios on the I and ii chords and the ♭9th over the V/ii and V chords. Use this idea over the first three bars of the first two A sections.

MM ____________________

7. This phrase outlines diminished passing chords and uses the ♭9th over the V/ii chord and a 3–5–7–9 arpeggio over the ii chord. Try this idea over the first four bars of the last A section.

MM ____________________

8. A Lee Morgan pattern that uses a ♯5th in bar 2 and a ♯9th, ♯5th, and ♭5th in bar 4. Use this pattern over the first five bars of the first two A sections (Curtis Fuller, *Slidin' Easy*).

MM ____________________

9. *Creative jazz improvisation*

a. The chords in the A section all revolve around one key center, and their related scales contain many common tones. When you improvise on the chord progression, think of the A section as one modal area or a dominant pedal point. You can play anything you want, as long as you resolve to the tonic chord at strategic points.

b. Improvise on rhythm changes in all twelve keys, using a metronome, a rhythm section, or Aebersold play-along volume 47, *I Got Rhythm*.

10. Make up your own patterns based on rhythm changes.

Improvising on Jazz Compositions Based on "Rhythm Changes" and Through-Composed Forms

Following is a partial list of jazz compositions based on "I Got Rhythm" changes or through-composed forms. These compositions are found in *The New Real Book*, vol. 1 (NRB), *The New Real Book*, vol. 2 (NR2), one of the volumes of Jamey Aebersold's *New Approach to Jazz Improvisation* (JA), or *Creative Beginnings: An Introduction to Jazz Improvisation* (CB). Memorize the most frequently played songs, and practice them in different keys.

Compositions Based on "Rhythm Changes" with a Cycle-of-4ths Bridge

"Anthropology"—Parker/Gillespie (NRB)
"Apple Jump"—Dexter Gordon (JA vol. 82)
"Bird Food"—Ornette Coleman (NRB)
"Lester Lept Out"—Scott Reeves (CB)
"Moose the Mooch"—Charlie Parker (JA vol. 69)
"Oleo"—Sonny Rollins (JA vols. 8 and 65)
"Shaw 'Nuff"—Parker/Gillespie (NRB)
"The Theme"—Miles Davis (JA vol. 7)
"Thrivin' from a Riff"—Charlie Parker (JA vol. 6)

Compositions Based on "Rhythm Changes" with a Modified Bridge

"Dexology"—Dexter Gordon (JA vol. 82)
"Gertrude's Bounce"—Richie Powell (JA vol. 53, NR2)
"Room 608"—Horace Silver (JA vol. 18)
"Serpent's Tooth"—Miles Davis (JA vol. 7)
"Third Rail"—Michael Brecker (JA vol. 61)

Compositions Based on Through-Composed Forms

"Blue in Green"—Evans/Davis (JA vol. 50)
"Dolphin Dance"—Herbie Hancock (JA vol. 11)
"Falling Grace"—Steve Swallow (NR2)
"Inner Urge"—Joe Henderson (JA vol. 38)

"Peri's Scope"—Bill Evans (JA vol. 45)
"Time Remembered"—Bill Evans (JA vol. 45, NR2)
"Turn Out the Stars"—Bill Evans (NR2)
"Unless It's You"—Bill Evans (NR2)

Charlie Parker's Improvised Solo on "Shaw 'Nuff"

Charlie Parker's improvised alto saxophone solo on the Parker/Gillespie composition "Shaw 'Nuff" was transcribed from the *Smithsonian Collection of Classic Jazz*, and can also be found on the CD or cassette accompanying *Jazz Styles* by Mark Gridley.[7] It was recorded in 1947 by Gillespie's All Stars, which included Al Haig on piano, Curley Russell on bass, and Sid Catlett on drums. It is interesting to hear Catlett, one of the great drummers from the swing era, play with such empathy behind beboppers Gillespie and Parker.

Compare this solo with Lester Young's solo on "Lester Leaps In," which is also based on rhythm changes (Chapter 5). Parker brings out the sound of each individual chord change to a much greater extent than Young. Bird not only articulates the basic changes but also implies many harmonic substitutions. In bars 3 and 11, he plays a D♭ minor 7th arpeggio in place of the G7 chord. During the B section, he arpeggiates both the standard changes and the chords a half-step above. This solo also contains a considerable amount of chromaticism, as seen in bars 4, 9, 11–12, 21–22, 25, 27–28, and 31. Altered chord tones are also common, such as the ♭9 over the dominant chord in bar 24. In contrast to earlier artists such as Coleman Hawkins or Don Byas (listen to Byas's solo on "I Got Rhythm" in the *Smithsonian Collection*), Bird uses a wider variety of accents, creating an underlying syncopation and fluidity that marks this as a bebop rather than a swing-era improvisation.

Every note in the solo seems to fit perfectly, despite the breakneck tempo (𝅗𝅥 = 144). After listening to the recording, practice the solo at different tempos with the metronome clicking on beats 2 and 4. Then continue improvising in the same style.[8]

[7] Mark Gridley, Jazz Styles, 5th ed. (Englewood Cliffs, NJ: Prentice Hall, 1994).

[8] A different version of this solo appears in The Charlie Parker Omnibook (Lynbrook, NY: Atlantic Music Corp., 1978).

Treble-clef C instruments:

B♭ instruments (Saxophone—8va where indicated):

E♭ instruments:

Bass-clef instruments:

12

Harmonic Structures and Coltrane Substitutions

"If you start judging what you
are writing or playing-
that puts another part of your brain in the
process, and it stops the creativity."

composer/pianist Jim McNeely[1]

The harmony of most jazz compositions can be classified as one of the following types:[2]

1. *Modal*—Compositions in which all the chords last at least four bars, with each chord typically constituting a complete section or phrase. A vamp between two or three chords whose scales contain the same notes may be considered as one modal area (e.g., Cmi7 to F7, or Cmi to D♭Ma7♭5).
2. *Chord Changes*—Compositions in which all the chords generally last less than four bars.
3. *Combination Modal/Changes*—Compositions in which some of the chords last more than four bars and some less than four. Often the modal area will delineate a separate section or phrase.
4. *Tonal Area*—Compositions in which there are no predetermined chord changes, yet a key center or tonal area is generally implied.
5. *Atonal* or *Nonharmonic*—Compositions in which there are no predetermined chord changes and no discernible key center or tonality. This may include pieces based on free atonality, systematic atonality (such as the twelve-tone system), or compositions that use sounds and textures instead of notes.

Although traditional forms of African music are primarily modal, the earliest styles of jazz drew on popular songs of the day, employing standardized European harmonic progressions, and the blues. Many early jazz musicians relied on the chord tones in their improvisations; the remaining notes were thought of as passing tones or approach tones. In the 1930s, this reliance on chord tones and arpeggios reached its culmination in Coleman Hawkins.[3] Lester Young offered an alternative to Hawkins' style by primarily playing on the scale, often merely alluding to the underlying chord changes. Most players find a balance

[1] Jim McNeely, personal conversation with author, Lake Placid Seminars, 8/20/98.
[2] David Baker, personal conversation with author, Indiana University, 1970.
[3] Listen to Coleman Hawkins's "Body and Soul" recording for another approach to creative chord change playing.

somewhere between these approaches. For example, in his *Giant Steps* period, John Coltrane relied heavily on chord arpeggios, Miles Davis in his *Kind of Blue* recording primarily emphasized melody, while Charlie Parker's improvisations seemed to draw equally on both melodic and harmonic considerations.

Early jazz compositions tended to employ strong harmonic progressions, with chords moving by major 2nds and perfect 4ths (although Jelly Roll Morton often stretched those boundaries). Dominant chords were usually not extended beyond the 7th, and major chords typically contained 6ths rather than major 7ths. Around 1940, Gillespie, Parker, Monk, and other beboppers began adding altered 9th and 5ths to dominant chords and the 7th and 9th to major chords, as well as employing numerous chord substitutions. Post-bop compositions added further extensions to chords, bitonal relationships, and chord progressions based on weak root movements, such as major and minor 3rds. Harmonic complexity reached its culmination in John Coltrane's composition "Giant Steps," which modulated by major 3rds every measure or two.

In the late 1950s, there was a new trend toward modality that appeared in the work of Ahmad Jamal, Gil Evans, and Miles Davis, which placed more emphasis on the melodic line. Miles's 1958 and 1959 recordings, *Milestones* and *Kind of Blue*, were particularly influential in popularizing this movement toward harmonic simplicity. Three tunes on these recordings relied exclusively on modal structures: "Milestones" (a 40-bar AABA song, not to be confused with an earlier chord-change composition of the same name), "So What" (a 32-bar AABA tune based on two dorian scales), and "Flamenco Sketches" (a through-composed composition in which each section remains on one mode for a length of time determined by the soloist). This concept was later explored in recordings such as Herbie Hancock's *Maiden Voyage* and *Empryean Isles*, as well as numerous compositions by John Coltrane, who had reached an impasse in his exploration of vertical structures.

Ornette Coleman's arrival on the jazz scene in the late 1950s offered another alternative to chord-change structures. His 1959 recording *The Shape of Jazz to Come* showed that improvisation could be based entirely on melody and rhythm, without any underlying harmonic structures. Ornette generally implied a key center or tonal area in his compositions (a reflection of his Texas-blues background and the inherently tonal nature of jazz), but felt free to leave that key center at any time. This method of improvising on a tonal area with no predetermined chord changes was referred to by Ornette as *harmolodic*; it influenced the work of such established artists as Sonny Rollins, John Coltrane, and Miles Davis. Tonal-area compositions were further explored by groups such as the World Saxophone Quartet and the Chicago Art Ensemble, as well as pianists Paul Bley and Keith Jarrett, saxophonist Eric Dolphy, and trombonist Albert Mangelsdorff.

Some compositions, such as *Abstractions* by Third-stream composer Gunther Schuller and portions of the recording, *Free Fall*, by the trio of Jimmy Guiffre, Paul Bley, and Steve Swallow, carefully avoided any key by working with tone rows, in a manner akin to twentieth-century classical composers. Others avoided key centers by using textures and sounds as their raw materials. These compositions with no discernible key center may be called *atonal* or *nonharmonic*. Some of the work of pianists Cecil Taylor and Sun Ra, composer Michael Mantler, and the early recordings of saxophonists Archie Shepp and Albert Ayler exemplified this style. Composer George Russell did not abandon tonality but used several key centers simultaneously. This approach is referred to as *polytonal* or, in Russell's word, *pantonal*, meaning "using all tonalities."

Coltrane Substitutions

The chord progression John Coltrane used in compositions such as "Giant Steps," "Satellite," and "Countdown" is a formula commonly known as *Coltrane substitutions*. It can be applied to any ii–V–I or I–vi–ii–V–I progression:

Standard ii-V-I Progression

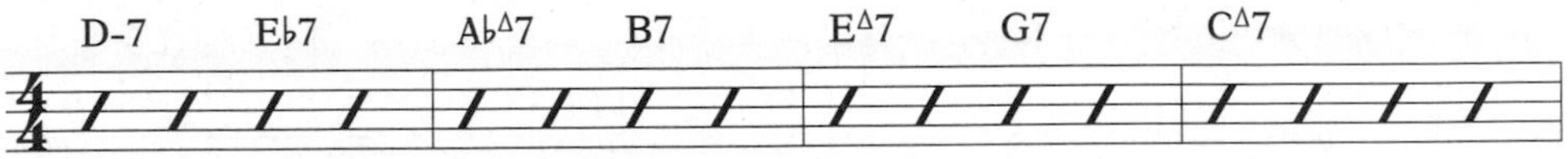

Coltrane Substitutions on ii-V-I Progression

In chord progressions beginning with a ii chord, the second chord moves up a half step to a V7 chord, which then resolves down a perfect 5th to a I chord. From there, the progression moves up a minor 3rd to another V7 chord, which resolves to its I chord. Moving up another minor 3rd brings us to the V7 chord of the original key, which subsequently resolves to the tonic chord. Coltrane applied this formula to the ii–V–I progressions found in standard tunes such as "But Not for Me" and "The Night Has a Thousand Eyes." He also used this formula, along with newly composed melodies, to transform Tadd Dameron's "Hot House" into "Fifth House" and Eddie Vinson's "Tune-Up" into "Countdown."

In "Giant Steps," the progression begins with a I chord and moves up a minor 3rd to a V7 chord, which resolves down a perfect 5th to a I chord. This same movement up a minor 3rd to a V7 with its resolution to I is repeated:

Opening Phrase of "Giant Steps"

Notice that the major 7th chords in Coltrane's formula produce key areas a major 3rd apart. The inspiration for this formula may have been derived from the bridge of the standard tune "Have You Met Miss Jones?," which also modulates through key centers a major 3rd apart:

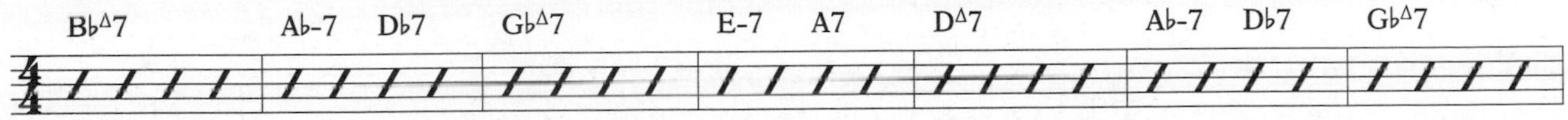

"Have You Met Miss Jones?," B Section

Although "Giant Steps" has a reputation as a difficult vehicle on which to improvise, knowing that all the chords are related to one of three key areas greatly simplifies the progression.

Later in his career, when Coltrane was no longer playing tunes like "Giant Steps" and "Countdown," you could still hear the influence of the these substitutions in his melodic lines within the context of his modal and atonal improvisations.

Theory/Ear Exercises

1. Pick any tune that uses ii–V–I or I–vi–ii–V–I progressions and apply Coltrane substitutions. You may have to alter parts of the melody to make it fit the new chords.
2. *Keyboard skills*: Play the chord progressions from this chapter on the piano.
3. *Harmonic structures*: Go through a fake-book or listen to several recordings, and categorize the harmonic structures of each tune as: 1) modal, 2) chord change, 3) combination modal/change, 4) tonal area, or 5) atonal.

Gaining Facility with Coltrane Substitutions

Practice the following exercises over the chord progression below, using either a metronome or Aebersold play-along volume 16, *Turnarounds, Cycles & II/V7s* (disc 2, track 7), or volume 68, *Giant Steps* (track 6).If you find yourself struggling with an exercise, slow it down, simplify it, or sing it while visualizing yourself playing it. After familiarizing yourself with the exercises, pick one or two to practice repeatedly, until you can play them without any conscious thought.

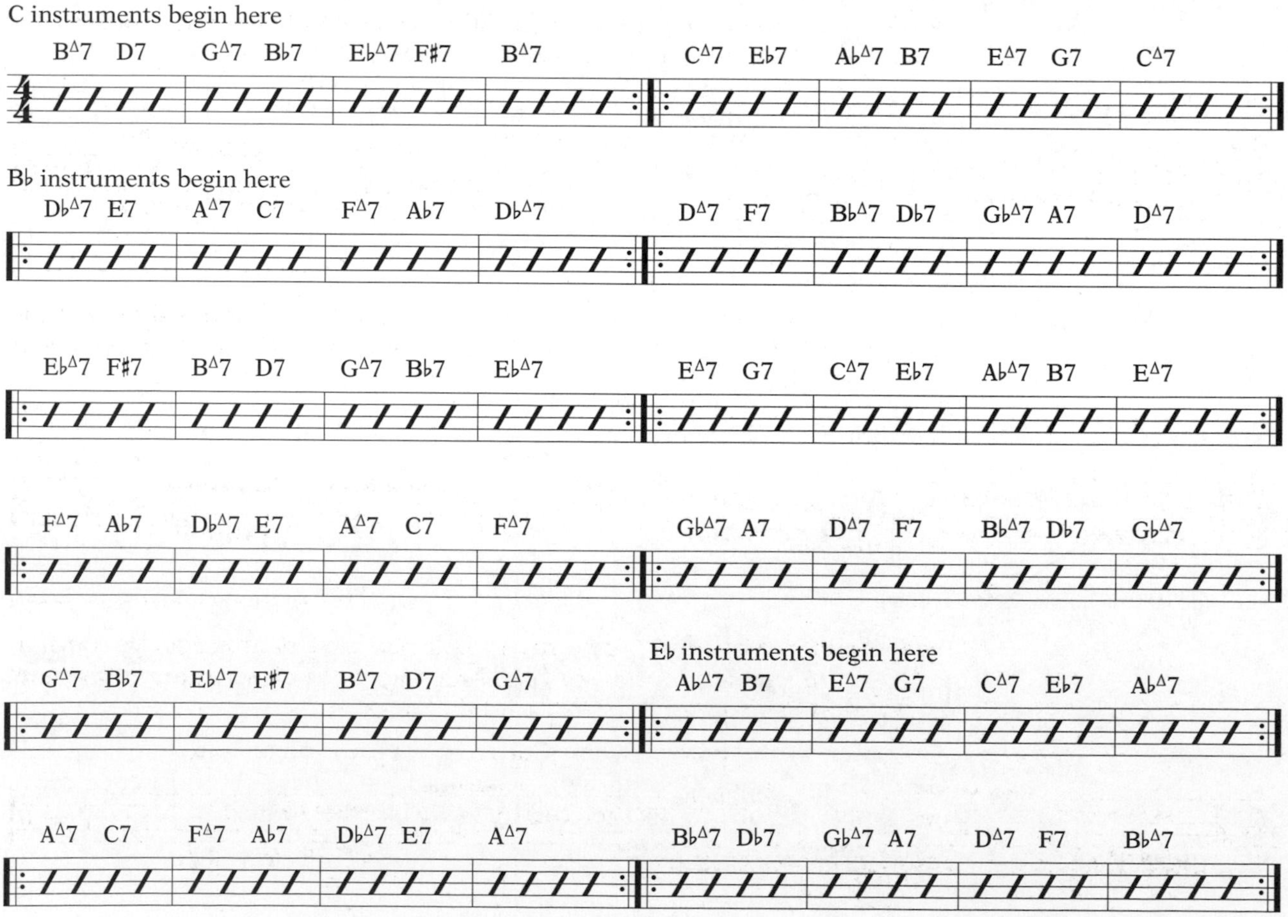

1. Outline the progression with the root, the 3rd, and the 5th of each chord.

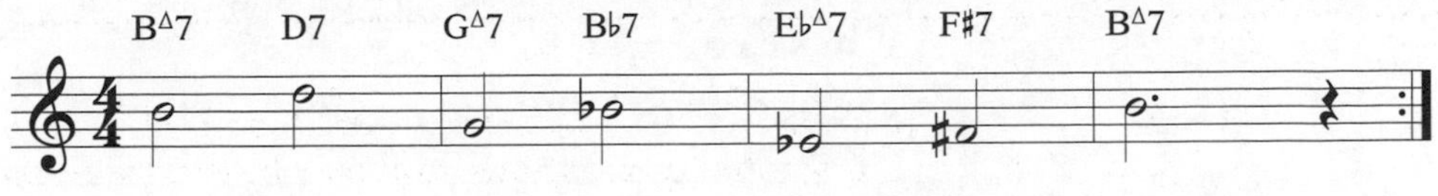

MM ____________________

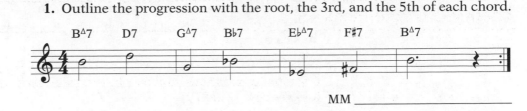

2. A guide-tone line that uses the 3rd of the major and minor chords and the 7th of the dominant chords. Create another guide-tone line based on the 7th of the major and minor chords and the 3rd of the dominant chords.

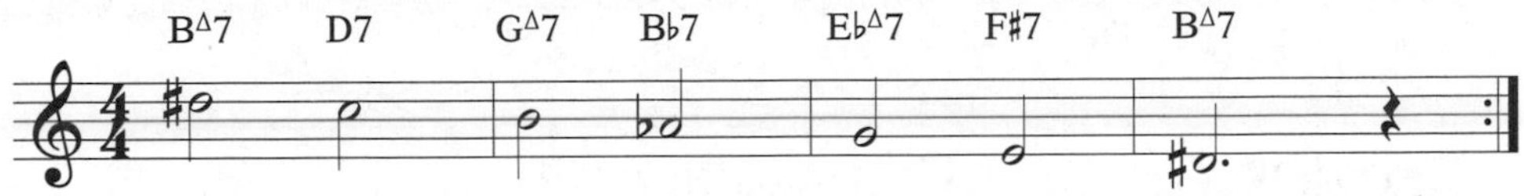

MM ____________________

3. Outline the progression by playing a 1–2–3–5 pattern in eighth notes over each chord.

MM ____________________

4. Outline the progression by alternating the 1–2–3–5 pattern with an 8–7–♭7–8 pattern on the dominant chords.

MM ____________________

5. This more complex approach to outlining the progression is similar to the approach Coltrane used in his "Giant Steps" solo (John Coltrane, *Giant Steps*, Atlantic 1311).

MM ____________________

6. Develop your ability to play melodically over the progression by continuing the direction of the line but changing to the closest note in the next scale at the beginning of each chord change.

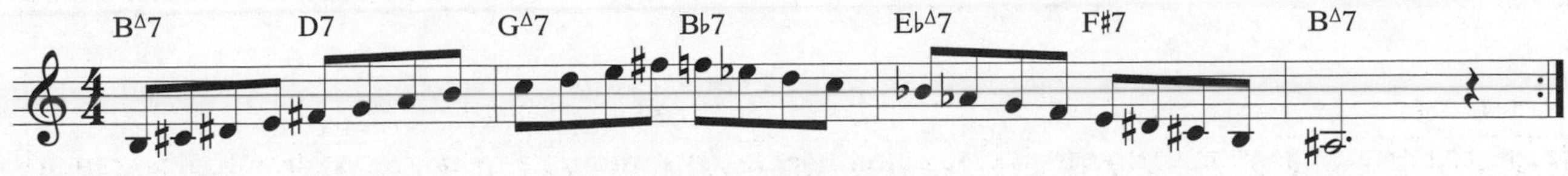

MM ____________________

7. *Creative jazz improvisation*: Improvise over the progression, practicing in only one register of the instrument. Find all you can in a given range, then move on.[4]
8. Make up your own approaches to outlining Coltrane substitutions.

MM ____________

MM ____________

Improvising on Jazz Compositions Based on Coltrane Substitutions

Following is a partial list of jazz compositions in which at least a portion of the Coltrane formula may be found. These compositions are found in *The New Real Book*, vol. 1 (NRB), *The New Real Book*, vol. 2 (NR2), one of the volumes of Jamey Aebersold's *New Approach to Jazz Improvisation* (JA), or *Creative Beginnings: An Introduction to Jazz Improvisation* (CB). Memorize the most frequently played songs, and practice them in different keys.

Compositions Based on Coltrane Substitutions

"Central Park West"—John Coltrane (JA vol. 75, NR2)
"Countdown"—John Coltrane (JA vols. 28 & 75)
"Dear John"—Freddie Hubbard (JA vol. 60)
"Down Time"—David Liebman (JA vol. 81)
"Exotica"—John Coltrane (JA vol. 75)
"Fee Fi Fo Fum"—Wayne Shorter (JA vol. 33)
"Fifth House"—John Coltrane (JA vol. 75)
"Giant Steps"—John Coltrane (JA vols. 28, 65, 68, and 75, NR2)
"Lazy Bird"—John Coltrane (JA vol. 38)
"Satellite"—John Coltrane (JA vol. 75)
"Step By Step"—Andy LaVerne (JA vol. 75)
"Training For Trane"—Andy LaVerne (JA vol. 75)
"26-2"—John Coltrane (JA vols. 28 and 75, NR2)
"Uncommon Tones"—Andy LaVerne (JA vol. 75)

Standards In Which Coltrane Substitutions Are Occasionally Used

"Body and Soul"—Heyman, Sour, Eyton, Green (JA vol. 75)
"But Not for Me"—Ira and George Gershwin (JA vol. 75)
"The Night Has A Thousand Eyes"—Bernier/Brainin (JA vol. 75)

John Coltrane's Improvised Solo on "Giant Steps"

John Coltrane's improvised tenor saxophone solo on his composition "Giant Steps" was transcribed from the 1959 landmark recording of the same name (Atlantic 1311). The album featured Tommy Flanagan or Wynton Kelly on piano,

[4] Joe Lovaro, personal conversation with author, Lake Placid Seminars, 8/21/98.

Paul Chambers on bass, Art Taylor or Jimmy Cobb on drums, and contained several compositions with extremely challenging chord-changes. "Countdown" was based on Coltrane substitutions on "Tune-Up," and "Giant Steps" further elaborated on this harmonic formula.

John Coltrane's playing has exerted a major influence on generations of musicians who followed him. Unlike many great artists who find their own voice and stay within that style, Coltrane continually evolved and changed during his career. He first came to prominence as a sideman during the mid-1950s as a member of Miles Davis's and Thelonious Monk's groups. At that time, his playing was rooted in the bebop tradition, but hinted at a new approach, with an emphasis on harp-like chord arpeggios (sometimes referred to as "sheets of sound") and a rhythmic style in which the eighth note was subdivided fairly evenly. His study of complex chord changes reached its apex in the album *Giant Steps*, but as a participant in Miles's classic *Kind of Blue* recording, Coltrane began to view *modal jazz* as an alternative direction. After forming his own group in 1960 with McCoy Tyner on piano, Steve Davis, Reginald Workman, or Jimmy Garrison on bass, and Elvin Jones on drums, he explored the use of modes, particularly pentatonic modes, to an unprecedented level. His rhythmic style continued to evolve, emphasizing the sixteenth note as the basic subdivision, as well as flurries of odd-numbered groupings. He and Elvin Jones also explored the use of polyrhythms, partially as an outgrowth of their interest in African drumming. In the last years of his life (1965–67), Coltrane became interested in the developments taking place in free jazz. He began to investigate the textural possibilities of the soprano and tenor saxophone, and used his considerable harmonic and rhythmic knowledge in new and less structured ways. Throughout his career, Coltrane's work always had a strong emotional content that reflected his spiritual concerns, but this intensified duing his latter years. His musical legacy strongly influenced the direction of the post-bop, free jazz, and jazz/rock fusion styles, and his saxophone technique had a marked effect on many of the leading players of the '70s and '80s, including Archie Shepp, Pharoah Sanders, David Liebman, Steve Grossman, Wayne Shorter, Charles Lloyd, and Michael Brecker.

"Giant Steps" is a sixteen-bar composition based on Coltrane substitutions. All the chords in the piece are ii, V, or I chords in one of three keys: B, G, or E♭ concert. In the first eight bars, the song modulates downward by major 3rds nearly every measure. The second eight-bar phrase modulates upward by major 3rds every two bars, giving the player a bit more time to negotiate the key centers.

Coltrane clearly outlines each of the chords, primarily with three- or four-note groupings too numerous to indicate. Some of the descending patterns include 5–3–1, 8–5–3, 5–3–1–♭7, 5–3–2–1, 8–5–3–1, 9–♭7–6–5, and 7–5–3–1 scale groupings. Ascending patterns include 1–3–5–7, 1–2–3–5, 3–5–8–10, 3–5–7–9, and 5–8–10 groupings. Patterns based on ascending and descending motion include 8–1–3–5, 10–5–8–10, 5–6–7–5, and 3–1–2–3 groupings. When time permits, Coltrane also employs a scalar approach, as in bars 4, 9, 12–14, 19, 30, 36, 42, 47–48, 52, 57, and 63–64. The only chord alterations are the ♭9th over the dominant chord in bar 5 and the augmented 5th over the dominant chord in bar 21. The tempo is brisk and swinging at 𝅗𝅥 = 148.

After listening to a recording of this solo, practice it at different tempos with the metronome clicking on beats 2 and 4. Then continue improvising on the chord progression in the same style. (Only the first four choruses of his solo have been transcribed.)[5]

[5]The remaining choruses may be found in a slightly different transcription by David Baker in *Downbeat* magazine, July 22, 1971.

Treble-clef C instruments:

32
Eb∆7 C#-7 F#7
3
B∆7 D7 G∆7 Bb7
36
Eb∆7 A-7 D7 G∆7 Bb7 Eb∆7 F#7
40
B∆7 F-7 Bb7 Eb∆7 A-7 D7
44
G∆7 C#-7 F#7 B∆7 F-7 Bb7
48
Eb∆7 C#-7 F#7
4
B∆7 D7 G∆7 Bb7
52
Eb∆7 A-7 D7 G∆7 Bb7 Eb∆7 F#7 B∆7
57
F-7 Bb7 Eb∆7 A-7 D7 G∆7
61
C#-7 F#7 B∆7 F-7 Bb7 Eb∆7

B♭ instruments (Trumpet—8va bassa where indicated):

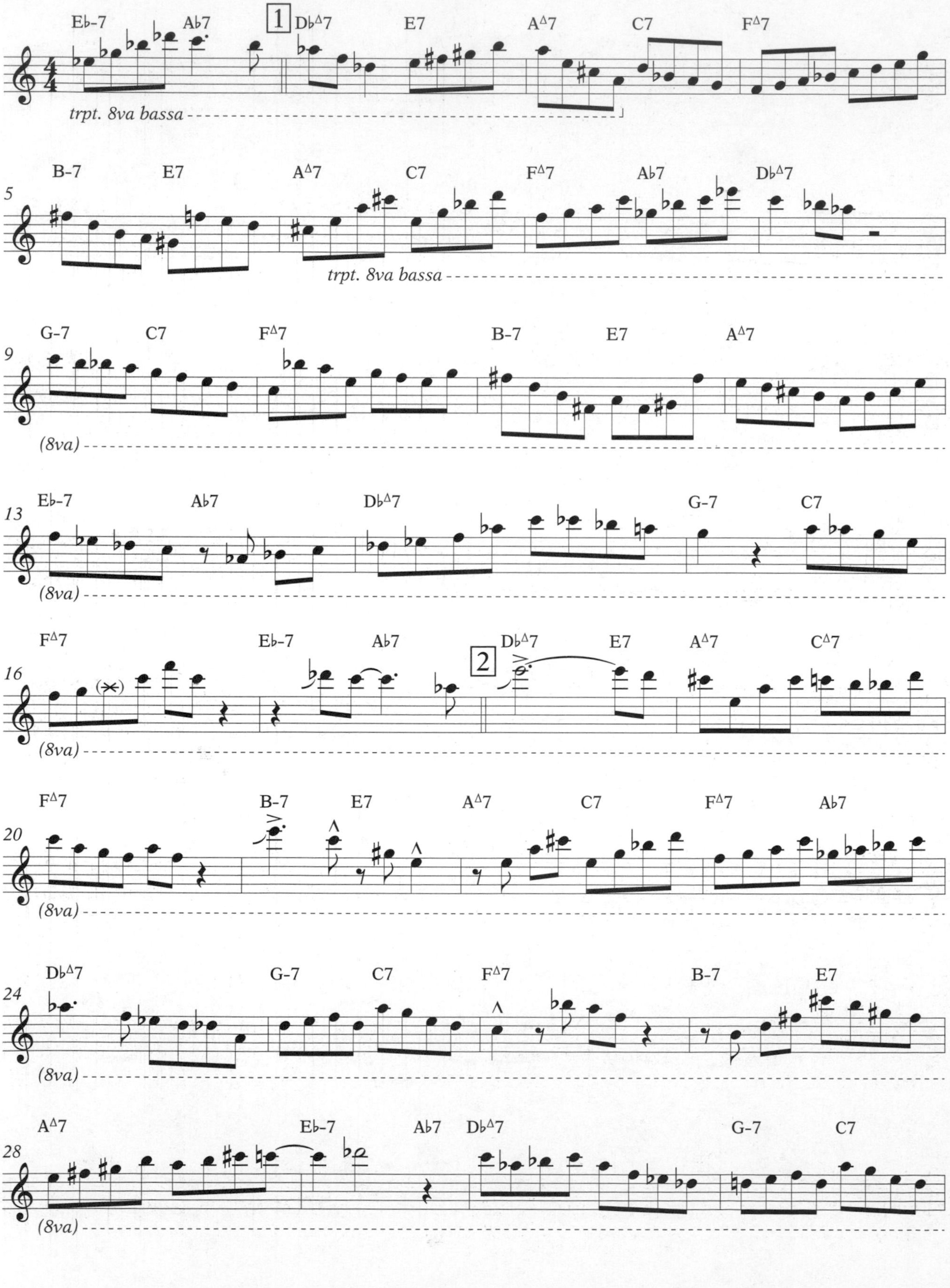

F^Δ7 E♭-7 A♭7 3 D♭^Δ7 E7 A^Δ7 C7
32
(8va)
F^Δ7 B-7 E7 A^Δ7 C7 F^Δ7 A♭7
36
trpt. 8va bassa
D♭^Δ7 G-7 C7 F^Δ7 B-7 E7
40
(8va)
A^Δ7 E♭-7 A♭7 D♭^Δ7 G-7 C7
44
(8va)
F^Δ7 E♭-7 A♭7 4 D♭^Δ7 E7 A^Δ7 C7
48
(8va)
F^Δ7 B-7 E7 A^Δ7 C7 F^Δ7 A♭7 D♭^Δ7
52
trpt. 8va bassa
G-7 C7 F^Δ7 B-7 E7 A^Δ7
57
(8va)
E♭-7 A♭7 D♭^Δ7 G-7 C7 F^Δ7
61
(8va)

E♭ instruments:

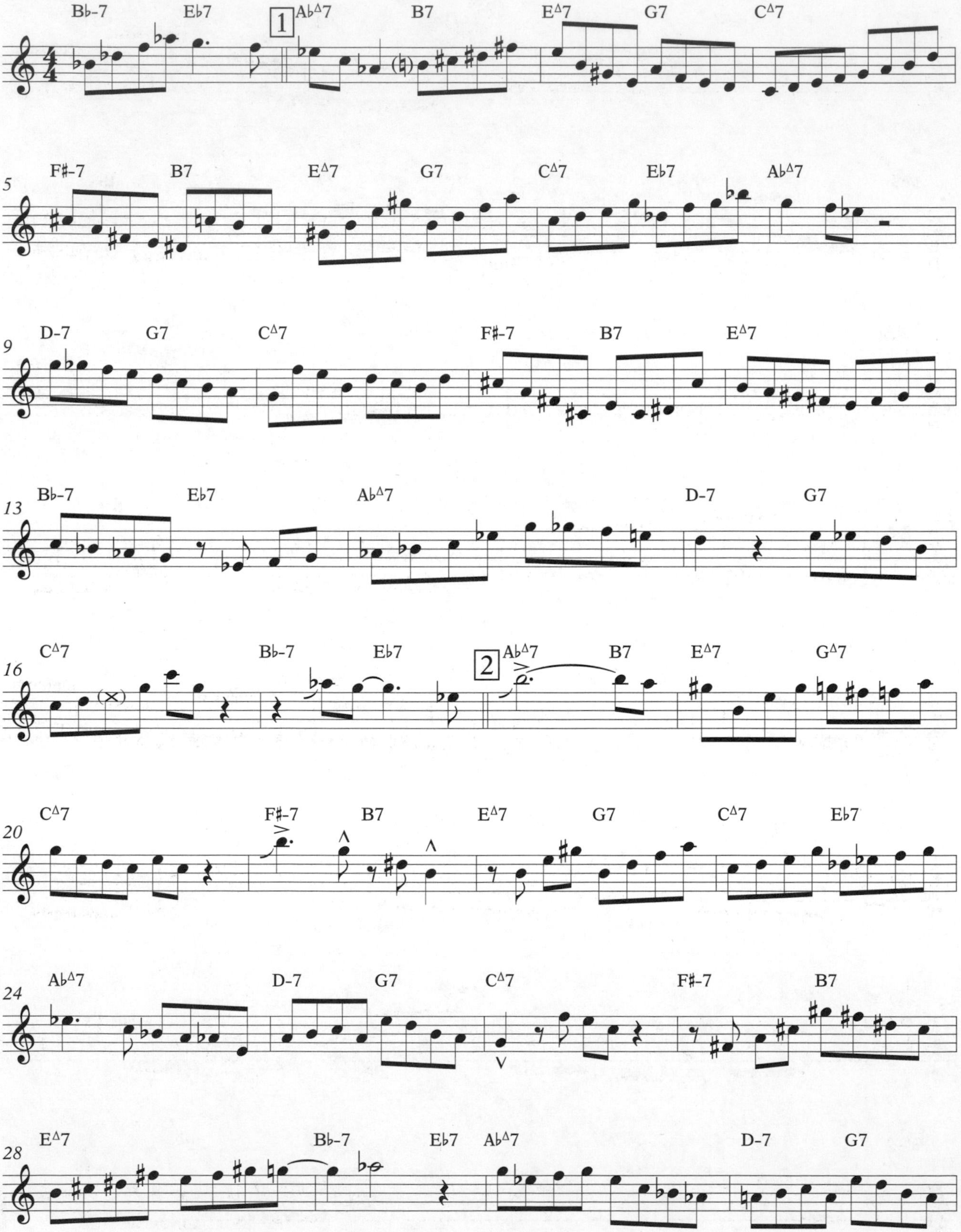

32 CΔ7 B♭-7 E♭7 3 A♭Δ7 B7 EΔ7 G7
36 CΔ7 F♯-7 B7 EΔ7 G7 CΔ7 E♭7
40 A♭Δ7 D-7 G7 CΔ7 F-7 B7
44 EΔ7 B♭-7 E♭7 A♭Δ7 D-7 G7
48 CΔ7 B♭-7 E♭7 4 A♭Δ7 B7 EΔ7 G7 CΔ7
53 F-7 B7 EΔ7 G7 CΔ7 E♭7 A♭Δ7
57 D-7 G7 CΔ7 F♯-7 B7 EΔ7
61 B♭-7 E♭7 A♭Δ7 D-7 G7 CΔ7

Bass-clef instruments:

32 E♭Δ7 C♯-7 F♯7 3 BΔ7 D7 GΔ7 B♭7
36 E♭Δ7 A-7 D7 GΔ7 B♭7 E♭Δ7 F♯7
40 BΔ7 F-7 B♭7 E♭Δ7 A-7 D7
44 GΔ7 C♯-7 F♯7 BΔ7 F-7 B♭7
48 E♭Δ7 C♯-7 F♯7 4 BΔ7 D7 GΔ7 B♭7 E♭Δ7
53 A-7 D7 GΔ7 B♭7 E♭Δ7 F♯7 BΔ7 opt. 8va
57 F-7 (8va) B♭7 E♭Δ7 A-7 D7 GΔ7
61 C♯-7 F♯7 BΔ7 F-7 B♭7 E♭Δ7

13
Free Forms

"I try to become an observer, rather than thinking what should come next."

trumpeter Tim Hagans [1]

Free improvisation, like the blues, is both a state of mind and a formal structure. Any piece of music can be played with an inner sense of freedom; in this respect, Louis Armstrong, Lester Young, and Sonny Rollins are all "free" players. This chapter, however, is concerned with the formal structure of free jazz. Free forms are those compositions in which none or few of the parameters (melody, chords, rhythm, and so forth) are predetermined. In general, there are two basic types of free forms: 1) a composition with a set melody, but no preexisting harmonic structure upon which to improvise, and 2) a spontaneously created piece devoid of any precomposed material (although a concept or basic plan may have been discussed beforehand). The first approach was initiated primarily by Ornette Coleman. This style, which Ornette called *harmolodic*, usually consisted of a composed melody in a traditional rhythmic context. It was free only in the sense that there were no predetermined chords. The soloists would improvise on fragments of the melody or develop new ideas, often adhering to one or more tonal areas. This was considered a revolutionary concept at the time, even though most of the parameters were fixed.

In the mid-1950s, Lennie Tristano, Cecil Taylor, and Sun Ra began experimenting with totally improvised compositions.[2] They were joined in the mid-1960s by groups associated with Chicago's Association for the Advancement of Creative Musicians (AACM) and St. Louis's Black Artists' Guild. These pieces could run the gamut from reliance on raw sound sources in lieu of notes, systematic atonality, implied tonal areas, or even the incorporation of traditional forms such as the blues, at the whim of the performers.

In the '60s and '70s, some musicians began composing extended works, which alternated between written themes and periods of free improvisation. Ornette Coleman's *Free Jazz* and *Skies of America*, John Coltrane's *Ascension* and *Om*, Don Cherry's *Complete Communion*, Wayne Shorter's *All Seeing Eye*, and Cecil Taylor's *Conquistador* were influential recordings in this genre.

Besides freeing the performer from the demands of a recurring chord structure, free improvisation also allows for a greater exploration of the emotional and timbre possibilities of each instrument. In this regard, many of the Free Jazz recordings are closer in spirit and technique to Early Jazz than to bebop styles.[3] Free Jazz, however, still demands that the musicians know their craft and be able to translate their feelings into sound on their instruments.

[1] Personal conversation, Lake Placid Seminars, 8/20/98.

[2] Listen to Lennie Tristano's "Intuition," or any early recordings by Cecil Taylor and Sun Ra.

[3] David Baker, personal conversation with author, Indiana University, 1981.

Gaining Facility with Free Improvisation

There is no chord progression or play-along recording for this chapter.

1. Improvise in a totally free manner, without any preconceptions. You may play anything that enters your mind, reacting to the music as pure sound. If you are improvising with other musicians, listen to them and respond.
2. *Harmolodic improvisation*: Improvise on a melody without any preexisting chord changes. Use fragments of the melody, rhythmic ideas, motivic development, or other creative ways of extending the melody.
3. Translate the following shapes into sound, using any notes, durations, or tempos that seem appropriate.

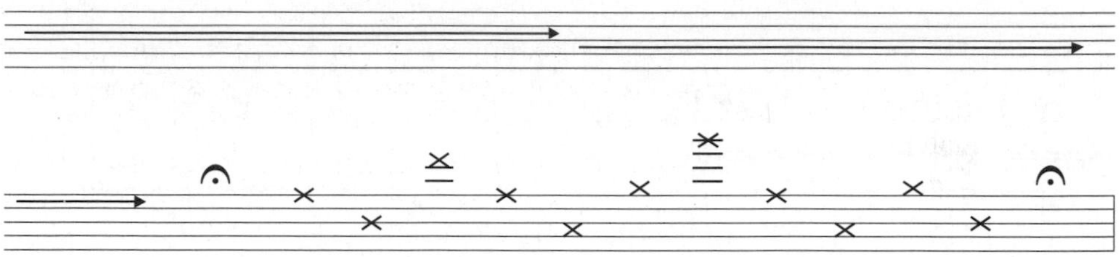

4. Improvise using the tone row below. You may use different versions of the row: retrograde (backwards), inversion (upside down), or retrograde inversion (upside down and backwards). You may also transpose the row to any pitch level. Use any durations or rhythms that seem appropriate.

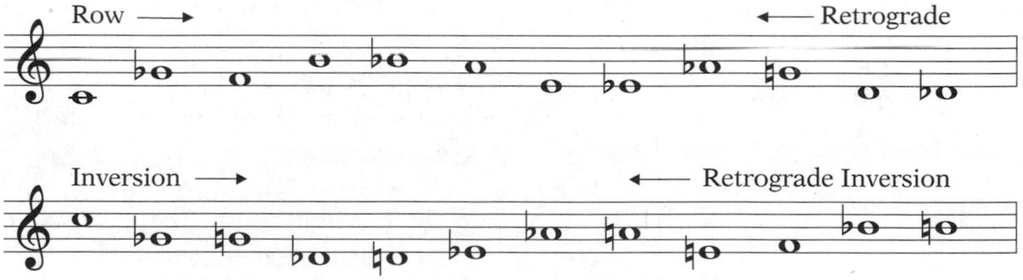

5. *Creative jazz improvisation*: Improvise on a tune with chord changes. Hear the chords in your head, but don't outline them. Let your fingers or hands move around the instrument, playing whatever they find, without any conscious control. Don't make any value judgments about "right" and "wrong" notes. Keep track of the form and periodically find resolutions in the harmony. Once you are comfortable with letting go of the need to play correct notes, apply this same approach to rhythm. Be aware of the underlying beat but don't feel obligated to play in the same meter. Occasionally resolve your ideas in time.[4]

[4] Based on the "third step exercise" by Kenny Werner, personal conversation with author, Scotch Plains, NJ, 1993.

6. Make up your own structures for free improvisation.

Improvising on Jazz Compositions Based on Free Forms

Following is a partial list of jazz composition based on free forms. These compositions are found in *The New Real Book*, vol. 1 (NRB), *The New Real Book*, vol. 2 (NR2), or one of the volumes of Jamey Aebersold's *New Approach to Jazz Improvisation* (JA).

"Bird Food" (free blues)—Ornette Coleman (NRB)

"Blues Connotation" (free blues)—Ornette Coleman (NRB)

"Expression"—John Coltrane (NR2)

"Freedom Jazz Dance"(originally a blues but performed with only a tonal area on Miles Davis's *Miles Smiles*)—Eddie Harris (NR2)

"Lookout Farm"—David Liebman (JA vol. 19)

"Off A Bird"—David Liebman (JA vol. 81)

To hear a wider cross section of compositions in this genre, listen to recordings by the following artists and groups. Please bear in mind that some of these musicians work primarily in the free jazz idiom, whereas others have made only occasional forays into this style: Muhal Richard Abrams, Geri Allen, Albert Ayler, Karl Berger, Tim Berne, Ed Blackwell, John Blake, Carla Bley, Paul Bley, Hamiet Bluiett, Jane Ira Bloom, Lester Bowie, Joanne Brackeen, Bobby Bradford, Anthony Braxton, Marion Brown, Don Byron, John Carter, Don Cherry, the Chicago Art Ensemble, Ornette Coleman, Steve Coleman, John Coltrane (1966-67), Chick Corea (1968-71), Marilyn Crispell, Andrew Cyrille, Anthony Davis, Miles Davis (1965-67), Eric Dolphy, Dave Douglas, Marty Ehrlich, the Fringe, George Garzone, Charles Gayle, Jimmy Guiffre, Charlie Haden, Tim Hagans, Herbie Hancock (1965-67), Graham Haynes, Julius Hemphill, Dave Holland, Keith Jarrett, Leroy Jenkins, Frank Lacy, Steve Lacy, Oliver Lake, George Lewis, David Liebman, Joe Lovano, Albert Mangelsdorff, Michael Mantler, Myra Melford, Pat Metheny, Roscoe Mitchell, Bobby Moses, David Murray, Sunny Murray, Amina Claudine Myers, James Newton, Bernie Nix, Orange-then-Blue, Oregon, Greg Osby, Evan Parker, Bobby Previte, Don Pullen,

Sun Ra, Dewey Redman, Sam Rivers, Sonny Rollins (*Our Man in Jazz*), Wallace Rooney, Kurt Rosenwinkle, Michele Rosewoman, Roswell Rudd, George Russell, Pharoah Sanders, Sonny Sharrock, Archie Shepp, Mathew Shipp, Wayne Shorter (1965-69), Cecil Taylor, Malachi Thompson, Henry Threadgill, Gianluigi Trovesi, Lennie Tristano (*Intuition*), Charles Tyler, Kenny Werner, Tony Williams (1965-71), the World Sax Quartet, John Zorn.

Transcribed Solos on Free Forms

For an examination of an improvised solo on a free form, listen to and play through Miles Davis's solo on "Petits Machins" in Chapter 21.

PART 4 Altered Chords, Diminished Modes, Whole-Tone and Harmonic Minor Scales, and Melodic Minor Modes

14

Diminished Scales, Diminished and Altered Dominant 7th Chords

"Many people train from a mind set
of trying to get better as fast as possible.
The irony of that is ... people skip some basic
issues that they should spend years on.
They think they are saving time, but in fact
they are dooming themselves to a certain
level which they'll never get out of."

pianist Kenny Werner[1]

Diminished scales alternate between half steps and whole steps. There are only two modes in this family—the scale that begins with a whole-step is called a *diminished (whole-step) scale*:

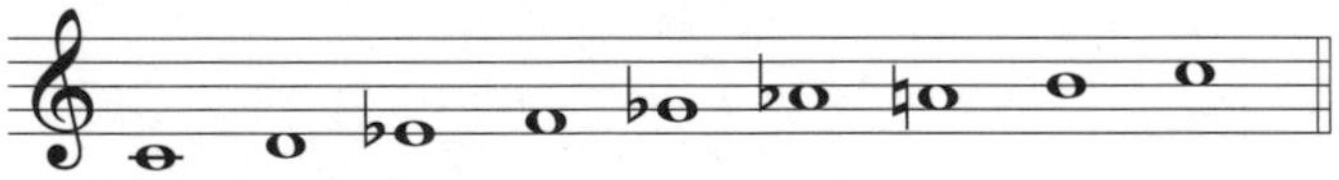

C Diminished (Whole-Step) Scale

If you begin with a half step, the resultant scale is called a *diminished (half-step) scale*:[2]

C Diminished (Half-Step) Scale

Because of their symmetrical alternation of half- and whole-steps, any of the diminished mode starting on C, E♭, G♭, or A will contain the same pitches (or their enharmonically equivalent). Likewise, the D, F, A♭, and B diminished modes, as well as the D♭, E, G, and B♭ diminished modes, all have the same pitches in common.

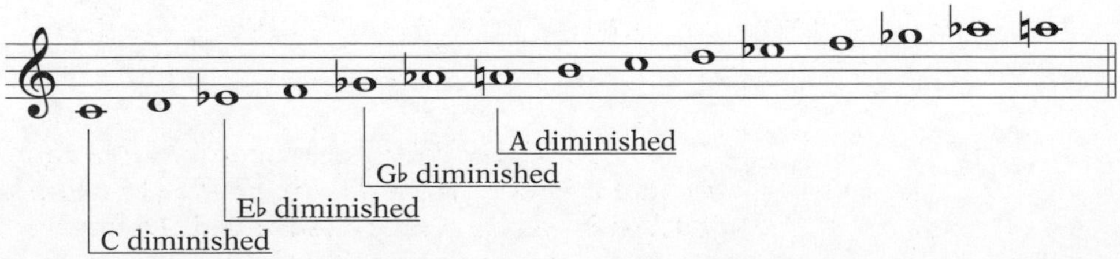

[1] Scott Reeves, "Two Conversations with Kenny Werner," *Jazz Educators Journal* (January 1999), 115.

[2] George Russell, in his *Lydian Chromatic Concept of Tonal Organization*, calls this scale an *auxiliary-diminished blues scale*. Most music theorists call it the *octatonic scale*.

The diminished (whole-step) scale is used when improvising on diminished triads, fully diminished 7th chords, diminished/major 7th chords, and a bitonal chord whose upper extensions form a triad a half step below the root, of the chord. Although a couple of the scale tones clash with the chord, the diminished (whole-step) scale may also be used with discretion over minor 7th and half-diminished 7th chords, especially when they resolve to an altered dominant 7th chord in the context of a ii–V progression.

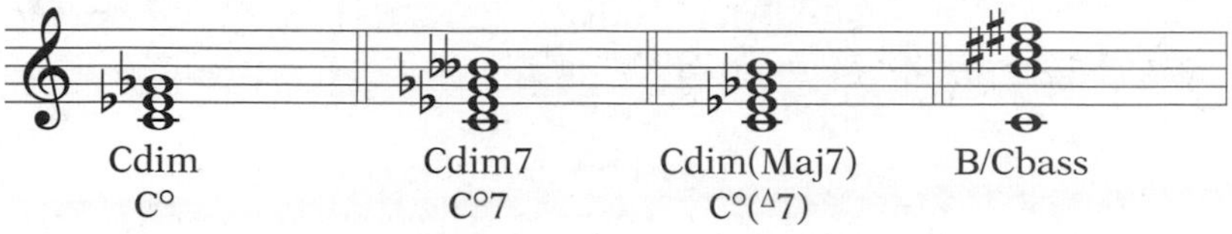

The *diminished triad* consists of a root, a minor 3rd, and a diminished 5th. A *fully-diminished 7th chord* is a diminished triad with a diminished (doubly flatted) 7th added, and a *diminished/major 7th chord* consists of a diminished triad with a major 7th added. Diminished chords usually function as passing chords between more stable sonorities:

All the notes in the diminished (whole-step) scale work well over the diminished 7th chord, with the 2nd, 4th, ♭6th, and major 7th having the most color.

The diminished (half-step) scale is used when improvising over a dominant 7th chord with a ♭9th, ♯9th, or ♭5th, particularly when the chord is functioning as a V chord in a major key. (In minor keys, V chords are best colored by the diminished/whole-tone scale—see Chapter 17.) The diminished (half-step) scale also may be used over two bitonal chords, one formed from a triad a diminished 5th above the root and another formed by a triad a major 6th above the root.

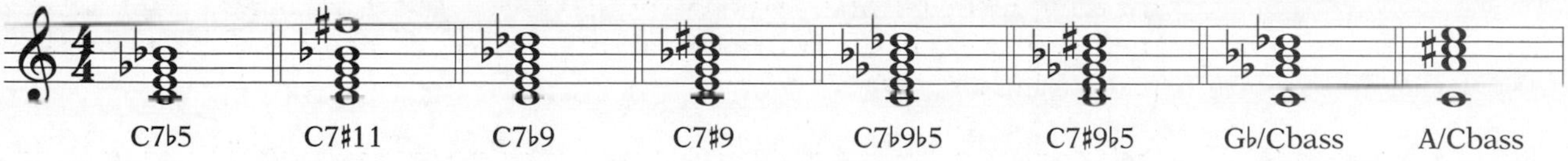

The *dominant 7th ♭5 chord* consists of a root, a major 3rd, a diminished 5th, and a minor 7th. A *dominant 7th ♯11 chord* consists of a dominant 7th chord with an augmented 11th added. Adding a minor 9th to a dominant 7th chord creates a *dominant 7th ♭9 chord,* while a *dominant 7th ♯9 chord* consists of a dominant 7th chord with an augmented 9th. All the notes in the diminished (half-step) scale work well over altered dominant chords; the melodic use of the ♯9–♭9th is highly characteristic of bebop and post-bop styles.

Theory/Ear Exercises

1. Write the diminished (whole-step) and diminished (half-step) scales in all twelve keys. Determine which of these scales use the same notes.
2. Write the fully diminished 7th, dominant 7♭9, dominant 7♯9, and dominant 7♭5 chords in all twelve keys.
3. *Keyboard skills*: Play diminished and altered dominant chords on the piano, and listen to their characteristic sound or color.
4. *Melodic and harmonic dictation*: Notate melodies based on diminished modes, and try to identify different alterations of dominant 7th chords when played on the piano.
5. *Transcription*: Transcribe a melody, a chord progression, or an improvised solo from a recording.

Gaining Facility with Diminished Scales

Practice the following exercises over the chord progression below, using either a metronome or the play-along recordings from *Creative Beginnings: An Introduction to Jazz Improvisation* (track 7) or volume 3, *The ii–V–I Progression* (track 2), of *A New Approach to Jazz Improvisation* by Jamey Aebersold. If you find yourself struggling with an exercise, slow it down, simplify it, or sing it while visualizing yourself playing it. After familiarizing yourself with the exercises, pick one or two to practice repeatedly, until you can play them without any conscious thought.

C instruments begin here

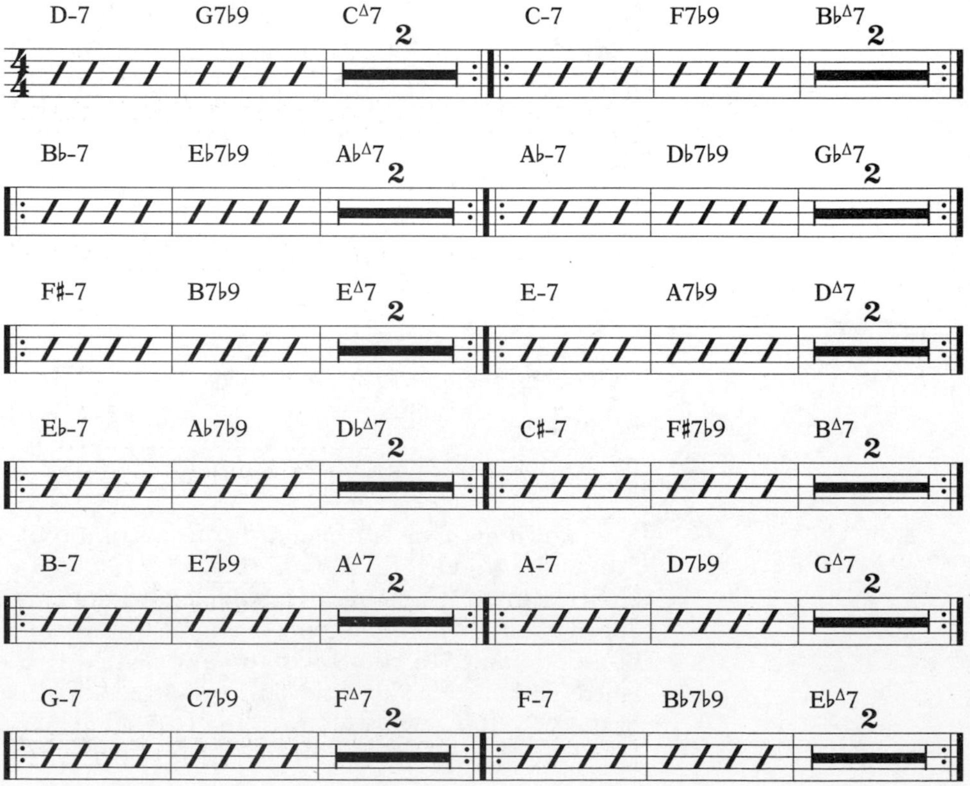

B♭ instruments begin here

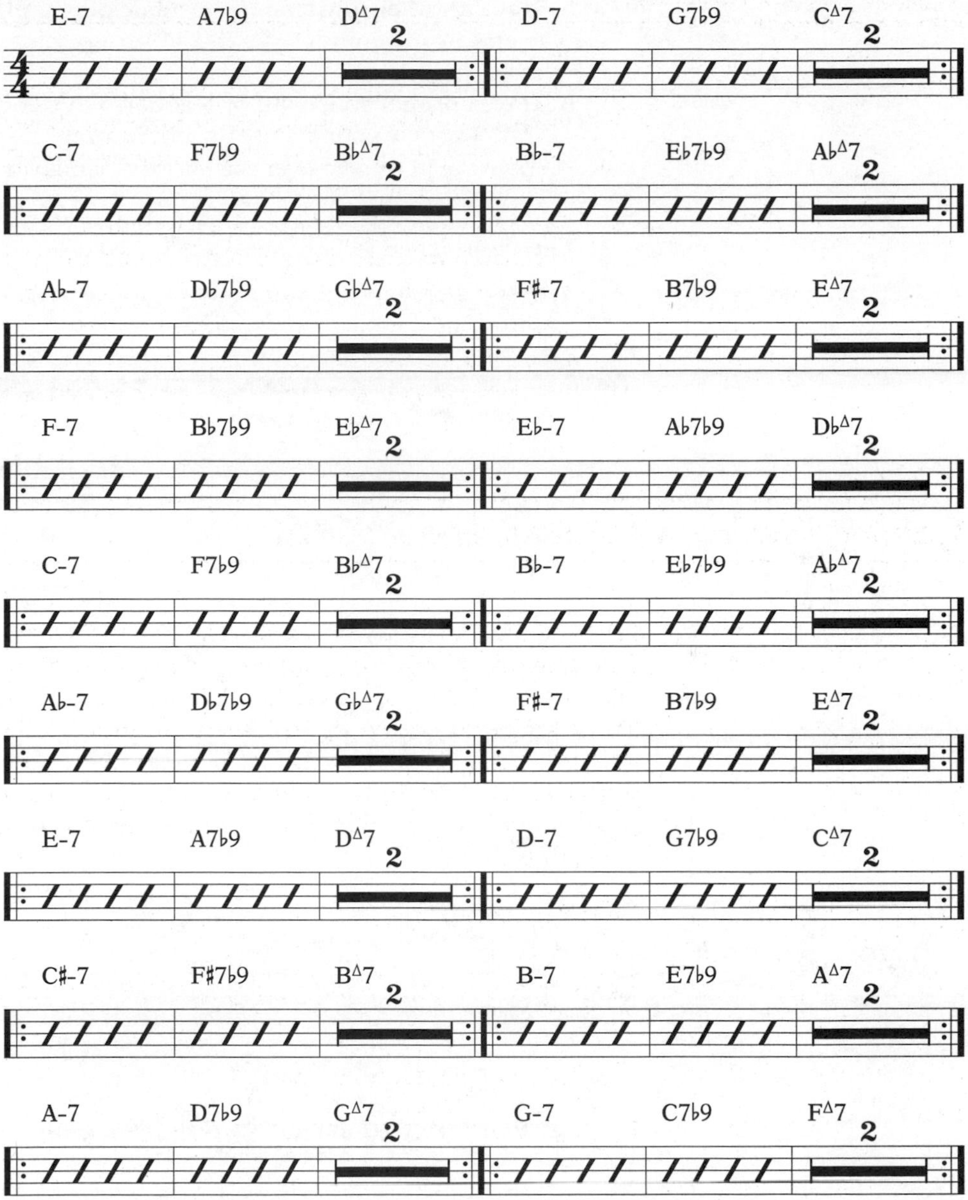

E♭ instruments begin here

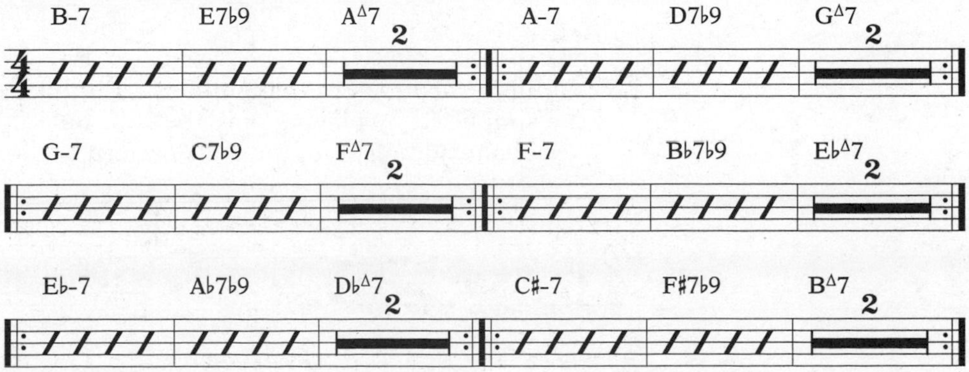

1. *Warmups*:
   a. Have another musician or teacher play a phrase based on diminished scales in the context of a ii–V–I progression. Play back the phrase you have just heard.
   b. Have another musician or teacher play random sequences of ii–V and ii–V–I progressions. Play the corresponding diminished scales on your instrument or solo over the chords, using your ear to determine the correct key area.
2. The diminished (whole-step) scale based on the root of the ii chord.

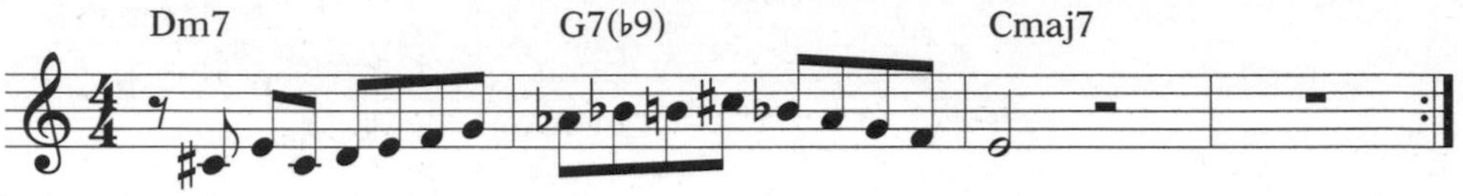

MM ____________________

3. The diminished (half-step) scale based on the root of the V chord.

MM ____________________

4. A David Baker pattern.

MM ____________________

5. A pattern used frequently by Miles Davis and J. J. Johnson in the 1950s.

MM ____________________

6. A diminished pattern that outlines a diminished chord. This pattern can be simplified by playing only the first note of each four-note grouping, gradually adding notes until the pattern is complete.

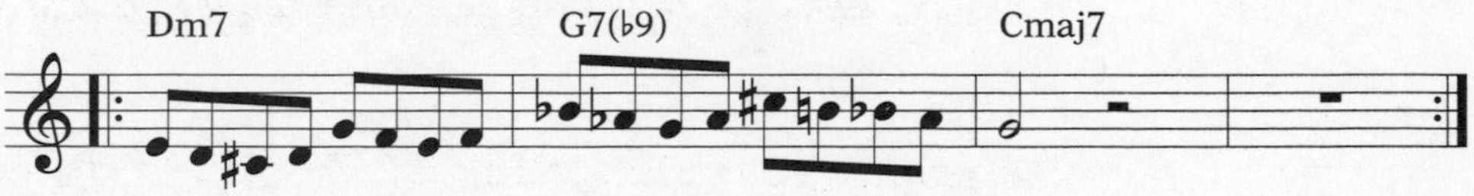

MM ____________________

7. A J. J. Johnson pattern from his "Aquarius" solo (*J. J. Inc.*, Columbia, AL 36808).

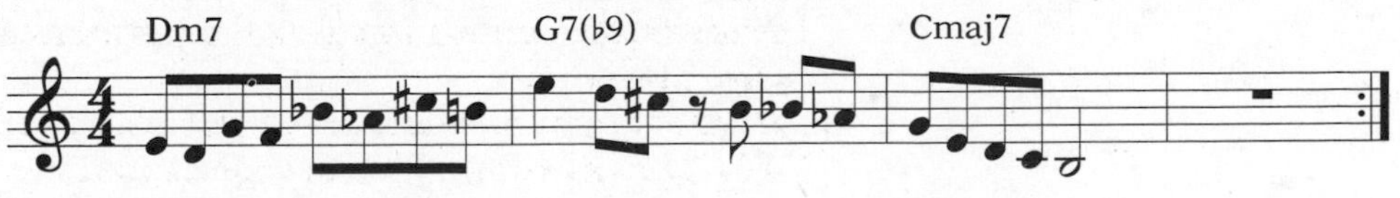

MM ____________________

8. Fully diminished 7th arpeggios.

MM ____________________

9. A Michael Brecker pattern that outlines triads descending by minor thirds.

MM ____________________

10. A diminished pattern using the interval of the major 7th. This pattern may be heard in Jerry Dodgion's composition "Thank You" (Thad Jones/Mel Lewis Orchestra, *New Life*, Horizon Sp 707).

MM ____________________

11. A Tom Harrell pattern that employs inverted 4ths descending by minor 3rds (Bob Berg, *New Life*, Xanadu 159).

MM ____________________

12. *Creative jazz improvisation*: Improvise over a ii–V–I progression in one key for thirty minutes or more. Experiment to see what you can discover. Tape record yourself and listen to the results. You may find new directions and ideas to practice that will help you discover your inner voice.

13. Make up your own patterns and melodic ideas based on the diminished modes.

a.

MM ____________________

b.

MM ____________________

Improvising on Jazz Compositions Based on Altered Dominant or Fully-Diminished Chords

Following is a partial list of jazz compositions that contain fully-diminished or dominant 7 ♯9 chords. These compositions are found in *The New Real Book*, vol. 1 (NRB), *The New Real Book*, vol. 2 (NR2), one of the volumes of Jamey Aebersold's *New Approach to Jazz Improvisation* (JA), or *Creative Beginnings: An Introduction to Jazz Improvisation* (CB). Memorize the most frequently played songs, and practice them in different keys.

Compositions In Which Fully Diminished Chords Occur Frequently

"Body & Soul"—Heyman/Sour/Eyton (JA vols. 25 and 74)
"Bye, Bye Blackbird"—Dixon/Henderson (JA vol. 65)
"Bye, Bye Blues"—Lowe/Gray/Bennett/Hamm (JA 79)
"Corcovado" ("Quiet Nights of Quiet Stars")—Antonio Carlos Jobim (JA vol. 31)
"Desafinado"—Mendonca/Jobim/Hendricks/Cavanaugh (JA vol. 74)
"Donna Lee"—Charlie Parker (JA vols. 6 and 69)
"Easy Living"—Robin/Rainger (JA vol. 59)
"Every Thing Happens to Me"—Adair/Dennis (JA vol. 23, NRB)
"How Insensitive"—Antonio Carlos Jobim (JA vol. 31)
"I Remember Clifford"—Benny Golson (JA vol. 14)
"Illegal Entrance"—David Baker (JA vol. 76)
"Imagination"—Van Heusen/Burke (JA vol. 58)
"Just Friends"—Davies, Klenner, Lewis (JA vol. 59)
"Like Someone in Love"—Burke/Van Heusen (JA vol. 23, NRB)
"Lover Come Back to Me"—Hammerstein/Romberg (JA vol. 41)
"Meditation"—Antonio Carlos Jobim (JA vol. 31, NRB)
"Napanoch"—David Liebman (NR2)
"Once I Loved"—Antonio Carlos Jobim (JA vol. 31, NRB)
"Sail Away"—Tom Harrell (JA vol. 63)
"September Song"—Weill/Anderson (JA vol. 65)
"Solitude"—Duke Ellington (JA vol. 12)
"Spring Is Here"—Hart/Rogers (JA vol. 34)
"The Hardbop Grandpop"—Horace Silver (JA vol. 86)
"The Song Is You"—Hammerstein/Kern (JA vol. 15)
"Upper Manhattan Medical Group"—Billy Strayhorn (JA vol. 66)
"Wave"—Antonio Carlos Jobim (JA vol. 31)
"Witchcraft"—Leigh/Coleman (JA vol. 44, NRB)

Compositions In Which Dominant 7 ♯9 Chords Occur Frequently

"Barbara"—Horace Silver (JA vol. 18)
"Blue in Green"—Evans/Davis (JA vol. 50)
"Caravan"—Ellington, Mills, Tizol (JA vol. 59)
"E.S.P."—Wayne Shorter (JA vol. 33, NRB)
"Have You Met Miss Jones?"—Hart/Rodgers (JA vols. 25 and 74)

"Hi-Fly"—Randy Weston (JA vol. 43, NR2)
"Le Miroir Noir"—David Baker (JA vol. 10)
"Invitation"—Kaper/Webster (JA vol. 59)
"Nuthouse"—Scott Reeves (CB)
"Peace"—Horace Silver (JA vol. 17, NR2)
"Stella By Starlight"—Washington/Young (JA vols. 59, 67, and 85)
"The Boy Next Door"—Martin/Blane (JA vol. 71)
"What It Is"—David Liebman (JA vol. 81)

J. J. Johnson's Improvised Solo on "Aquarius"

J. J. Johnson's improvised trombone solo on his composition "Aquarius" was transcribed from the album *J. J. Inc*. Originally issued by Columbia Records in 1961, it has been rereleased on Columbia's Jazz Odyssey series (Columbia AL 36808). The group features Freddie Hubbard on trumpet, Clifford Jordan on tenor sax, Arthur Harper on bass, Albert "Tootie" Heath on drums, and Cedar Walton on piano.

J. J. Johnson is generally acknowledged to be one of the first trombonists to successfully assimilate the bebop vocabulary, and was one of the few trombonists with whom Charlie Parker chose to record. He is also a master composer/arranger, and his improvised solos reflect his strong sense of construction and development. Like his friend and erstwhile employer Miles Davis, J. J. never uses unnecessary notes. Each note serves the purpose of bringing out colorful chord extensions or developing a melodic or rhythmic idea. He has a warm, clear sound on the trombone and plays effortlessly and cleanly at any tempo.

"Aquarius" is based on a modified blues form. Instead of progressing to a iv chord in the second phrase, the harmony moves down a major 2nd to the ♭vii chord for four bars. In the third phrase, the V/ii and ♭VI chords delay the occurrence of the ii$^{\varnothing}$7–V7–i cadence by one bar, but the twelve-bar structure still is preserved.

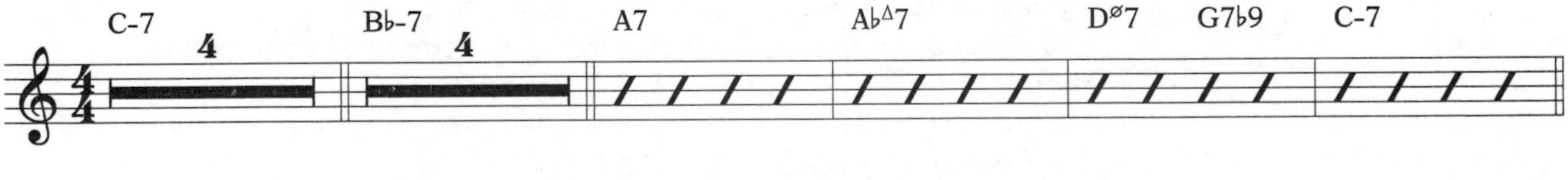

The composition is in 12/8, at ♩. = 84 m.m. The rhythm section maintains the 12/8 groove, but J. J. solos in 4/4, creating a three-against-two hemiola. He also plays with the time, speeding up and slowing down to create a floating feeling without changing the basic tempo. To simplify the reading of the solo, this transcription is notated in a double-time 4/4 meter, with the quarter note at 168 m.m., creating a 24-bar blues form.

J. J.'s penchant for bringing out colorful notes in the chord can be seen in bars 17–18, where he plays a C triad over the A7 chord, a bitonal relationship derived from the diminished (half-step) scale. In bars 25–27, he develops a rhythmic motive that emphasizes the 9th, 11th, and 13th of the tonic minor chord. He uses the diminished (half-step) scale once again in bars 41–42, drawing on a pattern based on major 2nds ascending by minor 3rds. At the end of his solo, J. J. demonstrates his sensitivity for harmonic color by ending on the 9th of the tonic minor chord.

After listening closely to a recording of this solo, practice it at different tempos with the metronome clicking on beats 2 and 4. Then continue improvising on the chord progression in the same style.

Treble-clef C instruments:

B♭ instruments (Trumpet—8va basso when necessary):

2nd chorus

E♭ instruments:

13
hold back
3
F#7(#9)
17
hold way back
3
Fmaj7
B∅7
21
E7(♭9)
Am7
2nd chorus
Am7
25
29
hold back
Gm7
33
3
36
40
F#7(#9)
Fmaj7
44
3
B∅7
E7(♭9)
Am7

Bass-clef instruments:

36
40
A7(♯9)
A♭maj7
44
3
D⌀7
G7(♭9)
Cm7

15
Whole-Tone Scales and Augmented Chords

"In the West, we tend to emphasize
how great we are,
this or that one is a great musician.
But in Africa, playing well is only
one part of the story.
You have to be respected by the community,
to be clean in mind and spirit.
If you play music,
you may have to cure someone,
and if you don't play the right note,
if your heart is not in the right place,
you can injure that person."

pianist Randy Weston[1]

The *whole-tone scale*, also known as the *auxiliary augmented scale*, consists entirely of whole steps. This gives the scale a very identifiable, exotic sound, to which certain composers like Claude Debussy and Thelonious Monk have been drawn. However, because all the adjacent intervals are major 2nds, the melodic possibilities are somewhat limited, and only one mode exists in this scale.

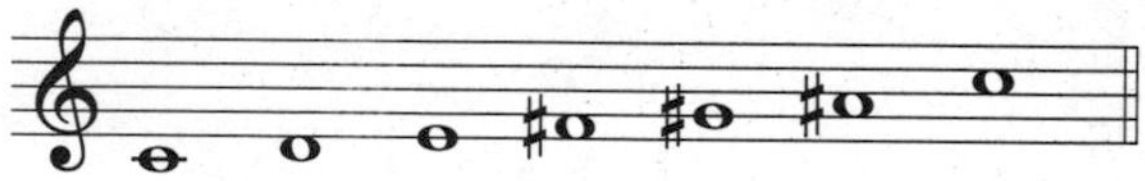

C Whole-Tone Scale

Since the scale is made up entirely of whole steps, the notes of the C, D, E, F♯ (G♭), G♯ (A♭), and A♯ (B♭) whole-tone scales are all *enharmonic*; that is, they sound the same even though they may be written differently. Likewise, the C♯ (D♭), D♯ (E♭), F, G, A, and B (C♭) whole-tone scales are enharmonic to each other.

The notes of the whole-tone scale may be used when improvising on augmented triads or dominant 7th chords with any combination of raised or lowered 5ths *and* major 9ths. You may also use the whole-tone scale over the minor 7th chord a perfect 4th below, although this will yield a certain amount of dissonance.[2]

[1] Ted Panken, "Randy Weston: African Soul," *Downbeat* (October 1998) 25.

[2] For an example of the use of a whole-tone scale over the minor 7th chord a perfect 4th below, listen to "Chim-Chim-Cheree" on *The John Coltrane Quartet Plays* (Impulse Records).

The *augmented triad* consists of a tonic, a major 3rd, and an augmented 5th. The *dominant 7th ♯5 chord* adds a minor 7th to the augmented triad, while the *dominant 7th ♭5 chord* replaces the augmented 5th with a diminished 5th. Adding a major 9th to the either chord creates *dominant 9th* ♭5 and *dominant 9th ♯5 chords*. (Notice that both the whole-tone and the diminished [half-step] scales contain diminished 5ths, but only the whole-tone scale contains an augmented 5th and a major 9th.) In general, every note in the whole-tone scale works well over these chords, with the augmented 5th giving the scale its characteristic sound.

Theory/Ear Exercises

1. Write the augmented triad, the dominant 7th ♭5 chord, and the dominant 9th ♯5 chord in all keys.
2. *Keyboard skills*: Play these chords on the piano, and listen to their characteristic sound or color.
3. *Harmonic identification*: Use your ear to differentiate among the different types of dominant 9th chords studied thus far: dominant 9th, dominant 7th ♭9, dominant 7th ♯9, dominant 9th ♭5, dominant 9th ♯5, dominant 7th ♭9 ♭5, dominant 7th ♯9 ♭5.
4. *Transcription*: Transcribe a melody, a chord progression, or an improvised solo from a recording.

Gaining Facility with Whole-Tone Scales

Practice the following exercises over the chord progression below, using a metronome. If you find yourself struggling with an exercise, slow it down, simplify it, or sing it while visualizing yourself playing it. After familiarizing yourself with the exercises, pick one or two to practice repeatedly, until you can play them without any conscious thought.

C instruments begin here

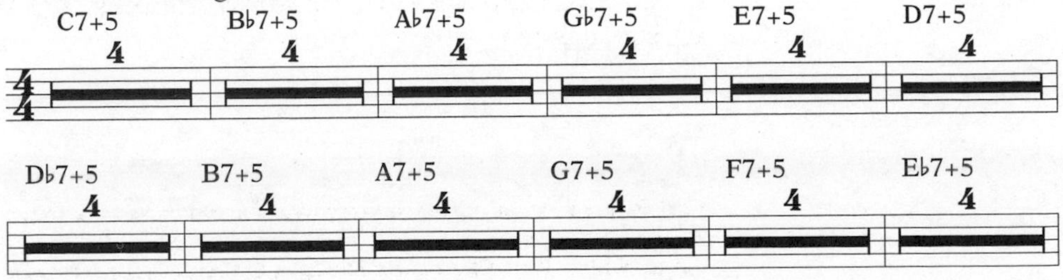

B♭ instruments begin here

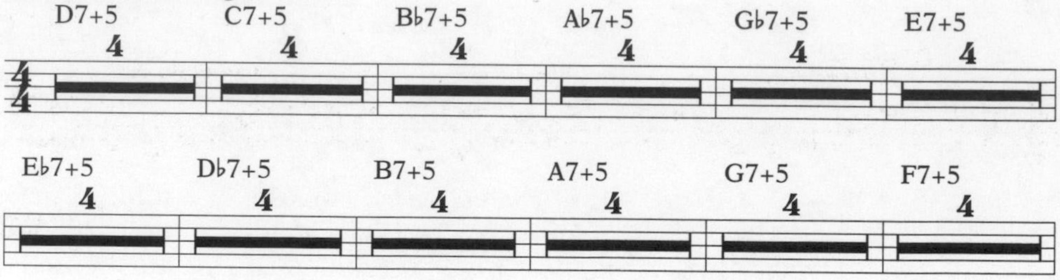

E♭ instruments begin here

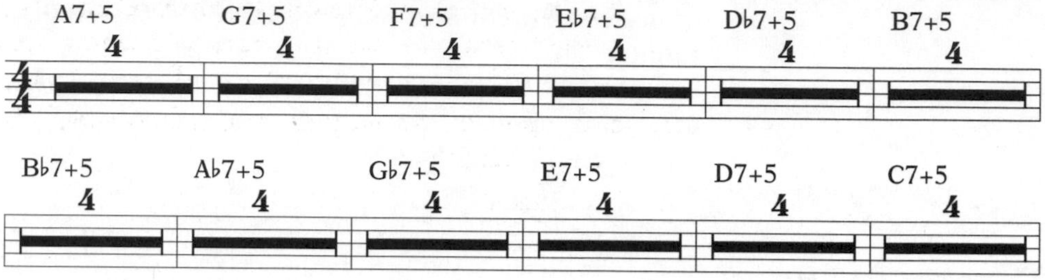

1. *Warmups*: Have another musician or your instructor play random sequences of chords. Play the corresponding scale on your instrument or solo over the chords, using your ear to determine the correct key.
2. The basic scale.

MM ____________

3. Major 3rds descending by whole steps.

MM ____________

4. Outlining the augmented triad.

MM ____________

5. A variation on exercise 2.

MM ____________

6. A paraphrase of a motive from John Coltrane's "One-Up, One-Down."

MM ____________________

7. *Creative jazz improvisation*: Improvise over the chord progression, focusing only on the contour of the phrases you are playing, instead of the notes. The dissonance inherent in augmented chords can be liberating, opening up the possibility that any note will work. This frees you up to concentrate on the shape and direction of your lines.
8. Make up your own patterns and melodic ideas based on whole-tone scales and augmented chords.

MM ____________________

Improvising on Jazz Compositions Based on Dominant 9 ♯5 Chords or Whole-Tone Scales

Following is a partial list of jazz compositions that contain dominant 9 ♯5 chords or whole-tone scales. These compositions are found in *The New Real Book*, vol. 1 (NRB), *The New Real Book*, vol. 2 (NR2), one of the volumes of Jamey Aebersold's *New Approach to Jazz Improvisation* (JA), or *Creative Beginnings: An Introduction to Jazz Improvisation* (CB). Memorize the most frequently played songs, and practice them in different keys.

Compositions Based Exclusively on Dominant 9 ♯5 Chords

"One-Up, One-Down"—John Coltrane
"Our Man Higgins"—Lee Morgan
"Spanning"—Charles Tolliver

Compositions In Which Dominant 9 ♯5 Chords Occur Frequently

"Body & Soul" (Coltrane version)—John Green (JA vol. 75)
"Desafinado"—Mendonca/Jobim/Hendricks/Cavanaugh (JA vol. 74, NRB)
"Exotica"—John Coltrane (JA vol. 75)
"Gregory Is Here"—Horace Silver (JA vol. 17, NR2)
"Jody Grind"—Horace Silver (JA vol. 17)
"Ju-Ju"—Wayne Shorter (JA vol. 33)
"Le Roi"—David Baker (JA vol. 10)
"Stella By Starlight"—Washington/Young (JA vols. 22 and 59)
"Take The 'A' Train"—Billy Strayhorn (JA vols. 12, 65, and 66, NRB)

Thelonious Monk's Improvised Solo on "Evidence"

Thelonious Monk's improvised piano solo on his composition "Evidence" illustrates many of his trademark devices, including angular melodic contours, unpredictable rhythms, tone clusters, and sixteenth-note runs comprised of whole-tone scales. This solo was transcribed from the *Smithsonian Collection of Classic Jazz,* but originally appeared on a 1948 Blue Note release (BLP 1509) that featured Monk's quartet of Milt Jackson on vibes, John Simmons on bass, and Shadow Wilson on drums.

Along with Charlie Parker and Dizzy Gillespie, Thelonious Monk was a pioneer in the formulation of the bebop style. His highly imaginative and frequently unpredictable style was uniquely personal and not easily imitated. He is considered one of jazz's greatest composers and his improvisations typically reflect his compositional sensibilities in their development of the melody and primary motives.

"Evidence" is based on the chord progression to a popular standard, "Just you, Just Me." Monk's unique and often quirky thought process is apparent even in his derivation of the title: just you, just me = just us = justice = evidence.[3] The melody to "Evidence" consists of very short motives which occur at unpredictable places in the rhythm. His penchant for working with motives can also be seen in his solo, particularly in bars 1, 6, 8, 11–12, 19–21, 23–24, and 27–28. Monk's delight in dissonance is quite apparent, as demonstrated by his use of the ♭5th of the chord in bars 3, 5, 10, 13, 27, and 29, the ♭9th in bars 10 and 28 and the tone-clusters in bars 1, 3, 6, 9, 10, 24, 27, 29, and 31–32. The whole-tone scale, his signature device, is used extensively in bars 4, 11–12, 17–18, 23–24, and 31–32.

After listening to a recording of this solo, practice it at different tempos with the metronome clicking on beats 2 and 4 (the original tempo is approximately ♩ = 166 m.m.). Then continue improvising in the same style.

[3] David Baker, personal conversation with author, Bloomington, IN, 1981.

Treble-clef C instruments:

B♭ instruments (Saxophone—8va where indicated):

E♭ instruments:

10
A7
D7♭5
12
G7+5
C7♭5
FΔ7
B♭7
15
D-7
G7
CΔ7
C7+5
19
FΔ7
F-7
B♭7
21
CΔ7
A7
23
D7♭5
G7+5
25
CΔ7
A7
D7♭5
28
G7♭9
C7♭5
FΔ7
B♭7
31
D-7
G7+5
CΔ7

Bass-clef instruments:

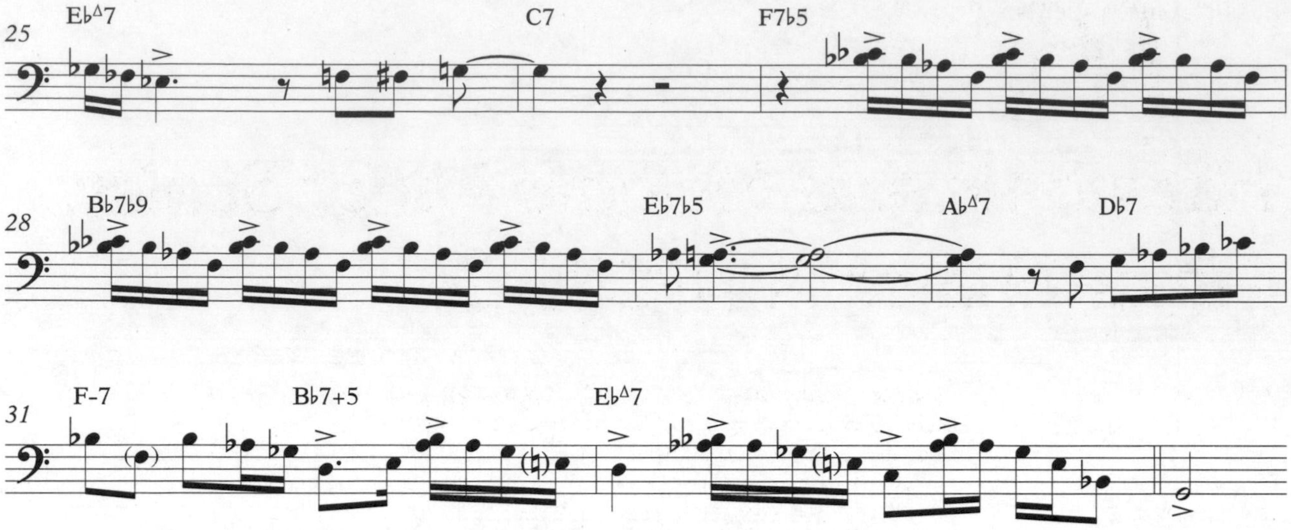
25
Eb∆7
C7
F7b5
28
Bb7b9
Eb7b5
Ab∆7
Db7
31
F-7
Bb7+5
Eb∆7

16

Harmonic and Melodic Minor Scales, Minor (Major 7th) Chords

"I sort of let the music take over by approaching it
through what you may call a Zen manner,
in that you close your mind—
you blank out your mind.
I've always done that when I was playing,
even when I started out,
without really knowing that I was doing Zen."

saxophonist Sonny Rollins[1]

The *harmonic minor scale* consists of the ascending pattern: whole step, half step, whole step, whole step, half step, augmented 2nd, half step. The interval of the augmented 2nd between the sixth and seventh notes gives this scale its characteristic exotic color.

C Harmonic Minor Scale

The notes in this scale may be used when improvising over minor triads, minor (major 7) chords, and minor 9 (major 7) chords.

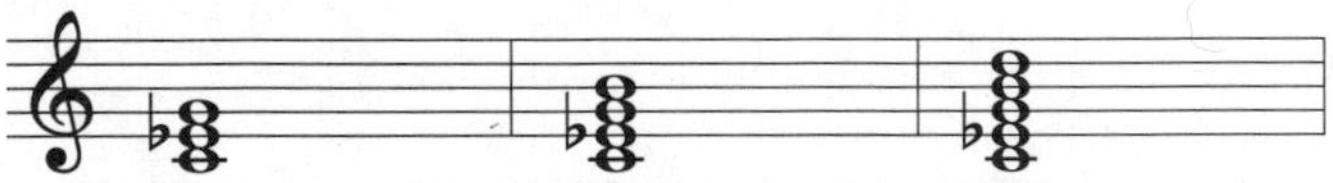

The *minor (major 7) chord* consists of a minor triad with a major 7th added. Adding a major 9th to this chord creates a *minor 9 (major 7) chord*. Typically, minor chords with major 7ths function as i or tonic chords in a minor key. The second and seventh notes in the harmonic minor scale are rich color tones when used over a minor chord. The flatted 6th is best used as a passing or neighbor tone to the 5th.

The *melodic minor scale* has a different sequence of notes when ascending than when descending. The ascending version, also known as the *jazz melodic minor scale* (the only version we will be concerned with), consists of the pattern: whole step, half step, whole step, whole step, whole step, whole step, half step.

[1] Mark Lewis, *San Diego.Sidewalk* MSN/Microsoft (May 1999).

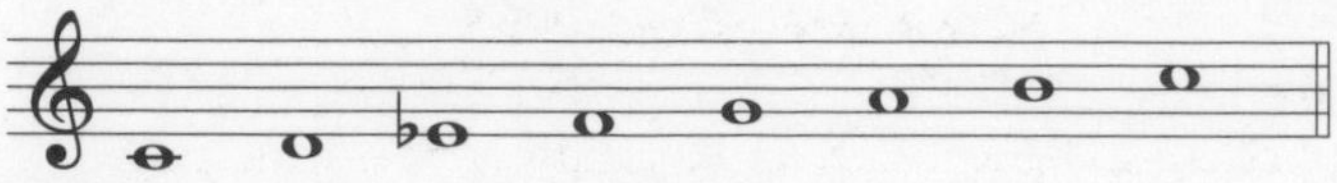

C Melodic Minor (Ascending Version)

It is the first mode in the family that includes the lydian augmented, lydian dominant, locrian ♯2, and diminished/whole-tone modes.[2] You may think of the melodic minor scale as a dorian scale with a major 7th or as a major scale with a minor 3rd. Like the harmonic minor scale, this scale may also be used when improvising on minor triads, minor (major 7) chords, and minor 9 (major 7) chords. All the notes in the scale work well over these chords, with the second, sixth, and seventh degrees having the richest color. Many players utilize the melodic tension created by the tritone that occurs between the minor 3rd and the major 6th.

Theory/Ear Exercises

1. Write the harmonic minor and jazz melodic minor scales in all twelve keys.
2. Compare these two scales with the minor scales previously studied (dorian, phrygian, and aeolian). How do these scales differ with regard to the sixth and seventh scale degrees? What notes do they have in common?
3. Write the minor/major 7th chords in all twelve keys.
4. *Keyboard skills*: Play the chord progressions from this chapter on the piano. How does the sound of the minor/major 7th differ from the minor 7th chord?
5. *Melodic and harmonic dictation*: Notate melodies and chord progressions based on the various types of minor scales and chords previously studied.
6. *Transcription*: Transcribe a melody, chord progression, or an improvised solo from a recording.

Gaining Facility with Melodic Minor Scales and Minor (Major 7th) Chords

Practice the following exercises over the chord progression below, using either a metronome or the play-along recording from *Creative Beginnings: An Introduction to Jazz Improvisation* (track 8). By ignoring the repeat signs, you can also use volume or vol. 21, *Gettin' It Together* (disc 2, track 13), of *A New Approach to Jazz Improvisation* by Jamey Aebersold. If you find yourself struggling with an exercise, slow it down, simplify it, or sing it while visualizing yourself playing it. After familiarizing yourself with the exercises, pick one or two to practice repeatedly, until you can play them without any conscious thought.

[2] See the Appendix for modes in the melodic minor scale.

C instruments begin here

B♭ instruments begin here

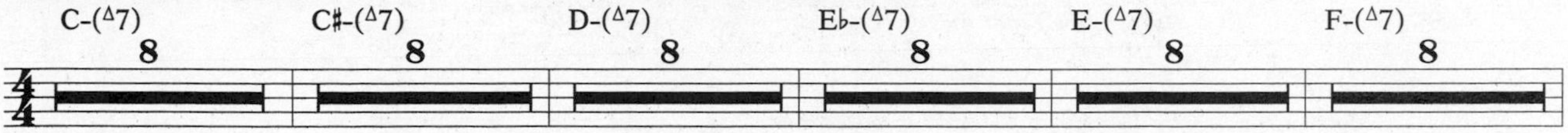

E♭ instruments begin here

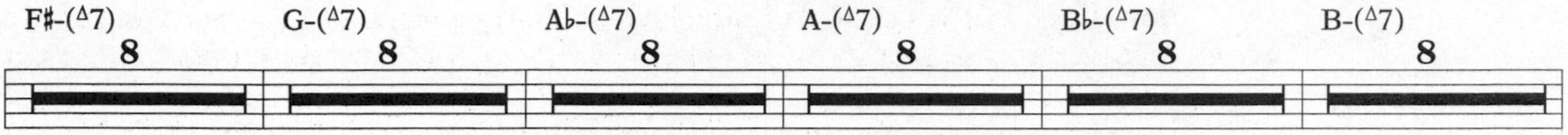

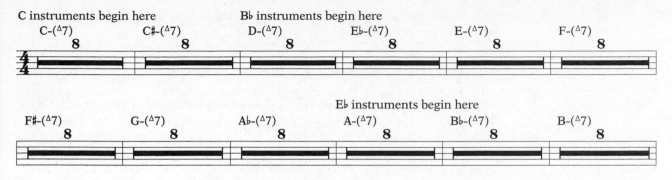

1. *Call and response warmups*: Have another musician or teacher play a phrase that fits over a minor/major 7th chord. Play back the phrase you have just heard.
2. The harmonic minor scale.

MM ____________________

3. The melodic minor scale.

MM ____________________

4. A minor 9th/major 7th arpeggio pattern.

MM ____________________

5. The arpeggio to the 11th.

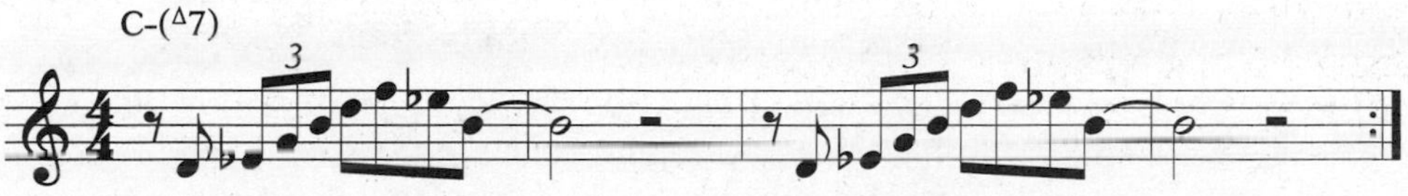

MM ____________________

6. A Freddie Hubbard line based on a melodic minor scale, which ends with the tritone that occurs between the ♭3rd and the 6th (J. J. Johnson, "Shutterbug", *J. J. Inc.*, Columbia AL 36808).

MM ____________________

7. A Sonny Rollins pattern from his "Airegin" solo (Miles Davis, *Miles Davis and the Modern Jazz Giants,* Prestige 7150).

MM ____________________

8. *Creative jazz improvisation*:

a. *Your inner voice*: Scat sing a solo into a tape recorder while playing the chord progression on the piano. Transcribe what you sang and play it on your instrument.

b. *Vocalizing your improvisation*: Using your instrument, improvise over the chord progression without looking at the chord symbols. Imagine that your melodies have words set to them.

9. Make up your own patterns and melodic ideas based on harmonic and melodic minor scales or minor/major 7th chords.

a.

MM ____________________

b.

MM ____________________

Improvising on Jazz Compositions Based on Minor (Major 7th) Chords

Following is a partial list of jazz compositions that contain minor/major 7th chords, or tonic minor 7th chords that lend themselves to the use of melodic and harmonic minor scales. These compositions are found in *The New Real Book*, vol. 1 (NRB), *The New Real Book*, vol. 2 (NR2), one of the volumes of Jamey Aebersold's *New Approach to Jazz Improvisation* (JA), or *Creative Beginnings: An Introduction to Jazz Improvisation* (CB). Memorize the most frequently played songs, and practice them in different keys.

Compositions In Which Minor/Major 7th Chords or Tonic Minor 7th Chords Occur Frequently

"Airegin"—Sonny Rollins (JA vol. 8, NRB)
"All or Nothing at All"—Lawrence/Altman (JA vol. 44)
"Alone Together"—Dietz/Schwartz (JA vol. 41)
"Angel Eyes"—Brent/Dennis (JA vol. 23, NRB)
"Chelsea Bridge"—Billy Strayhorn (JA vol. 32, NRB)
"Daahoud"—Clifford Brown (JA vol. 53)
"Double Entendre"—Scott Reeves (CB)
"Harlem Nocturne"—Rogers/Hagen (NR2)
"In a Sentimental Mood"—Duke Ellington (JA vol. 12)
"In Walked Bud"—Thelonious Monk (JA vol. 56, NRB)
"Invitation"—Kaper/Webster (JA vols. 34 and 59)

"It Don't Mean A Thing"—Ellington/Mills (JA vol. 59)
"Mindanao"—Cal Tjader (JA vol. 64)
"My Funny Valentine"—Rodgers/Hart (JA vol. 25)
"Nardis"—Miles Davis (JA vol. 50)
"Nica's Dream"—Horace Silver (JA vols. 18 and 65, NR2)
"Out of This World"—Mercer/Arlen (JA vol. 46, NRB)
"Round Midnight"—Thelonious Monk (JA vol. 40)
"Sky Dive"—Freddie Hubbard (JA vol. 60)
"Solar"—Miles Davis (JA vol. 7, NRB)
"This Masquerade"—Leon Russell (NRB)
"Yesterdays"—Jerome Kern (NRB)
"You Don't Know What Love Is"—Raye/DePaul (JA vol. 32)

Sonny Rollins's Improvised Solo on "Airegin"

Sonny Rollins's improvised tenor saxophone solo on his composition "Airegin" was transcribed from the Miles Davis album *Miles Davis and the Modern Jazz Giants* (Prestige 7150). The recording session took place in 1954 with a group that included Miles on trumpet, Sonny on tenor, Horace Silver on piano, Percy Heath on bass, and Kenny Clarke on drums.

Sonny Rollins and John Coltrane are considered to be the most influential tenor saxophonists of their generation. Rollins's early style was modeled after Charlie Parker, but he soon found his own voice. His first jobs were with J. J. Johnson and Miles Davis, and he was an important component of the Clifford Brown–Max Roach Quintet during the mid-1950s. As a leader, he has explored a wide variety of styles, including the post-bop mainstream, free jazz (*Our Man in Jazz,* with trumpeter Don Cherry), Latin and Caribbean rhythms, as well as the best of the pop music genre. Rollins has a predilection for taking ordinary songs typically avoided by jazz artists, and turning them into to vehicles for his boundless creativity. His solos are marked by rhythmic inventiveness, a total command of the harmonic/melodic language, and a spirit of freedom, spontaneity, and abandon.

"Airegin" ("Nigeria" spelled backwards) starts in the key of F minor concert, but ends in the relative major key of A♭. The form is A–B–A–C, with the B section being comprised of a twelve-bar phrase—resulting in a thirty-six measure form, instead of the usual thirty-two. The chords in the A section center around the keys of F minor and B♭ minor, while the B section modulates through the keys of D♭, C, B, B♭ and A♭ major. Rollins easily negotiates these harmonic changes, even at the brisk tempo (♩ = 126).

Over the tonic minor chords, Rollins frequently uses harmonic and melodic minor scales. Bars 2–4, 7–8, 20–26, and 61–63 are primarily based on harmonic minor scales, while bars 27–28 (with its emphasis on the tritone between the ♭3rd and the 6th), 26–40, and 73 all draw on melodic minor scales. Rollins also uses a great deal of chromaticism, as demonstrated in bars 6, 18, 29, 34–36, 47, 54, 57–60, and 68. The solo's construction is very imaginative in its contrasting of short, syncopated motives with long eighth-note phrases.

There are some interesting melodic ideas well worth excerpting and practicing, particularly the ii–V patterns in bars 17–19, 31–32, and 33–35, as well as the major 7th chord arpeggio in bars 15–16. After listening to a recording of this solo, practice it at different tempos with the metronome clicking on beats 2 and 4. Then continue improvising in the same style. (Only the first two of Sonny's three improvised choruses appear here.)

Treble-clef C instruments:

35 A♭Δ7 Gø7 C7♭9 2 F-
38 C7+9 F- F7 B♭-
42 F7+9 B♭- B♭7 D♭Δ7 D-7 G7
47 CΔ7 C♯-7 F♯7 BΔ7
50 C-7 F7 B♭Δ7 B♭-7
54 E♭7 A♭Δ7 Gø7 C7♭9
57 F- C7+9 F-
60 F7 B♭- F7+9 B♭-
64 B♭7 D♭Δ7 Dø7 G7♭9 Cø7

B♭ instruments (Trumpet—optional 8va basso as necessary):

29
E♭Δ7
Eø7
A7♭9
Dø7
3
32
G7♭9
Cø7
F7♭9
35
B♭Δ7
Aø7
D7♭9
2
G-
38
D7+9
G-
G7
C-
42
G7+9
C-
C7
E♭Δ7
E-7
A7
47
DΔ7
3
3
E♭-7
A♭7
D♭maj7
50
D-7
G7
CΔ7
C-7
3
54
F7
B♭Δ7
3
Aø7
D7♭9
3
57
G-
D7+9
G-

E♭ instruments:

20 E⌀7 A7♭9 D- A7+9 D-
24 D7 G- D7+9 G- G7
29 B♭Δ7 B⌀7 E7♭9 A⌀7
32 D7♭9 G⌀7 C7♭9
35 FΔ7 E⌀7 A7♭9 2 D-
38 A7+9 D- D7 G-
42 D7+9 G- G7 B♭Δ7 B-7 E7
47 AΔ7 B♭-7 E♭7 A♭Δ7
50 A-7 D7 GΔ7 G-7

Bass-clef instruments:

13
BΔ7
CΔ7
F7
B♭Δ7
3
3
17
B♭-7
E♭7
A♭Δ7
20
Gø7
C7♭9
F-
C7+9
F-
24
F7
B♭-
F7+9
B♭-
B♭7
29
D♭Δ7
Dø7
G7♭9
Cø7
3
32
F7♭9
B♭ø7
E♭7♭9
35
A♭Δ7
Gø7
C7♭9
2
F-
38
C7+9
F-
F7
B♭-
42
F7+9
B♭-
B♭7
D♭Δ7
D-7

47
C△7
C#-7
F#7
B△7
50
C-7
F7
Bb△7
Bb-7
54
Eb7
Ab△7
Gø7
C7b9
57
F-
C7+9
F-
60
F7
Bb-
F7+9
Bb-
64
Bb7
Db△7
Dø7
G7b9
Cø7
68
F7b9
Bbø7
Eb7b9
71
Ab△7
Gø7
C7b9
3
F-

17

Locrian ♯2 and Diminished/Whole-Tone Scales, and Minor iiø7–V7–i Progressions

"I always like people who have developed
through introspection and a lot of dedication.
I think that what they arrive at is usually
deeper and more beautiful
than the person who seems to have that ability
and fluidity from the beginning."

pianist Bill Evans[1]

The *locrian ♯2 scale* consists of the ascending pattern: whole step, half step, whole step, half step, whole step, whole step, whole step.

A Locrian ♯2 Mode

The locrian ♯2 scale is the sixth mode in the melodic minor family and contains the same notes as the melodic minor scale a major 6th below (or a minor 3rd above). You may also think of the locrian ♯2 scale as a locrian scale with a raised second degree. Like the locrian scale, the locrian ♯2 scale may be used when improvising over half-diminished 7th chords. Because the second degree of the scale is a major rather than minor second above the tonic, this scale allows us to extend the half-diminished chord to include the 9th and the 11th.

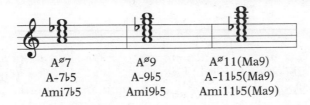

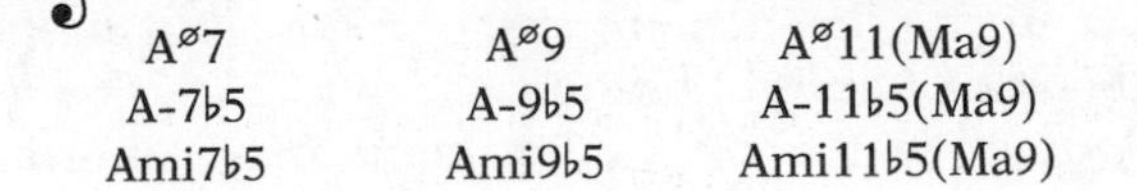

The *half-diminished 7th chord* consists of a root, a minor 3rd, a diminished 5th, and a minor 7th. Adding a major 9th to this chord creates a *half-diminished 9th chord*. A *half-diminished 11th chord* consists of a half-diminished

[1] Martin Williams, "Homage to Bill Evans," *The Complete Riverside Recordings*—accompanying booklet, *Fantasy Recordings* (1984).

9th chord with a perfect 11th added. These chords function as ii$^{\varnothing}$7 chords in a minor ii$^{\varnothing}$7–V7–i cadence or as vii$^{\varnothing}$7 chords in a major keys. Every note in the scale works well over the preceding chords.

The *diminished/whole-tone scale,* also known as the *super locrian scale* or the *altered scale*, consists of the ascending pattern: half step, whole step, half step, whole step, whole step, whole step, whole step.

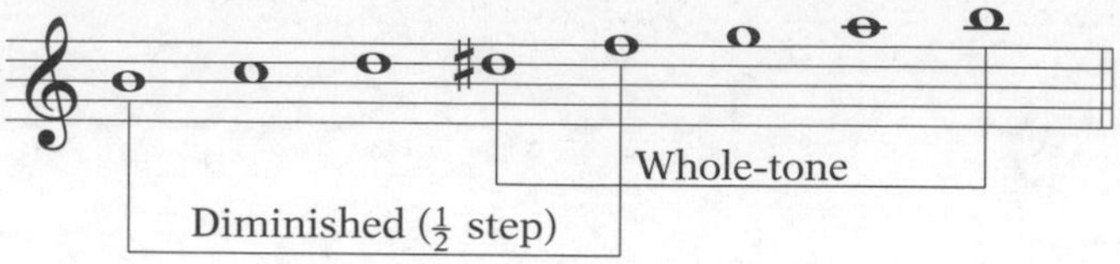

B Diminished/Whole-Tone or Super-Locrian Mode

The diminished/whole-tone mode is the seventh mode in the melodic minor family and contains the same notes as the melodic minor scale a minor 2nd above. (Notice that it has the same relationship to melodic minor as does the locrian scale to the major scale.) With the possible exception of the melodic minor scale, it is the most widely used mode in the melodic minor family. The notes of this scale may be used when improvising over altered dominant 7th chords that include any combinations of raised and lowered 5ths and 9ths: dominant 7 ♭5; dominant 7 ♯5; dominant 7 ♭5♭9; dominant 7 ♭5♯9; dominant 7 ♯5♭9; and dominant 7 ♯5♯9, (the dominant 7th ♯5♯9 being the most commonly used alteration.) Some of these chord alterations form bitonal structures over the basic chord.

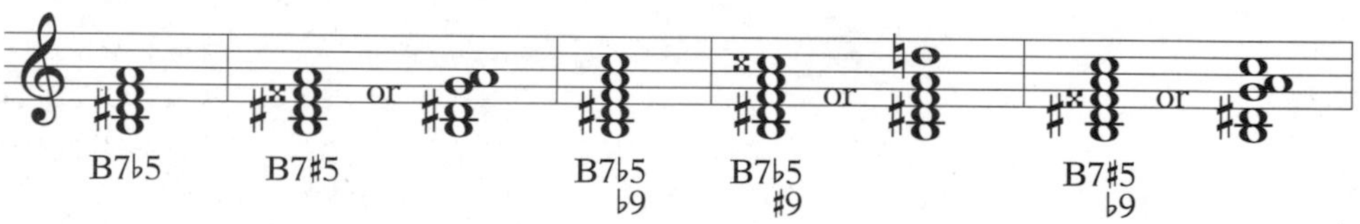

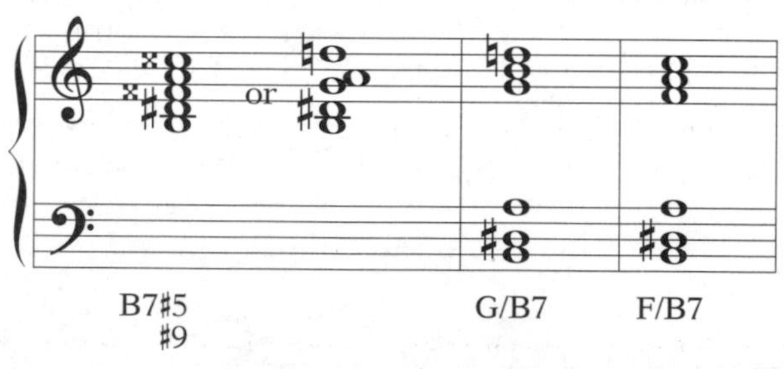

Dominant 7th ♭5, *dominant 7th ♭5♭9*, and *dominant 7th ♭5♯9* chords were described in Chapter 14, and the *dominant 7th ♯5* chord in Chapter 15. The *dominant 7th ♯5♭9* chord (a dominant 7th ♯5 chord with a minor 9th) and the *dominant 7th ♯5♯9* chord (a dominant 7th ♯5 chord with an augmented 9th) are both formed exclusively from the diminished/whole-tone scale. These chords usually function as V7 chords in both major and minor ii–V–I progressions. Every note in the rdiminished/whole-tone scale works well over the preceding chords, with the ♯9th, ♭9th, and the ♯5th giving the scale its characteristic sound.

In a minor ii$^{\varnothing}$7–V7–i progression, the ii$^{\varnothing}$7 chord is half-diminished, the V7 chord typically contains alterations of the 9th and the 5th, and the i chord is minor, with either a minor 7th or a major 7th added. In improvising over this progression, the locrian or the locrian ♯2 scale may be used over the iiø7 chord, the diminished/whole-tone scale over the V chord, and either the aeolian, harmonic minor, or melodic minor scales over the i chord, depending on type of 7th used.

Theory/Ear Exercises

1. Write the locrian ♯2 and diminished/whole-tone scales in all twelve keys.
2. Write the dominant 7th ♯5♭9 and dominant 7th ♯5♯9 chords in all twelve keys.
3. In one key, write out all the scales for dominant 7th chords, including the mixolydian, the Bebop 7th, the diminished (half-step), the whole-tone, the diminished/whole-tone, and the lydian dominant (see Chapter 18). What notes do they have in common and which notes are different? Combine all of the notes from these scales. What does that tell you about the potential of the dominant 7th chord?
4. *Keyboard skills*: Play the chord progressions from this chapter on the piano.
5. *Transcription*: Transcribe a melody, a chord progression, or an improvised solo from a recording.

Gaining Facility with Minor iiø7–V7–i Progressions

Practice the following exercises over the chord progression below, using either a metronome or the play-along recordings from *Creative Beginnings: An Introduction to Jazz Improvisation* (track 9) or volume 3, *The ii–V–I Progression* (track 5), of *A New Approach to Jazz Improvisation* by Jamey Aebersold. If you find yourself struggling with an exercise, slow it down, simplify it, or sing it while visualizing yourself playing it. After familiarizing yourself with the exercises, pick one or two to practice repeatedly, until you can play them without any conscious thought.

C instruments begin here

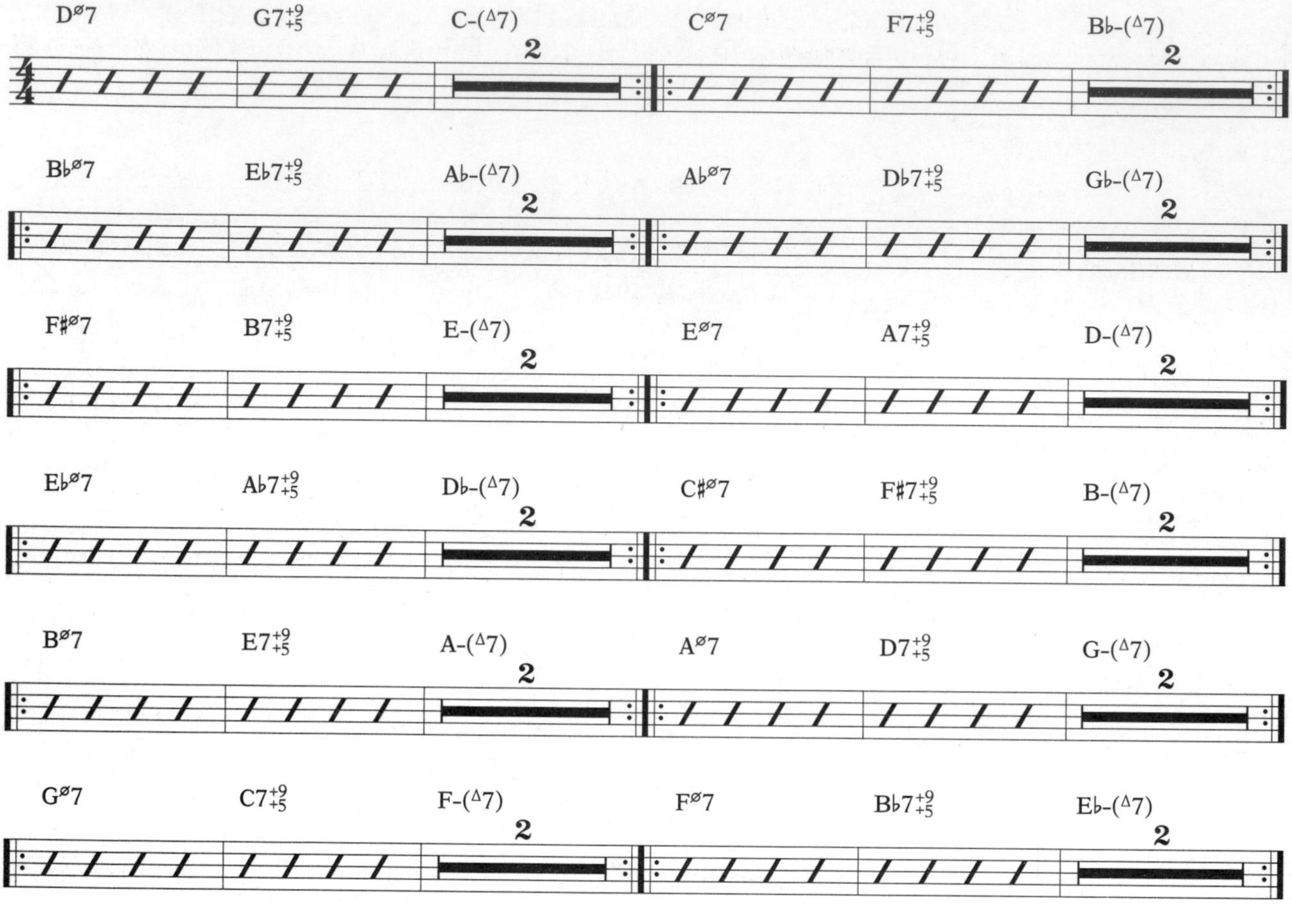

B♭ instruments begin here

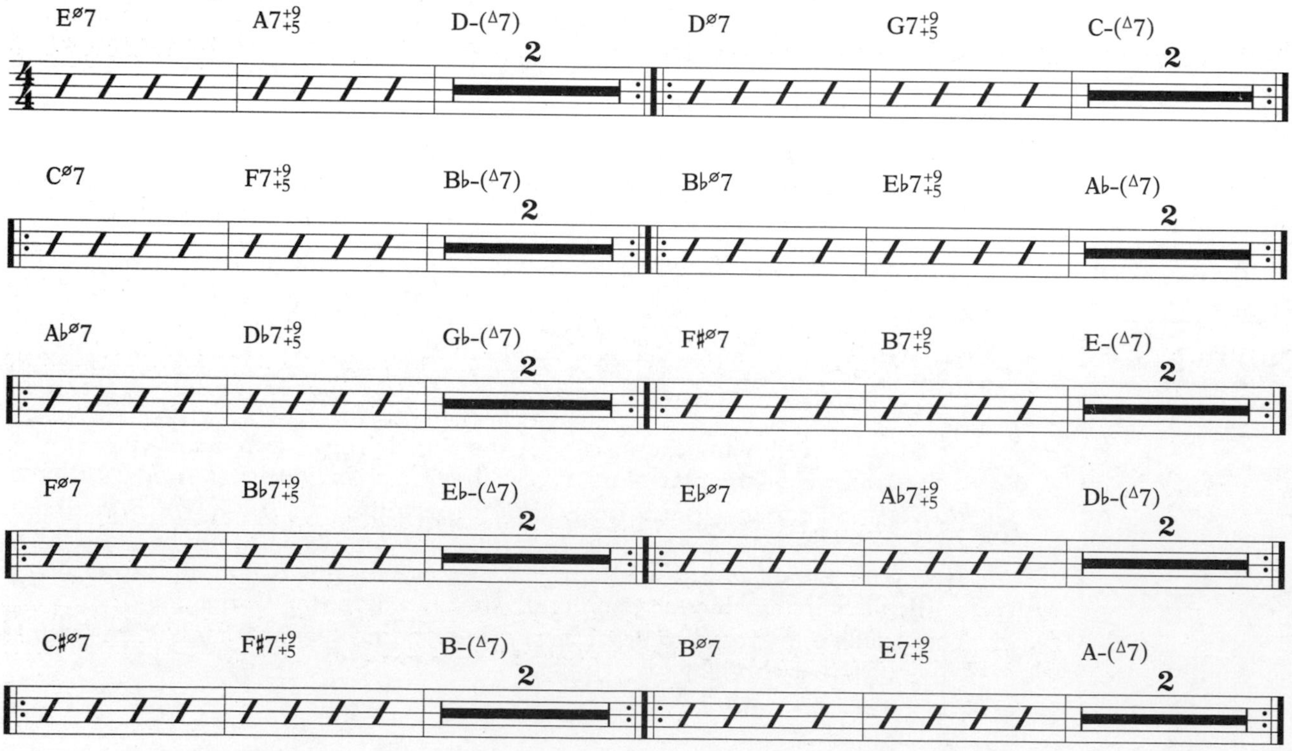

E♭ instruments begin here

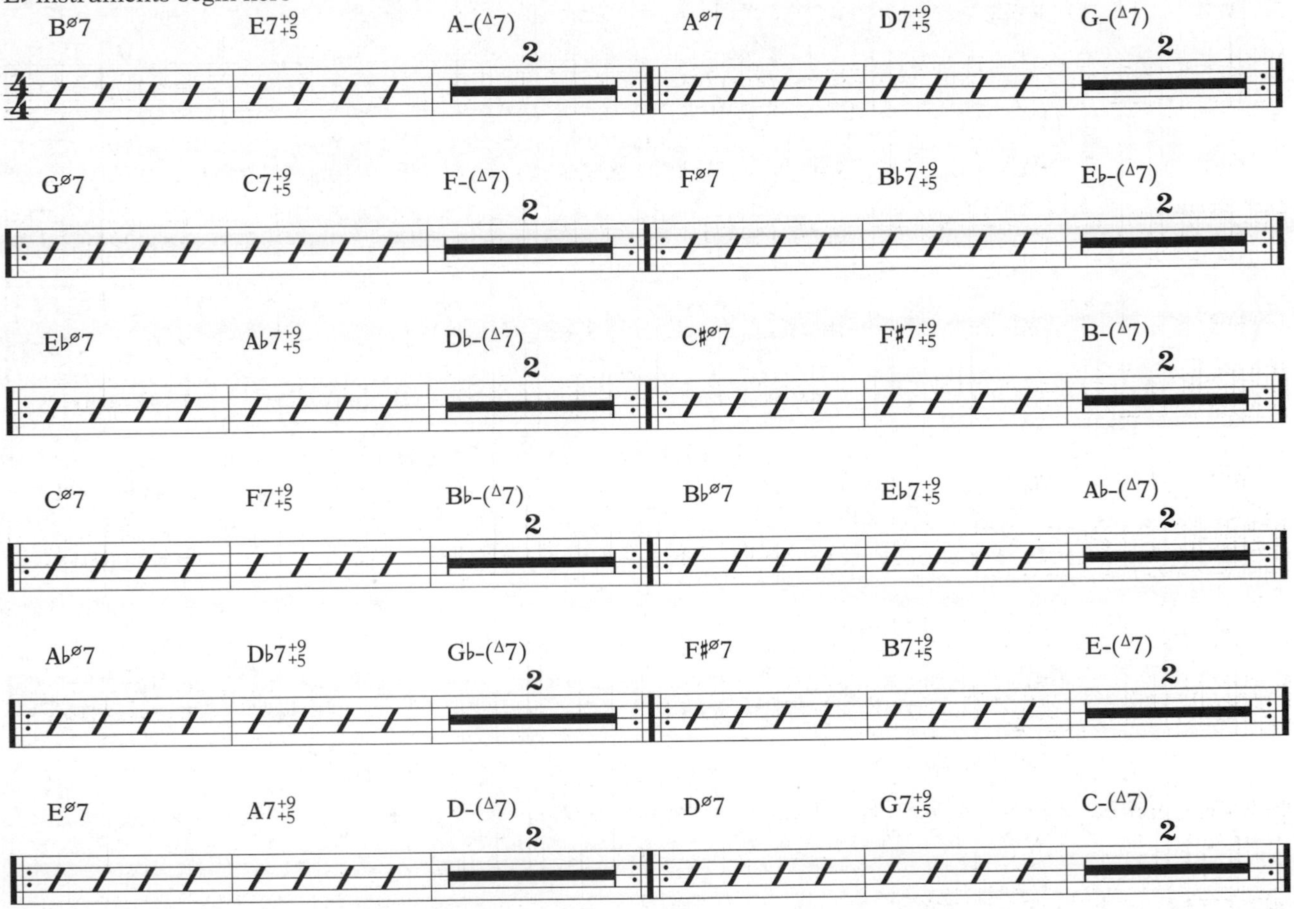

1. *Warmups*:
   a. Have another musician or teacher play a phrase that fits over a minor ii∅7–V7–i progression. Play back the phrase you have just heard.
2. A pattern based on locrian ♯2 and diminished/whole-tone scales.

MM ______________________

3. The locrian ♯2, diminished/whole-tone, and melodic minor scales.

MM ______________________

4. A pattern that uses the locrian ♯2 scale on the ii chord and emphasizes the ♯9, the ♭9, and the ♯5 on the V chord.

MM ____________

5. A post-bop pattern that emphasizes the ♯9, the ♭9, and the ♯5 over the V chord, similar to that used by Woody Shaw in his "Softly As In A Morning Sunrise" solo (*Larry Young: Unity*, Blue Note #4221).

MM ____________

6. A Jamey Aebersold pattern from his "Freddieish" solo, which uses the locrian scale over the ii chord, the diminished whole-tone scale over the V chord, and the melodic minor scale over the i chord (*Jazz Clinicians Quartet Plays for You*, JA 1975).

MM ____________

7. A Bill Evans motive based on quarter-note triplets ("Autumn Leaves," *Bill Evans: Portrait In Jazz*, Riverside RLP 315).

MM ____________

8. A variation on another Bill Evans idea from his "Autumn Leaves" solo (*Bill Evans: Portrait In Jazz*, Riverside RLP 1162).

MM ____________

9. *Creative jazz improvisation*:

a. Along with a drummer, play lines comprised mainly of eighth notes without basing your improvisation on a predetermined chord progression. Don't worry about the notes, just concentrate on the time.

b. Improvise over the chord progression from this chapter. Try to maintain that same feeling of freedom you experienced in the previous exercise. Since altered dominant chords contain a great deal of dissonance, a melodic line with a strong rhythm will sound convincing, no matter which notes are played.

10. Make up your own patterns and melodic ideas based on ii–V–I progressions.

a.

MM ____________________

b.

MM ____________________

Improvising on Jazz Compositions Based on Half-Diminished 7th and Altered Dominant Chords

Following is a partial list of jazz compositions that contain ii$^{\varnothing}$7–altered V7–i progressions. These compositions are found in *The New Real Book*, vol. 1 (NRB), *The New Real Book*, vol. 2 (NR2), one of the volumes of Jamey Aebersold's *New Approach to Jazz Improvisation* (JA), or *Creative Beginnings: An Introduction to Jazz Improvisation* (CB). Memorize the most frequently played songs, and practice them in different keys.

Compositions Based Exclusively on ii$^{\varnothing}$7–altered V7–i Progressions

"Ease Away Walk"—Benny Golson (JA vol. 14)

Compositions In Which ii$^{\varnothing}$7–altered V7–i Progressions Occur Frequently

"Alone Together"—Dietz/Schwartz (JA vol. 41)
"Autumn Leaves"—Mercer/Kosma (JA vol. 44, NRB)
"Beautiful Love"—King/Young (NRB)
"Blood Count"—Billy Strayhorn (JA vol. 66)
"Blue in Green"—Evans/Davis (JA vol. 50)
"Blood Count"—Billy Strayhorn (JA vol. 66)
"Caravan"—Ellington, Mills, Tizol (JA vol. 59)
"Catalonian Nights"—Dexter Gordon (JA vol. 82)
"Crescent"—John Coltrane (JA vol. 27)
"Crisis"—Freddie Hubbard (JA vols. 38 and 60)
"Don't Blame Me"—Fields/McHugh (JA vol. 74)
"How Insensitive"—Antonio Carlos Jobim (JA vol. 31)
"I Fall In Love Too Easily"—Kahn/Styne (JA vol. 59)
"Invitation"—Bronislav Kaper (JA vol. 34)
"Johnny Come Lately"—Billy Strayhorn (JA vol. 66)
"Laurie"—Bill Evans (JA vol. 45)
"Little Boat"—Roberto Menescal (JA vol. 31)
"Little Dancer"—Tom Harrell (JA vol. 63)
"Love for Sale"—Cole Porter (JA vol. 40)

"Lullaby Of The Leaves"—Petkere/Young (JA vol. 58)
"Magic Morning"—Dan Haerle (JA vol. 4)
"Montmartre"—Dexter Gordon (JA vol. 82)
"My One and Only Love"—Wood/Mellin (JA vol. 51)
"Nuthouse"—Scott Reeves (CB)
"Old Folks"—Hill/Robinson (JA vol. 71)
"Peace"—Horace Silver (JA vol. 17)
"Road Song"—Wes Montgomery (JA vol. 62)
"Round Midnight"—Thelonious Monk (JA vol. 40)
"Sail Away"—Tom Harrell (JA vol. 63)
"Saudade"—Walter Booker (JA vol. 13)
"Scooter"—Dan Haerle (JA vol. 4)
"Softly As in a Morning Sunrise"—Richard Rodgers (JA vol. 40)
"Soul Eyes"—Mal Waldron (JA vols. 32 and 74)
"Summer Samba"—Marcos/Valle (JA vol. 31)
"The Shadow of Your Smile"—Webster/Mandel (JA vols. 34 and 59)
"The Touch Of Your Lips"—Ray Noble (JA vol. 71)
"Turn Out the Stars"—Bill Evans (JA vol. 45)
"Upper Manhattan Medical Group"—Billy Strayhorn (JA vol. 66)
"What Is This Thing Called Love?"—Cole Porter (JA vols. 15, 41, and 74)
"What's New"—Burke/Haggart (JA vols. 41 and 74, NRB)
"Wise One"—John Coltrane (NR2)
"Woody'n You" ("Algo Buena")—Dizzy Gillespie (JA vol. 65, NR2)
"Yours Is My Heart Alone"—Smith/Lehar (JA vol. 41)
"Yardbird Suite"—Charlie Parker (JA vol. 6)
"Yesterdays"—Harbach/Kern (NRB)

Bill Evans's Improvised Solo on "The Autumn Leaves"

Bill Evans's improvised piano solo on the Johnny Mercer standard, "The Autumn Leaves," is a wonderful example of the use of diminished and diminished/whole-tone scales, long melodic lines, inventive motivic development, and intricate permutations of rhythm. It was transcribed from the Bill Evans album *Portrait in Jazz* (Riverside RLP 1162), which was recorded in December 1959 and was subsequently rereleased as *Spring Leaves* (Milestone M-4703). This recording showcased Bill Evans's classic trio, which included Scott LaFaro on bass and Paul Motian on drums, a group that revolutionized the concept of the piano trio through its intimate conversational interplay among the musicians. Due in part to LaFaro's prodigious technical skills as a bassist, as well the the open nature of Evans's and Motian's styles, the music created by the trio often seemed more like a dialogue than that of a soloist with rhythm section accompaniment.

After formative studies of classical piano at Louisiana State and informal work with jazz composer/theorist George Russell, Evans's earliest recordings revealed the prevailing influence of pianist Bud Powell. After a brief apprenticeship with Miles Davis (including an appearance on the classic *Kind of Blue* recording), he began to forge a uniquely personal approach that subsequently inspired and influenced numerous pianists, including Herbie Hancock, Chick Corea, Keith Jarrett, Fred Hersch, and Kenny Werner. Through his introspective personality, colorful harmonies, refined touch and sound concept, inner moving voices, and subtle rhythmic ideas, Evans often transformed well-worn standards and popular show tunes into vehicles of almost transcendental musings. His own compositions were typically through-composed tone poems, which avoided the common 32-bar AABA or ABAC formulas.[2] Evans continued to perform and record, primarily in the piano trio format, until his premature death in 1980.

One interesting aspect of this solo is the implication of polyrhythms through his use of quarter-note and eighth-note triplets. In the first six bars of the second chorus, he develops and subsequently fragments an eighth-note triplet motive, while in bars 47–56 and 60–63, he accents eighth-triplets in groupings of twos, implying a 3 against 2 hemiola. His use of quarter-note triplets in bars 42, 57–58, 69–74, and 85–87, as well as the syncopations in bars 93–94, verge on suggesting another meter.

His choice of scalar/harmonic material is also quite rich. The diminished/whole-tone scale, with its alterations of the 5ths and 9ths, is used over the altered dominant chords in bars 6, 42, 50, 58, 66, 70, 73, and 86. He frequently uses diminished modes, particularly in measures 25–26, 33–34, 54, 69–70, 81–82. The melodic minor scale is his preferred scale choice over most of the tonic minor chords in the minor ii^{ø}7–V7–i progressions. Of special interest is his use of bitonal substitutions, including the G♭ triad over the E♭7 chord in bar 17, the F triad over the D7 chord in bar 18, the F triad over the E♭7 ♯9 in bar 57, as well as the use of quartal harmony in bar 58.

Although Evans frequently played ballads and mood pieces, this performance demonstrates his ability to swing (the tempo is 𝅗𝅥 = 104). After listening closely to a recording of this solo, practice it at different tempos with the metronome clicking on beats 2 and 4. Then continue improvising on the chord progression in the same style.

[2] Refer to the list of through-composed jazz compositions in Chapter 11; most of them are Evans's compositions.

Treble-clef C instruments:

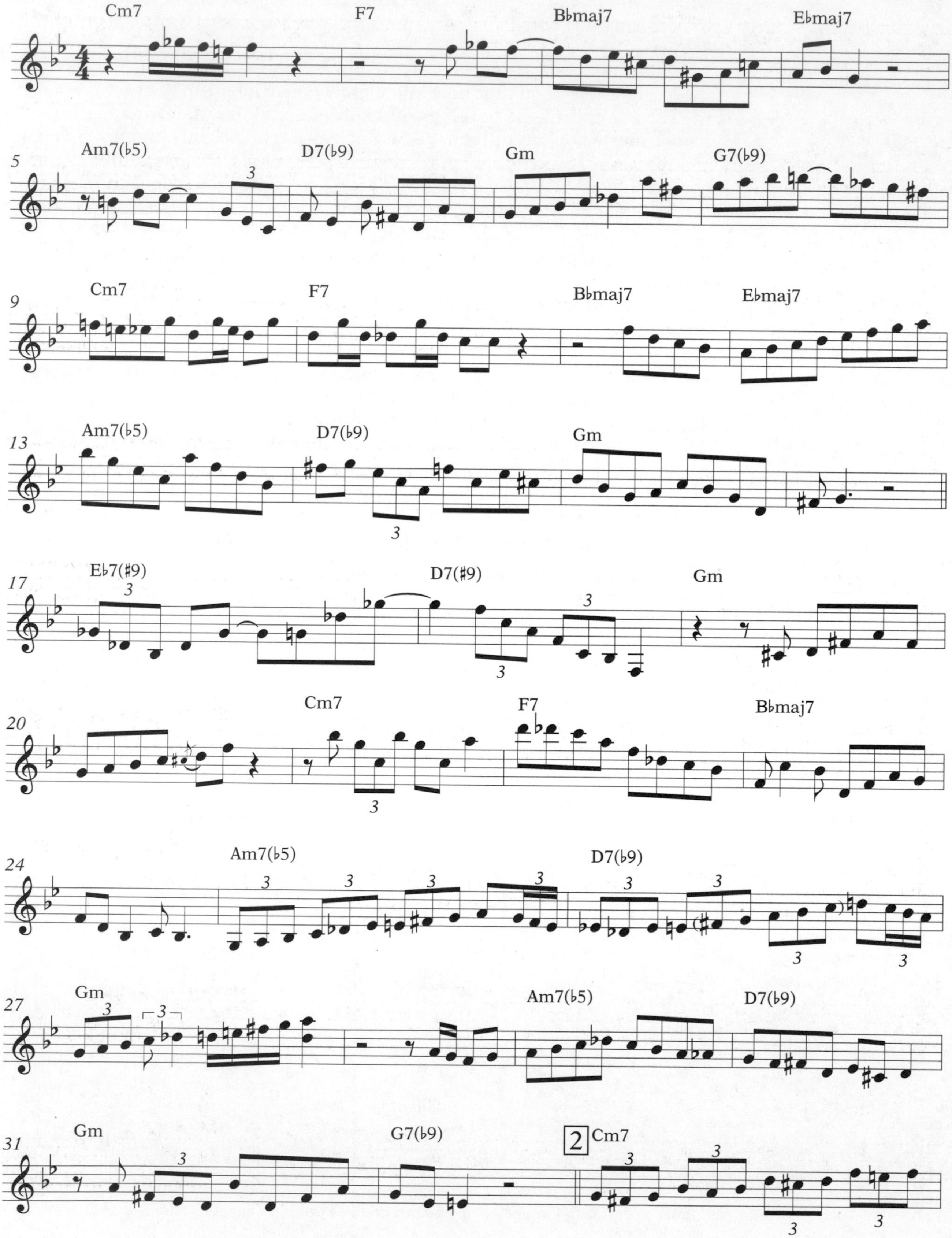

34
F7(♭5)
B♭maj7
E♭maj7
Am7(♭5)
38
D7(♭9)
Gm
8va
Cm7
(8va)
42
F7(♭5♯9)
B♭maj7
E♭maj7
Am7(♭5)
46
D7(♭9)
Gm
49
Am7(♭5)
D7(♭9)
Gm
52
Cm7
F7(♭9)
55
B♭maj7
E♭7(♯9)
58
D7(♭9)
Gm
61
Am7(♭5)
D7(♭9)
Gm
G+7

3
8va
65
Cm7
F7(♭5♯9)
B♭maj7
(8va)
68
E♭maj7
Am7(♭5)
D7(♭9)
Gm
(8va)
72
Cm7
F7(♭5♭9)
B♭maj7
(8va)
76
E♭maj7
Am7(♭5)
D7(♭9)
(8va)
79
Gm
E♭7(♯9)
D7(♭5♭9)
8va
83
Gm
Cm7
F7(♭5♯9)
(8va)
87
B♭maj7
Am7(♭5)
D7(♭9)
91
Gm
Am7(♭5)
94
D7(♭9)
Gm
G7(♭9)
Cm7

B♭ instruments (Saxophone—8va where indicated):

34
G7(♭5)
Cmaj7
Fmaj7
Bm7(♭5)
38
E7(♭9)
Am
Dm7
42
G7(♭5♯9)
Cmaj7
Fmaj7
Bm7(♭5)
46
E7(♭9)
Am
49
Bm7(♭5)
E7(♭9)
Am
52
Dm7
G7(♭9)
55
Cmaj7
F7(♯9)
58
E7(♭9)
Am
61
Bm7(♭5)
E7(♭9)
Am
A+7

3
65 Dm7
G7(♭5♯9)
Cmaj7
68 Fmaj7
Bm7(♭5)
E7(♭9)
Am
72 Dm7
G7(♭5♭9)
Cmaj7
sax. 8va
76 Fmaj7
(8va)
Bm7(♭5)
E7(♭9)
79 (8va)
Am
F7(♯9)
E7(♭5♭9)
83 Am
sax. 8va
Dm7
G7(♭5♯9)
87 Cmaj7
Bm7(♭5)
E7(♭9)
91 Am
Bm7(♭5)
94 E7(♭9)
Am
A7(♭9)
Dm7

E♭ instruments:

34
D7(♭5)
Gmaj7
Cmaj7
F♯m7(♭5)
38
B7(♭9)
Em
opt. 8va bassa
Am7
42
D7(♭5♯9)
loco
Gmaj7
Cmaj7
F♯m7(♭5)
46
B7(♭9)
Em
49
F♯m7(♭5)
B7(♭9)
Em
52
Am7
D7(♭9)
55
Gmaj7
C7(♯9)
58
B7(♭9)
Em
61
F♯m7(♭5)
B7(♭9)
Em
E+7

opt. 8va bassa
3
65
Am7
D7(♭5♯9)
loco
Gmaj7
68
Cmaj7
F♯m7(♭5)
B7(♭9)
Em
72
Am7
D7(♭5♭9)
Gmaj7
76
Cmaj7
F♯m7(♭5)
B7(♭9)
79
Em
C7(♯9)
B7(♭5♭9)
83
Em
opt. 8va bassa
Am7
D7(♭5♯9)
87
Gmaj7
loco
F♯m7(♭5)
B7(♭9)
91
Em
F♯m7(♭5)
94
B7(♭9)
Em
E7(♭9)
Am7

Bass-clef instruments:

34
F7(♭5)
opt. 8va bassa
B♭maj7
E♭maj7
loco
Am7(♭5)
38
D7(♭9)
Gm
Cm7
42
F7(♭5♯9)
B♭maj7
E♭maj7
Am7(♭5)
46
D7(♭9)
Gm
49
Am7(♭5)
D7(♭9)
Gm
52
Cm7
F7(♭9)
55
B♭maj7
E♭7(♯9)
opt. 8va bassa
58
D7(♭9)
Gm
loco
61
Am7(♭5)
D7(♭9)
opt. 8va bassa
Gm
G+7

3
Cm7
loco
F7(♭5♯9)
B♭maj7
E♭maj7
Am7(♭5)
D7(♭9)
Gm
Cm7
F7(♭5♭9)
B♭maj7
E♭maj7
Am7(♭5)
D7(♭9)
Gm
E♭7(♯9)
D7(♭5♭9)
Gm
Cm7
F7(♭5♯9)
B♭maj7
Am7(♭5)
D7(♭9)
Gm
Am7(♭5)
D7(♭9)
Gm
G7(♭9)
Cm7

18

Lydian Augmented and Lydian Dominant Scales, and Major 7th ♯5 and Dominant 9th ♯11 Chords

"What improvising really means isn't
just to play a solo,
it's creating a solo at the moment,
creating a dialogue with the musicians
you're playing with.
It's not just playing notes.
It's telling a story."

saxophonist Joe Lovano[1]

The *lydian augmented scale* consists of the ascending pattern: whole step, whole step, whole step, whole step, half step, whole step, half step.

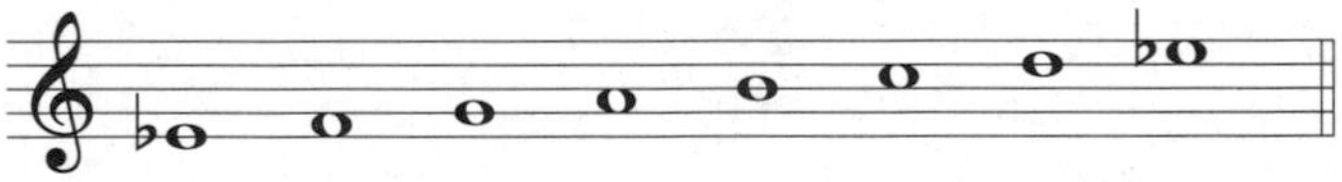

E♭ Lydian Augmented Scale

The lydian augmented scale is the third mode in the melodic minor family and contains the same notes as the melodic minor scale a minor 3rd below. The lydian augmented scale may also be thought of as a lydian scale with a raised 5th degree. The notes of the lydian augmented scale may be used when improvising over an augmented major 7th chord (major 7th ♯5), which is often notated as a bitonal chord (III triad/I bass).

E♭Ma7♯5
E♭$^{\Delta}$7♯5
G triad/E♭bass

The *augmented major 7th chord* consists of a tonic, a major 3rd, an augmented 5th, and a major 7th. This chord usually functions as an altered I chord in a major key or an altered III chord in a minor key; occasionally, it functions as a ♭VI chord (a tritone substitute for V7/V). Every note in the lydian augmented scale works well over the augmented major 7th chord.

[1] Michael Bourne, "Blindfold Test," *Downbeat* (September 1997) 70.

The *lydian dominant scale*, also known as the *overtone scale*, consists of the ascending pattern: whole step, whole step, whole step, half step, whole step, half step, whole step.

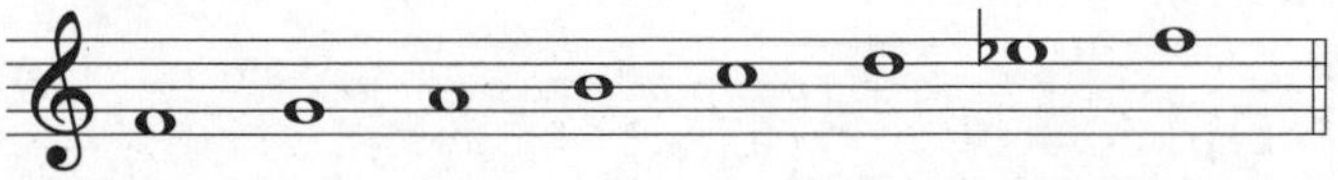

F Lydian Dominant

The lydian dominant scale is the fourth mode in the melodic minor family and contains the same notes as the melodic minor scale a perfect 4th below. You may also think of it as a mixolydian scale with a raised 4th degree or a lydian scale with a lowered 7th degree. The lydian dominant scale is frequently used as an alternative to the whole-tone scale, and may be used when improvising over dominant 7th ♭5, dominant 9th ♭5, dominant 9th ♯11, and dominant 13th ♯11 chords. The dominant 13 ♯11 chord may be also notated as a bitonal chord.

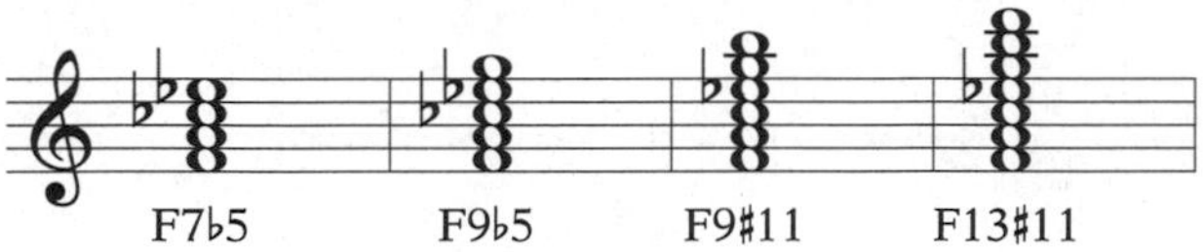

Dominant 7th ♭5 and *dominant 9th ♭5* chords were discussed in Chapter 15. *Dominant 9th ♯11 and dominant 13th ♯11 chords* consist of a dominant 9th chord with an augmented 11th or major 13th added. These chords typically function as either V7 chords, tritone substitutes for V7, secondary dominant 7ths (often V7/V), or tonic chords—as in the case of the blues progression.[2] Every note in the lydian dominant scale works well over the preceding chords, with the second, fourth, and sixth degrees lending a bitonal sound to the improvisation. When using this scale, it may be helpful to think of improvising on the triad a whole step above the root of the dominant chord.

Theory/Ear Exercises

1. Write the lydian augmented and lydian dominant modes in all twelve keys.
2. Write the major 7th ♭5 and dominant 9th ♯11 chords in all twelve keys.
3. In one key, write out all the scales for major 7th chords, including the major, lydian, and lydian augmented. Which notes do they have in common? Which notes are different?
4. *Keyboard skills*: Play the chord progressions from this chapter on the piano.
5. *Transcription*: Transcribe a melody, a chord progression, or an improvised solo from a recording.

[2] The first chord of Horace Silver's "Gregory Is Here" is a 7 ♭5 chord functioning a tritone substitute for V7; the second chord of Billy Strayhorn's "Take the 'A' Train" is a 7 ♭5 functioning as secondary dominant chord (V7/V); the first chord of Sonny Rollins' "Blue Seven" is a 7 ♭5 chord serving as a tonic chord.

Gaining Facility with Lydian Augmented and Lydian Dominant Scales and Major 7th ♯5 and Dominant 9th ♯11 Chords

Play the following exercises over the chord progression below, using a metronome. If you find yourself struggling with an exercise, slow it down, simplify it, or sing it while visualizing yourself playing it. After familiarizing yourself with the exercises, pick one or two to practice repeatedly, until you can play them without any conscious thought.

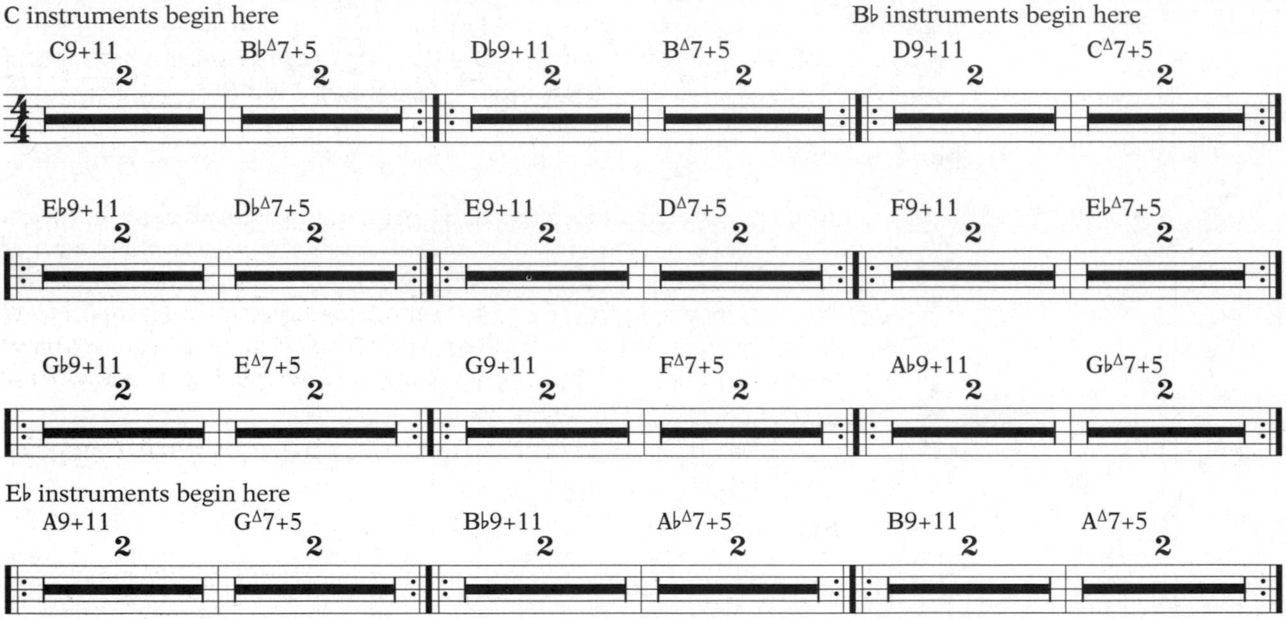

1. *Warmups*:
   a. Have another musician or teacher play a phrase that fits over dominant 9th ♯11 or major 7th ♯5 chords. Play back the phrase you have just heard.
   b. Sing (or silently imagine) a phrase that fits over a dominant 9th ♯11 or major 7th ♯5 chord while visualizing yourself playing it on your instrument. Play what you have just sung.
2. The lydian dominant and lydian augmented modes.

MM ______________

3. The dominant 13th ♯11 and major 7th ♯5 arpeggios.

MM ______________

4. A pattern beginning on the 13th of the dominant chord and ending on the ♯5th of the major chord.

MM ______________________

5. A pattern based on lydian dominant and lydian augmented modes.

MM ______________________

6. *Creative jazz improvisation*: When you practice, practice listening. Listen to the click of the metronome, the sounds in the room, and the sound of your instrument. If you are playing in public, listen to the sound of other musicians, the sounds in the room, and the sound of the audience. Don't be seduced by listening to yourself and thinking about what you are playing. Step outside the confines of your ego and simply listen. Allow your body to react to what you hear.

7. Make up your own patterns and melodic ideas based on lydian dominant and lydian augmented modes.

a.

MM ______________________

b.

MM ______________________

Improvising on Jazz Compositions Based on Dominant 9th ♯11 or Major 7th ♯5 Chords

Following is a partial list of jazz compositions that contain 9th♯ 11 chords or major 7th♯ 5 chords. These compositions are found in *The New Real Book*, vol. 1 (NRB), *The New Real Book*, vol. 2 (NR2), and one of the volumes of Jamey Aebersold's *New Approach to Jazz Improvisation* (JA). Memorize the most frequently played songs, and practice them in different keys.

Compositions In Which Dominant 9♯ 11 Chords Occur Frequently

"A Flower Is A Lovesome Thing"—Billy Strayhorn (JA vol. 66)
"Blue Seven"—Sonny Rollins (JA vol. 8)

"Chelsea Bridge"—Billy Strayhorn (JA vols. 32 and 66, NRB)
"Days of Wine and Roses"—Mercer/Mancini (JA vol. 40)
"Desafinado"—Antonio Carlos Jobim (JA vols. 31 and 74, NRB)
"Ecaroh"—Horace Silver (JA vol. 18, NR2)
"Girl from Ipanema"—Antonio Carlos Jobim (JA vol. 31)
"Gregory Is Here"—Horace Silver (JA vol. 17, NR2)
"Introspection"—Thelonious Monk (JA vol. 56)
"Isfahan"—Strayhorn/Ellington (JA vol. 66, NR2)
"Jody Grind"—Horace Silver (JA vol. 17)
"Katerina Ballerina"—Woody Shaw (JA vol. 9)
"Lush Life"—Billy Strayhorn (JA vols. 32 and 66, NRB)
"Mary Lou"—Horace Silver (JA vol. 86)
"Moonglow"—Delange, Hudson, Mills (JA vol. 59)
"Moonlight in Vermont"—Blackburn/Suessdorf (JA vol. 65, NRB)
"Off-Minor"—Thelonious Monk (JA vol. 56)
"One Note Samba"—Antonio Carlos Jobim (JA vol. 31)
"Pensativa"—Claire Fischer "Crisis" (JA vol. 60)
"Soul Eyes"—Mal Waldron (JA vol. 32)
"Speak Low"—Weill/Nash (JA vol. 65)
"Stella By Starlight"—Washington/Young (JA vols. 22 and 59)
"Sweet And Lovely"—Arnheim, Tobias, Lemare (JA vol. 59)
"Take The 'A' Train"—Billy Strayhorn (JA vols. 12, 65, and 66, NRB)
"Tenderly"—Lawrence/Gross (JA vol. 44, NRB)
"The Midnight Sun"—Mercer/Hampton/Burke (NRB)
"Tokyo Blues"—Horace Silver (JA vol. 86)
"We'll Be Together Again"—Laine/Fischer (NRB)
"Will You Still Be Mine"—Adair/Dennis (JA vol. 23, NR2)

Compositions In Which Major 7th ♯ 5 Chords Occur Frequently

"Easy 'Nuff"—David Liebman (JA vol. 81)
"Elm"—Richard Beirach (NRB)
"Falling Stones"—David Liebman (JA vol. 81)
"For Lydia"—Caris Visentin (JA vol. 81)
"Hope Street"—Tom Harrell (JA vol. 63)
"Naima"—John Coltrane (JA vol. 27, NR2)
"Natural Selection"—Richard Beirach (NR2)
"Sail Away"—Tom Harrell (JA vol. 63)
"Wind Sprint"—John Patitucci (NR2)

Sonny Rollins's Improvised Solo on "Blue Seven"

Sonny Rollins's improvised tenor saxophone solo on his composition "Blue Seven" was transcribed from the *Smithsonian Collection of Classic Jazz*, but was originally released in 1956 on *Saxophone Colossus* (Prestige 7326). The group included Tommy Flanagan on piano, Doug Watkins on bass, and Max Roach on drums.

"Blue Seven" is a 12-bar blues based on a descending two-note motive comprised of an augmented 4th. This motive frequently serves as raw material for Sonny's solo, as seen bars 1–8, 13–14, 20, 21–24, 27–28, 39–40, and 49–56. The endless variations he spontaneously creates on this simple idea are astounding. In between episodes of motivic and rhythmic development, Sonny connects his ideas with double-time bebop lines (measures 10–12, 25–27, 34–39, and 42–48). There are no unnecessary notes in this solo—virtually every note either refers to the primary motive or is part of a connecting line.

An interesting feature of this improvisation is the use of the dominant 9th ♯11 chord and the lydian dominant scale. The ♯11th (or ♭5th) figures prominently in the melody and is used throughout the solo. Variations on the dominant 9th ♯11 arpeggio appear in bars 10, 20, 22, 38, and 46, and the entire lydian dominant mode is used in bars 29–32. Other alterations of the dominant chord include the use of the ♯5th in measures 11, 41, and 53 and the ♯9th and ♭9th in bar 59.

For contrast, Sonny also employs other scale choices, including the bebop 7th scale (bars 8–11, 25, and 44–45) and the blues scale (bars 61–62). Also worth noting is the pattern Sonny plays in measure 47. It is derived from Charlie Parker's "signature" lick, a double-time figure which Bird played frequently. Rollins, as well as other saxophonists influenced by Parker, subsequently adopted this pattern as part of their vocabulary (refer to the exercises in Chapter 7).

After listening closely to a recording of this solo, practice it at different tempos with the metronome clicking on beats 2 and 4. Continue improvising on the chord progression in the same style. The tempo is moderate at ♩ = 132.

Treble-clef C instruments:

35 F7 hold back B♭7 C-7 F7
4
38 B♭7 E♭7 B♭7
41 vib. E♭7
44 B♭7
46 F7 C-7 F7
48 B♭7 F7 5 B♭7 E♭7
52 B♭7 vib. E♭7
56 B♭7 C-7 F7
60 B♭7 F7 6 B♭7

B♭ instruments (Trumpet—8va bassa where indicated):

35
G7
hold back
3
C7
D-7
G7
4
C7
38
F7
C7
41
vib.
3
F7
44
C7
trpt. 8va bassa
46
G7
D-7
G7
(8va)
48
C7
G7
5
C7
F7
(8va)
52
C7
vib.
3
F7
56
C7
D-7
G7
3
3
60
C7
G7
6
C7
3

E♭ instruments:

35 D7
hold back
G7
A-7
D7
4
38 G7
C7
G7
41
vib.
C7
44 G7
46 D7
A-7
D7
48 G7
D7
5 G7
C7
52 G7
vib.
C7
56 G7
A-7
D7
60 G7
D7
6 G7

Bass-clef instruments:

35
F7
hold back
B♭7
C-7
F7
4
38
B♭7
E♭7
B♭7
41
vib.
E♭7
44
B♭7
46
F7
C-7
F7
48
B♭7
F7
5
B♭7
E♭7
52
B♭7
vib.
E♭7
56
B♭7
C-7
F7
60
B♭7
F7
6
B♭7

19

Pentatonic Scales

"The highest form of musical execution
on a musical instrument is JAZZ.
We know what we're doing and
we know it's the truth..."

drummer Art Blakey[1]

Pentatonic scales contain exactly five notes, exclusive of the octave. Pentatonic scales are commonly used in music from African and Asian.[2] Some jazz artists, particularly Yusef Lateef and John Coltrane, have incorporated pentatonic scales from other cultures into their work. However, the pentatonic scales most commonly used in jazz are the major and minor pentatonic scales:

C Major Pentatonic Scale

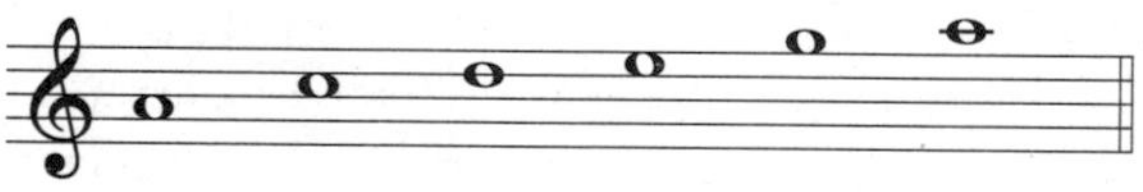

A Minor Pentatonic Scale

Major and minor pentatonic scales belong to the same modal family, with the minor pentatonic scale containing the same notes as the major pentatonic scale a minor 3rd above.

The *major pentatonic scale*, also known as the *diatonic pentatonic scale*, consists of the ascending pattern: whole step, whole step, minor 3rd, whole step, minor 3rd. It may also be thought of as a major scale with the fourth and seventh notes omitted. Major pentatonic scales may be used over major 7th and dominant 7th chords. For major 7th chords, there are three options: 1) the major pentatonic scale built on the root of the chord, 2) the major pentatonic scale built on the 5th of the chord, and 3) the major pentatonic scale built on the 9th of the chord. The first choice contains the smallest number of chord extensions, the latter choice the greatest, including the ♯11 of the chord:

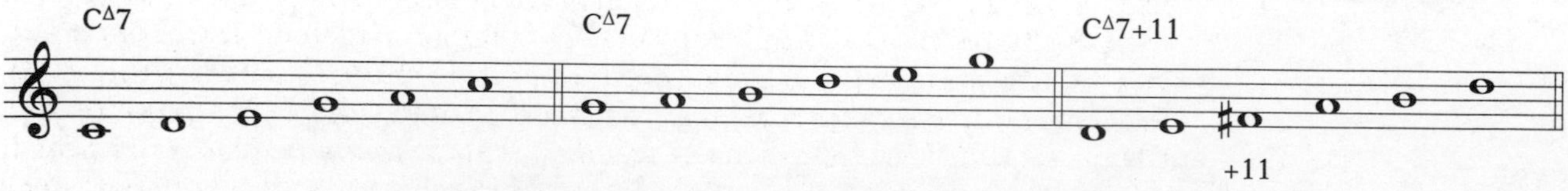

[1] "Art Blakey—the Jazz Messenger," Public Broadcasting System, 1987.

[2] Examples of Asian pentatonic scales include the Pelog (1, ♭2, ♭3, 5, ♭6), the Hirajoshi (1, 2, ♭3, 5, ♭6), and the Kumoi (1, 2, ♭3, 5, 6).

When using the pentatonic scale over unaltered dominant 7th chords, the major pentatonic scale built on the root of the chord is the best choice; when improvising on dominant chords with altered 5ths and 9ths, the major pentatonic scale a tritone (diminished 5th) away from the root of the chord works best. This option contains alterations of both the 5th and the 9th:

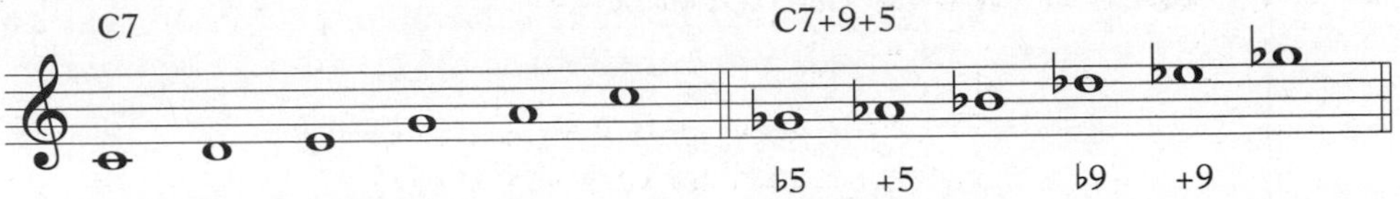

Major pentatonic scales also may be used when improvising over ii–V–I progressions. If the V chord is unaltered, the major pentatonic built on the root of the I chord or the V chord may be used over all three chords in the progression:

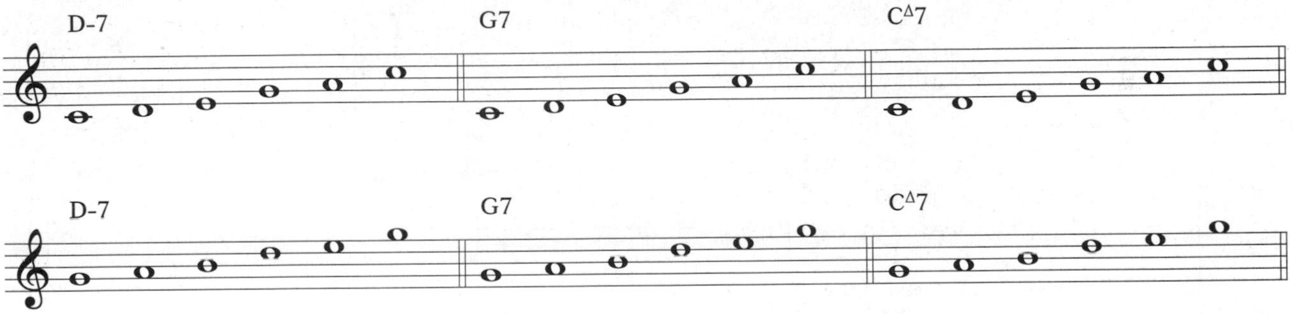

If the dominant chord is altered, the major pentatonic scale a tritone away from the root of the dominant chord should be used over the V chord:

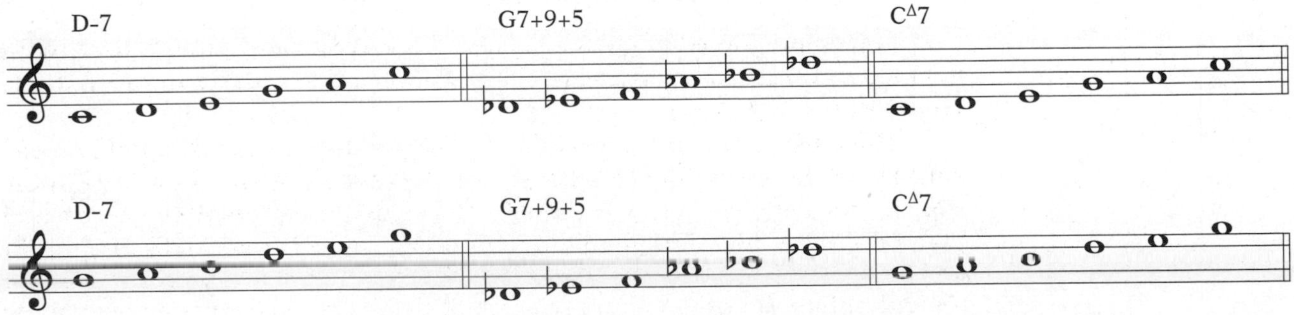

The *minor pentatonic scale* consists of the ascending pattern: minor 3rd, whole step, whole step, minor 3rd, whole step. You may think of the scale as an aeolian or dorian scale with the second and sixth notes omitted, or a blues scale with the flatted fifth omitted. When using the minor pentatonic scale over minor 7th chords, you have the same three options as the major pentatonic scale: 1) the minor pentatonic scale built on the root of the chord, 2) the minor pentatonic scale built on the 5th of the chord, and 3) the minor pentatonic scale built on the 9th of the chord. The scale built on the root of the chord is best used when the chord is functioning as a i chord in a minor key; the scales built on the 5th and the 9th of the chord are best used when the chord is functioning as a ii chord in a major key:

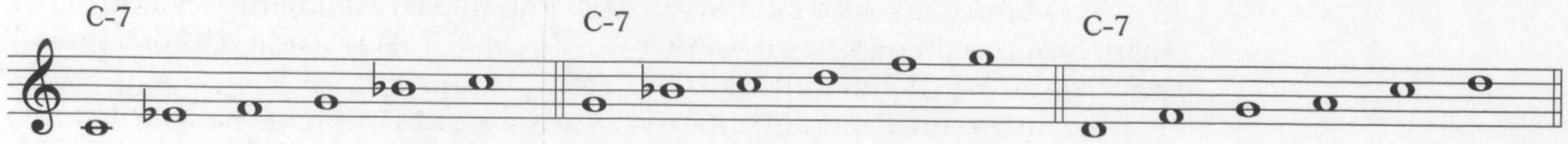

When using the minor pentatonic scale to improvise over minor 7th ♭5 or half-diminished chords, the minor pentatonic scales a whole step below or a perfect 4th above the root of the chord may be used:

In the contemporary era, pentatonic scales are often used to intentionally violate, or go "outside," the normal coloration of the chords. In the right situation, this can create exciting, dissonant relationships. Generally, the player will start with the "correct" scale, move "outside" in the middle of the phrase, and resolve to an "inside" sound at the end of the phrase or cadence.[3] When improvising on major 7th chords, the most consonant options are those that do not violate the major 7th of the chord.[4] For example, over a C major 7th chord, you may use the "inside" choices of C major pentatonic, G major pentatonic, and D major pentatonic, as well as the "outside" choices of A major pentatonic, E major pentatonic, and B major pentatonic:

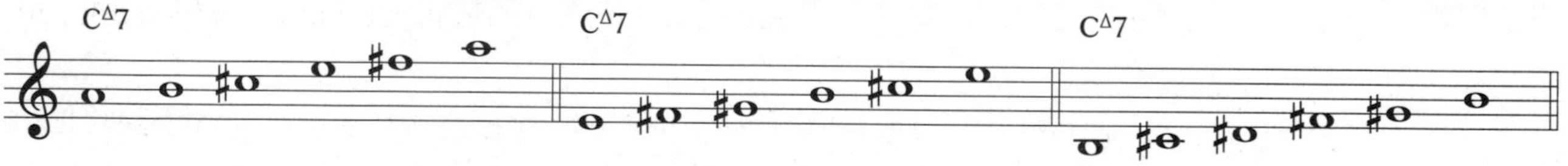

Minor and dominant 7th chords seem to absorb dissonance better than major 7th chords. Virtually any pentatonic scale may be used to go "outside" these chords, the scales a half step and a minor 3rd above the root being the most frequently used choices:

Sometimes referred to as "side-slipping," this technique was developed primarily by John Coltrane, McCoy Tyner, and their followers.

A variant of the minor pentatonic scale, referred to by this author as the *minor/added 6th pentatonic*, uses the major 6th in place of the minor 7th degree.

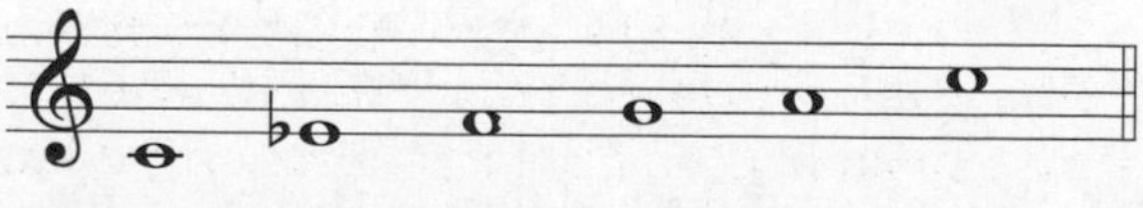

C Minor/Added 6th Pentatonic

[3] Woody Shaw, private lesson, San Francisco, 1973.

[4] Gary Peacock, "Winning in Music Seminar," Seattle, 1979.

This scale was used extensively by John Coltrane in the early 1960s in his improvisations on such compositions as "Equinox," "Your Lady," "Impressions," and "Softly as in a Morning Sunrise."

The minor/added 6th pentatonic scale consists of the ascending pattern: minor 3rd, whole step, whole step, whole step, minor 3rd. This scale can be used when improvising over minor 7th, minor 7th ♭5 (half-diminished), and unaltered dominant 7th chords. When using the minor/added 6th pentatonic scale over minor 7th chords, the scale built on the root of the chord is the best choice, particularly when that chord is functioning as a ii chord in a major key or in a modal context. When using a minor/added 6th pentatonic scale over minor 7th ♭5 chords, the scale a minor 3rd above the root of the chord is the preferred option. Over unaltered dominant chords, the minor/added 6th pentatonic a perfect 4th below the root of the chord is used:

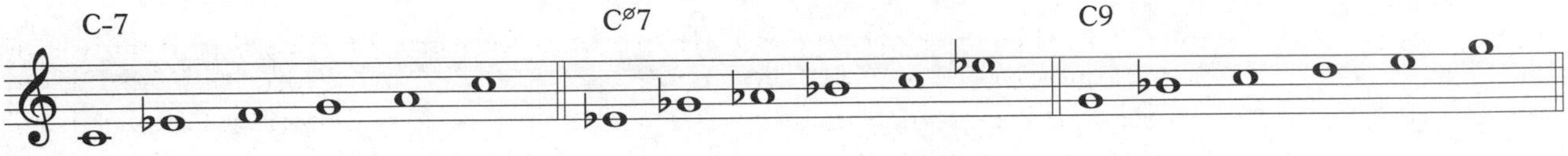

Theory/Ear Exercises

1. Write the major pentatonic, minor pentatonic, and minor/added 6th pentatonic scales in all twelve keys.
2. Create new pentatonic scales derived from scales previously studied, such as the diminished and melodic minor modes.
3. *Analysis of jazz composers*: Look over all the lists of jazz compositions in this text. Make special note of composers having two or more songs represented in a particular chapter. For instance, what types of scales and forms did Charlie Parker, Chick Corea, Billy Strayhorn, Wayne Shorter, Bill Evans, Thelonious Monk, and Horace Silver tend to use in their compositions?
4. *Transcription*: Transcribe a melody, a chord progression, or an improvised solo from a recording.

Gaining Facility with Major Pentatonic Scales

Practice the following exercises over the chord progression below, using either a metronome or the play-along recordings from *Creative Beginnings: An Introduction to Jazz Improvisation* (track 7) or volume 3, *The ii–V–I Progression* (track 2), of *A New Approach to Jazz Improvisation* by Jamey Aebersold. If you find yourself struggling with an exercise, slow it down, simplify it, or sing it while visualizing yourself playing it. After familiarizing yourself with the exercises, pick one or two to practice repeatedly, until you can play them without any conscious thought.

C instruments begin here

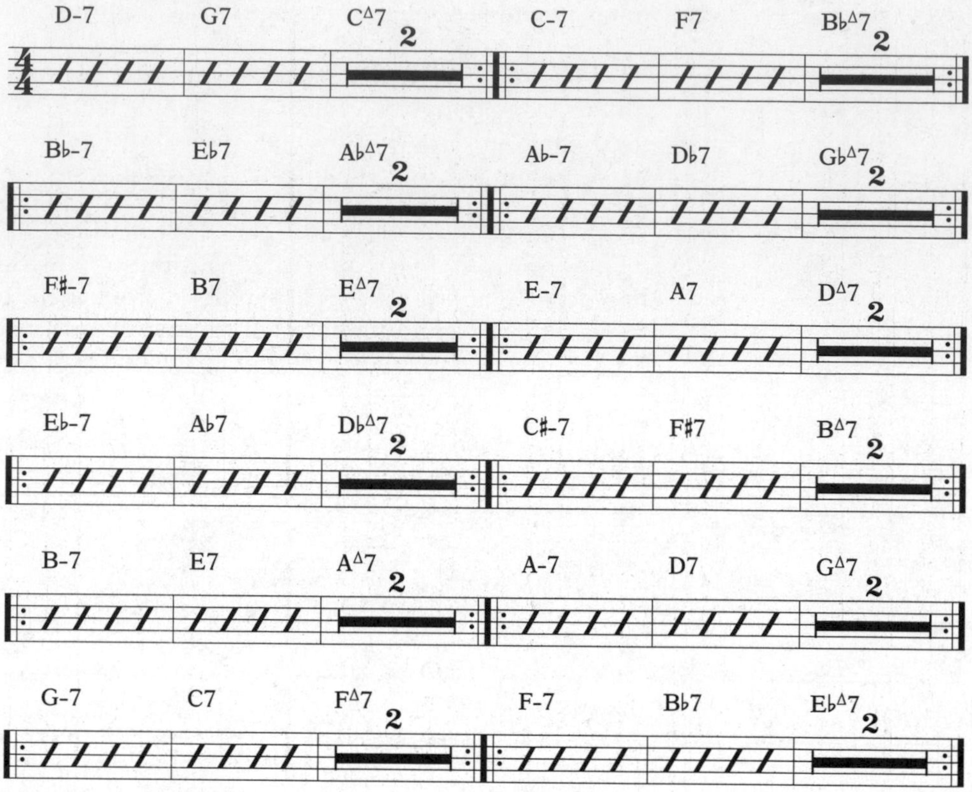

B♭ instruments begin here

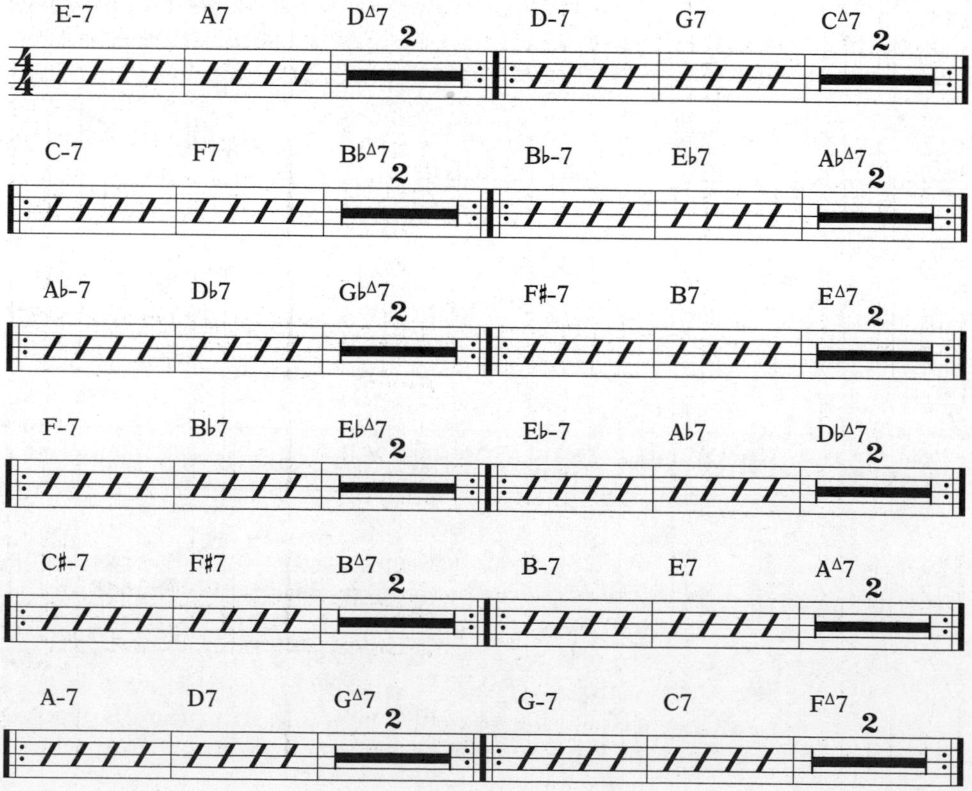

E♭ instruments begin here

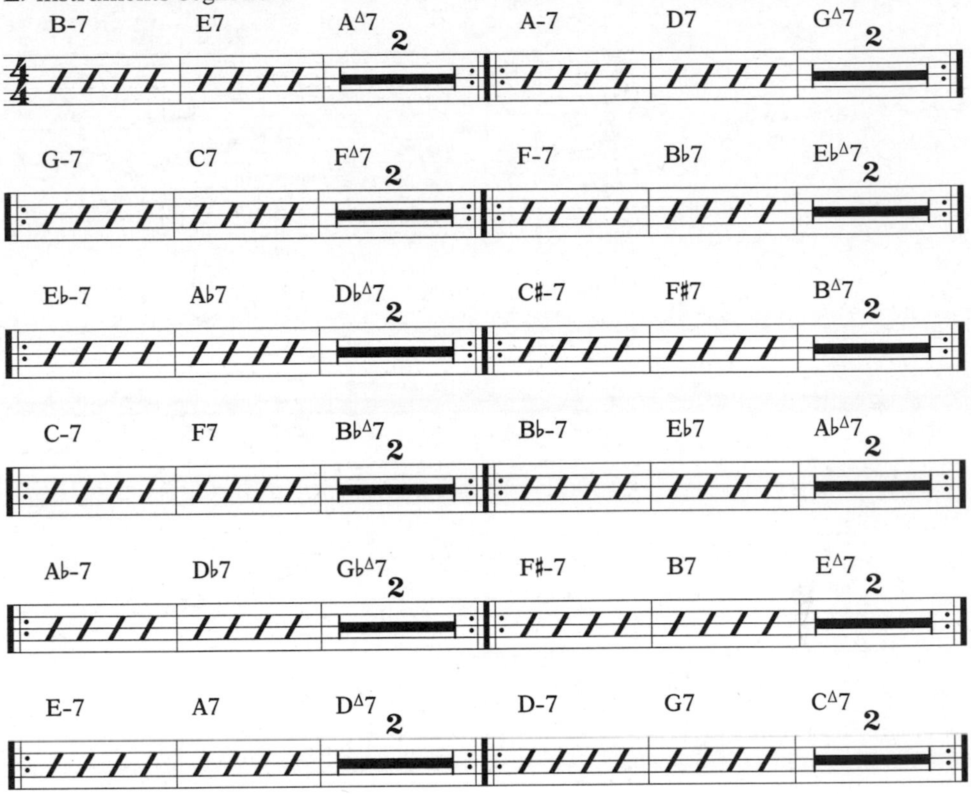

1. *Warmups*:
   a. Have another musician or teacher play a phrase that fits over a ii–V–I progression. Play back the phrase you have just heard.
   b. Have another musician or teacher play random sequences of ii–V and ii–V–I progressions. Play the corresponding pentatonic scales on your instrument or solo over the chords, using your ear to determine the correct key area.

2a. Using the major pentatonic scale built on the tonic.

MM ____________________

2b. Using the major pentatonic scale built on the dominant.

MM ____________________

2c. Using the major pentatonic scale built on the tonic over the ii and V chords, and the major pentatonic scale built on supertonic over the I chord.

MM ____________________

3a. The major pentatonic scale built on the tonic, played stepwise.

MM ____________________

3b. The major pentatonic scale built on the dominant, played stepwise.

MM ____________________

4. A Woody Shaw phrase from his "Child's Dance" solo, based on the pentatonic scale a perfect 5th above the root of a major chord (Art Blakey, *Child's Dance*, Prestige 10047).

MM ____________________

5. A Jamey Aebersold pattern from his "Freddieish" solo (*Jazz Clinicians Quartet Plays for You*, Aebersold Records JA 1975).

MM ____________________

6. A pattern based on the pentatonic scale built on the dominant.

MM ____________________

7. The same pattern, using the tritone substitution for the V chord.

MM ______________

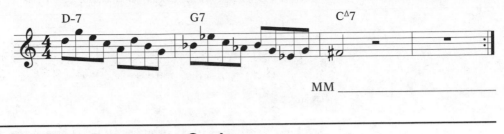

Gaining Facility with Minor Pentatonic Scales

Practice the following exercises over the chord progression below, using either a metronome or the play-along recordings from *Creative Beginnings: An Introduction to Jazz Improvisation* (track 10) or vol. 21, *Gettin' It Together* (disc 2, track 4), of *A New Approach to Jazz Improvisation* by Jamey Aebersold. If you find yourself struggling with an exercise, slow it down, simplify it, or sing it while visualizing yourself playing it. After familiarizing yourself with the exercises, pick one or two to practice repeatedly, until you can play them without any conscious thought.

C instruments begin here

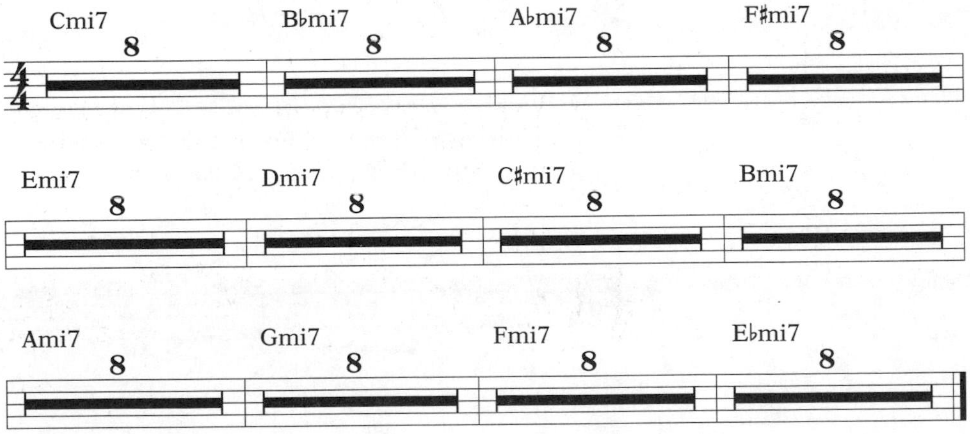

B♭ instruments begin here

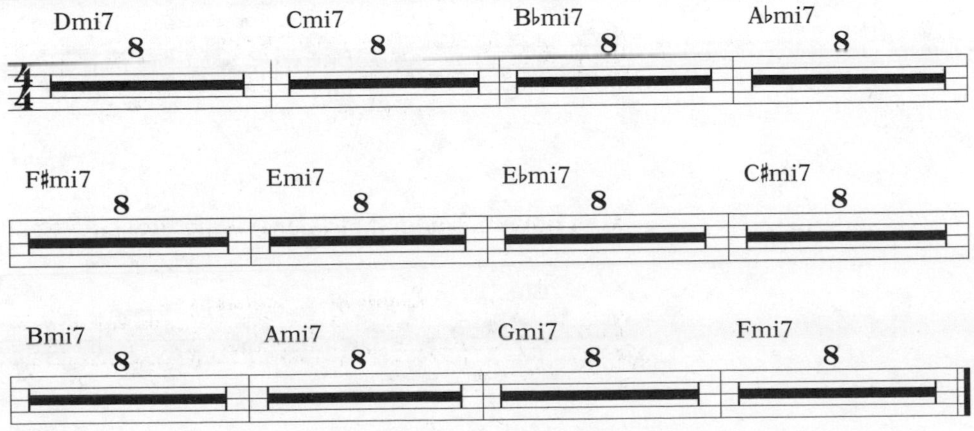

E♭ instruments begin here

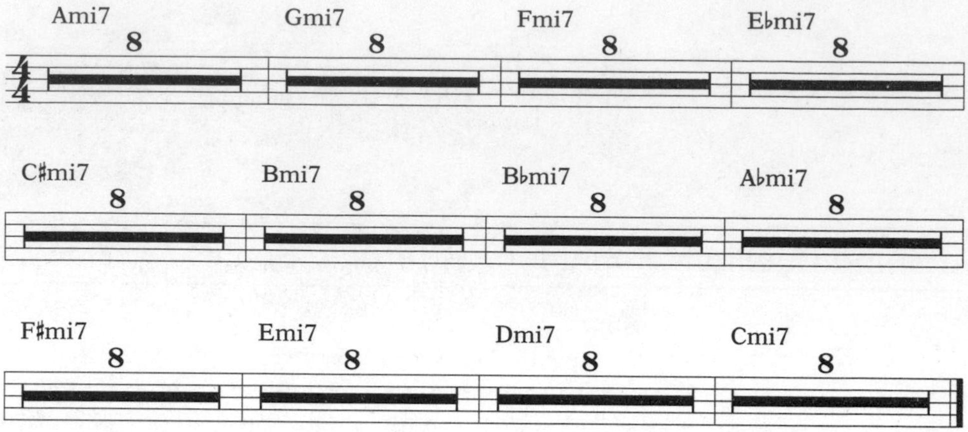

1. A motive from John Coltrane's composition "Blues Minor" (*Africa/Brass*, Impulse 6).

MM ______________________

2. The minor pentatonic scale. Play this exercise starting on the root and a perfect 5th above the root of each chord.

MM ______________________

3. The minor/added 6th pentatonic scale.

MM ______________________

4. The minor/added 6th pentatonic descending stepwise.

MM ______________________

5. A Randy Brecker stepwise pattern from his "Loran's Dance" solo (Idris Muhammad, *Power of Soul*, Kudu P698).

MM ______________

6. A McCoy Tyner stepwise pattern from his "Salvadore de Samba" solo (*Fly With the Wind*, Milestone 9067).

MM ______________

7. The minor pentatonic scale alternating in 4ths and 3rds, with every other grouping inverted. Play this exercise starting on the root and a perfect 5th above the root of each chord.

MM ______________

8. A Woody Shaw line from his "Moontrane" solo that uses the minor pentatonic scale a perfect 5th above the chord, alternating in 4ths (Larry Young, *Unity*, Blue Note 4221).

MM ______________

9. A David Liebman line from his solo on "Float," which uses both the minor pentatonic and the minor/added 6th pentatonic. The first twelve notes can be practiced separately (David Liebman, *Lookout Farm*, ECM 1039ST).

MM ______________

10. A 1–4–5–8 pattern, stepwise descending. This pattern is used in the opening of Woody Shaw's composition "The Goat and the Archer" (Woody Shaw, *Song of Songs*, Contemporary).

MM ______________

11. *Creative jazz improvisation*:

a. *Exploring alternatives*: Improvise over the chord progressions from this chapter while looking at the chord symbols. Experiment with the sound of the pentatonic scales based on the root of the chord, a perfect 5th above the root, and a major 2nd above the root of the chord. Then try experimenting with "outside" pentatonic scales by starting with one of the "normal" scale choices, shifting to a pentatonic scale outside of the key, and resolving back to the chord.

b. *Developing mastery*: When practicing, try to make every thing you play feel as easy as a middle-register whole-note. Until you achieve that level of ease, you will not be able to use that material in a solo without consciously thinking about it or trying too hard.[5]

12. Make up your own patterns and melodic ideas based on pentatonic scales.

a.

MM ______________

b.

MM ______________

Improvising on Jazz Compositions Using Pentatonic Scales

Pentatonic scales may be used when improvising on any compositions that contain major 7th, minor 7th, dominant 7th or half-diminished 7th chords. However, the following compositions lend themselves particularly well to the use of

[5] Kenny Werner, personal conversation with author, Scotch Plains, NJ, 1995.

pentatonic scales. These compositions are found in *The New Real Book*, vol. 1 (NRB), *The New Real Book*, vol. 2 (NR2), one of the volumes of Jamey Aebersold's *New Approach to Jazz Improvisation* (JA), UNC Jazz Press publications (UNC), or *Creative Beginnings: An Introduction to Jazz Improvisation* (CB). Memorize the most frequently played songs, and practice them in different keys.

Compositions for the Use of Major Pentatonic Scales

"Brite Piece"—David Liebman (JA vol. 19)
"Dear Lord"—John Coltrane (JA vol. 28, NR2)
"Fantasy in D"—Cedar Walton (JA vol. 35)
"Freddieish"—Jamey Aebersold (JA vol. 5)
"In a Sentimental Mood" (uses a major pentatonic scale in the melody)—Duke Ellington (JA vol. 12)
"In Case You Haven't Heard"—Woody Shaw (JA vol. 9)
"India"—John Coltrane (JA vol. 81)
"Little Red's Fantasy"—Woody Shaw (JA vol. 9)
"Little Sunflower"—Freddie Hubbard (JA vol. 60)
"Loft Dance"—David Liebman (JA vol. 19)
"Master of the Obvious"—David Liebman (JA vol. 81)
"Naima"—John Coltrane (JA vol. 27)
"Oasis"—David Liebman (JA vol. 19)
"Piccadilly Lilly"—David Liebman (JA vol. 19)
"St. Thomas"—Sonny Rollins (JA vols. 8 and 74, NRB)
"The Moontrane"—Woody Shaw (JA vol. 9)
"The Night Has a Thousand Eyes"—Weisman/Garrett/Wayne (JA vol. 52)
"Tomorrow's Expectation"—David Liebman (JA vol. 19)
"Yes or No"—Wayne Shorter (JA vol. 33, NRB)

Compositions for the Use of Minor Pentatonic or Minor/Added 6th Pentatonic Scales

"A Love Supreme"—John Coltrane (JA vol. 28)
"African Skies"—Michael Brecker (JA vol. 83)
"Beauty and the Beast"—Wayne Shorter (NR2)
"Blues for Wood"—Woody Shaw (JA vol. 9)
"Blues to Woody"—Scott Reeves (UNC)
"Bolivia"—Cedar Walton (JA vol. 35, NR2)
"Cantaloupe Island"—Herbie Hancock (JA vols. 11, 54, and 85)
"Class B Tavern Serenade"—Scott Reeves (UNC)
"Cold Duck Time"—Eddie Harris (NR2)
"El Corazon"—Scott Reeves (CB)
"Fire"—Joe Henderson (NRB)
"Footprints"—Wayne Shorter (JA vol. 33, NRB)
"Full House"—Wes Montgomery (JA vol. 62)
"Funky Sea, Funky Dew"—Randy Brecker (JA vol. 83)
"Impressions"—John Coltrane (JA vols. 28 and 54, NR2)
"Invitation"—Kaper/Webster (JA vols. 32 and 59)
"Little Sunflower"—Freddie Hubbard (JA vol. 60)
"Mahjong"—Wayne Shorter (NR2)
"Maiden Voyage"—Herbie Hancock (JA vols. 11 and 54)
"Mr. Clean"—Weldon Irvine (NRB)
"Mr. P.C."—John Coltrane (JA vol. 27, NR2)
"Nutville"—Horace Silver (JA vol. 17, NR2)

"Philadelphia Mambo"—Tito Puente (JA vol. 64)
"Picadillo"—Tito Puente (JA vol. 64)
"Recordame"—Joe Henderson (JA vol. 38)
"Red Clay"—Freddie Hubbard (JA vol. 60)
"Sea Journey"—Chick Corea (NR2)
"Softly, As In A Morning Sunrise"—Hammerstein/Romberg (JA vols. 40 and 85)
"Some Skunk Funk"—Randy Brecker (JA vol. 83)
"Song for Barry"—Michael Brecker (JA vol. 83)
"Song for My Father"—Horace Silver (JA vols. 17 and 54, NR2)
"Song for Shelby"—Scott Reeves (UNC)
"Spiritual"—John Coltrane (JA vol. 27)
"Sponge"—Randy Brecker (JA vol. 83)
"Strap Hangin'"—Randy Brecker (JA vol. 83)
"The Jody Grind"—Horace Silver (JA vol. 17)
"The Promise"—John Coltrane (JA vol. 27, NR2)
"Tomorrow's Destiny"—Woody Shaw (JA vol. 9)

Woody Shaw's Improvised Solo on "Child's Dance"

Trumpeter Woody Shaw's improvised solo on the Ramon Morris composition "Child's Dance" was transcribed from drummer Art Blakey's album of the same name (Prestige 10047). It was recorded in 1972 with a group that also included Ramon Morris on tenor sax, Manny Boyd on flute, George Cables on piano, Stanley Clarke on bass, and Ray Mantilla on congas.

Woody Shaw was one of the most significant trumpeters in the post-bop idiom. He was the first brass player to employ the pentatonic scales and wide intervals used by reed players such as John Coltrane and Eric Dolphy. Rooted in the bebop tradition but seeking new types of harmonic expression, he was equally comfortable playing "inside" and "outside" the chord changes. Although he did not receive the public recognition he deserved, legions of young trumpet players are indebted to his pioneering work.

"Child's Dance" is based on an AABA form. Each section is comprised of a ii–V vamp, with the B section being a minor 3rd above the A section. Since the harmonies are static, the tune may be regarded as essentially modal. Throughout, Woody primarily relies on major pentatonic scales. The F♯ major pentatonic scale is used over the C♯ mi–F♯7 vamp in bars 1–15, 33–47, and 57–66, while he colors the Emi7–A7 vamp in bars 17–24, 49–52, and 53–56 with A and D major pentatonic scales.

The entire solo is beautifully constructed and highly melodic. In bars 1–12 Woody extends his opening motive by expanding it and framing it with space. In bars 17–24 he develops a second idea through rhythmic variation. A third idea unfolds in bars 25–31 via a series of descending 5-note motives. Similar areas of development also occur at the beginning of the second chorus. Also worth noting is Woody's warm tone on the trumpet and the way he contrasts long tones with short, staccato notes. After much restraint and space, he ends with a flurry of sixteenth notes, just to let you know he can "burn" when he wants to. An even eighth-note Latin beat underpins the rhythm at 𝅗𝅥 = 82m.m. After listening closely to a recording of this solo, practice it at different tempos with the metronome clicking on beats 2 and 4. Continue improvising on the chord progression in the same style.

Treble-clef C instruments:

B♭ instruments (Saxophone—8va where indicated):

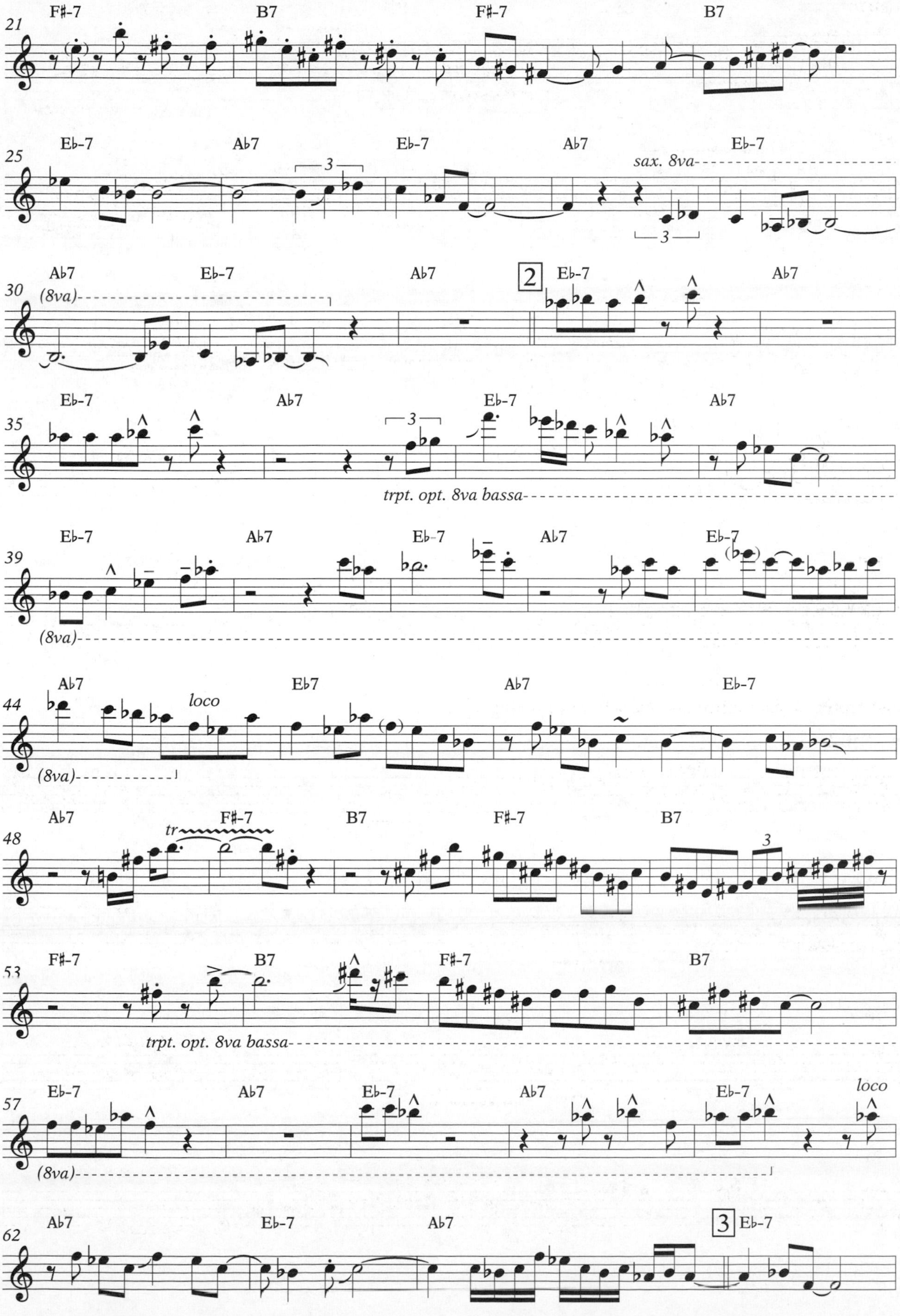
21 F♯-7 B7 F♯-7 B7
25 E♭-7 A♭7 E♭-7 A♭7 E♭-7
sax. 8va
30 A♭7 E♭-7 A♭7 2 E♭-7 A♭7
(8va)
35 E♭-7 A♭7 E♭-7 A♭7
trpt. opt. 8va bassa
39 E♭-7 A♭7 E♭-7 A♭7 E♭-7
(8va)
44 A♭7 E♭7 A♭7 E♭-7
loco
(8va)
48 A♭7 F♯-7 B7 F♯-7 B7
tr
53 F♯-7 B7 F♯-7 B7
trpt. opt. 8va bassa
57 E♭-7 A♭7 E♭-7 A♭7 E♭-7
loco
(8va)
62 A♭7 E♭-7 A♭7 3 E♭-7

E♭ instruments:

Bass-clef instruments:

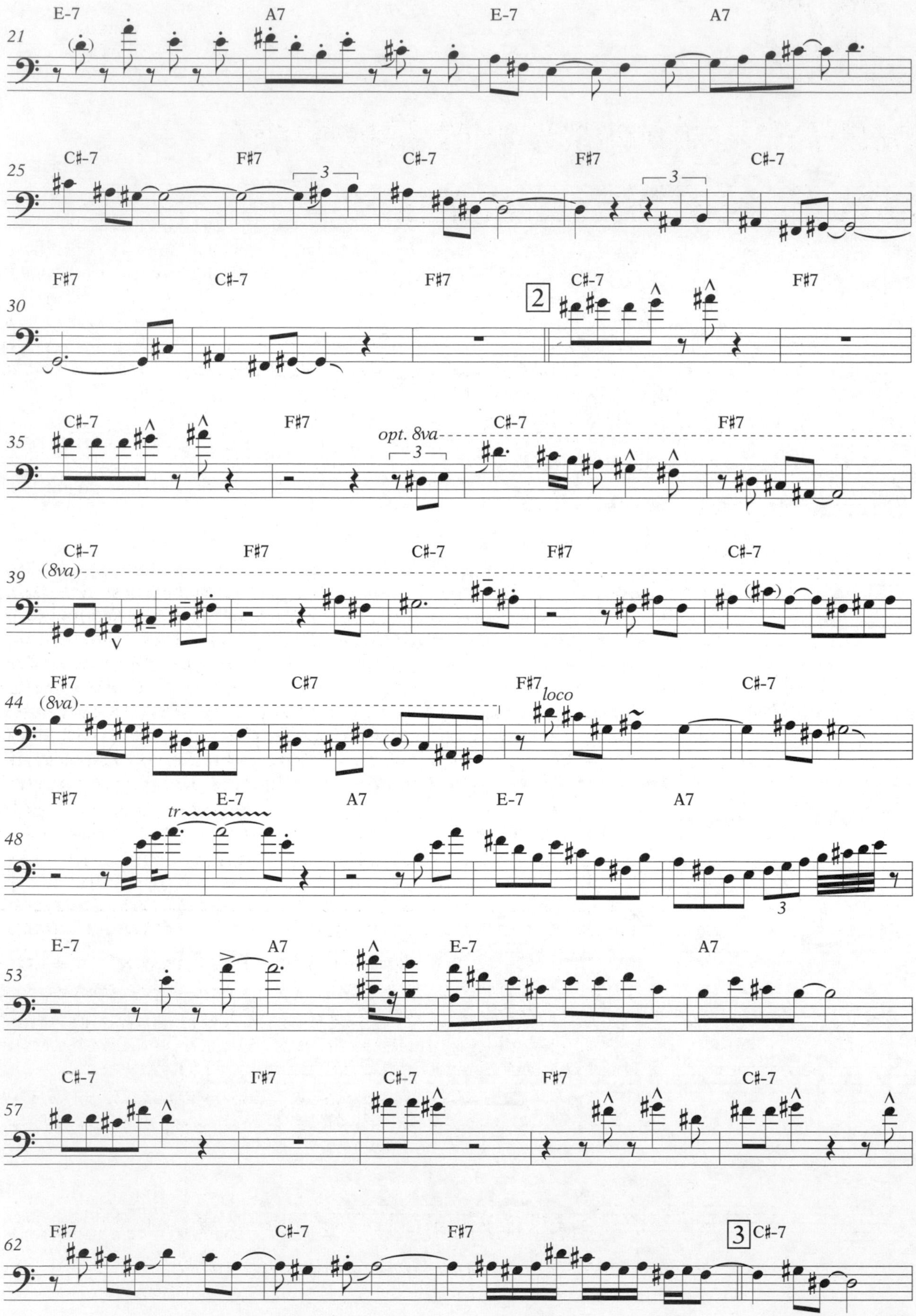
21 E-7 A7 E-7 A7
25 C#-7 F#7 C#-7 F#7 C#-7
30 F#7 C#-7 F#7 2 C#-7 F#7
35 C#-7 F#7 opt. 8va C#-7 F#7
39 C#-7 (8va) F#7 C#-7 F#7 C#-7
44 F#7 (8va) C#7 F#7 loco C#-7
48 F#7 tr E-7 A7 E-7 A7
53 E-7 A7 E-7 A7
57 C#-7 F#7 C#-7 F#7 C#-7
62 F#7 C#-7 F#7 3 C#-7

20

Four-Note Groupings Derived from Pentatonic Scales

"It's a given that ... you have to play hip notes,
have to play with a good groove,
play deep inside the change,
play over the changes.
Some people make careers out of the fundamentals—
but I think (that) to go to the next level
you have to find your own way
of looking at music, thinking about melody, sound
and what music is to you.

guitarist Pat Metheny[1]

Often jazz musicians will improvise with groupings comprised of four eighth notes, instead of complete scales. In a tonal context, these four-note groupings may be used to delineate a chord change. In previous chapters, we have used the 1–2–3–5 grouping to outline major and dominant chords and the 1–2–♭3–5 grouping to outline minor chords. In contemporary improvisation, however, four-note groupings are often used to go outside the key center. This is often accomplished by *sequencing* a four-note grouping through foreign key centers, before resolving back to the correct key. This technique is often applied to modal tunes, where the improviser has time to establish the sound of the correct chord, leave the key center, and come back to the original chord. However, artists such as Woody Shaw and McCoy Tyner also employ this approach on tunes with standard chord progressions. In this situation, the improviser will usually clearly delineate the chord changes at the beginning of the phrase, then use four-note groupings to play "outside" on the transitional and passing chords in the middle of the phrase, and resolve to the correct chord at the *cadence* at the end of the phrase. This creates a feeling of tension and release, rather than simply sounding "wrong."

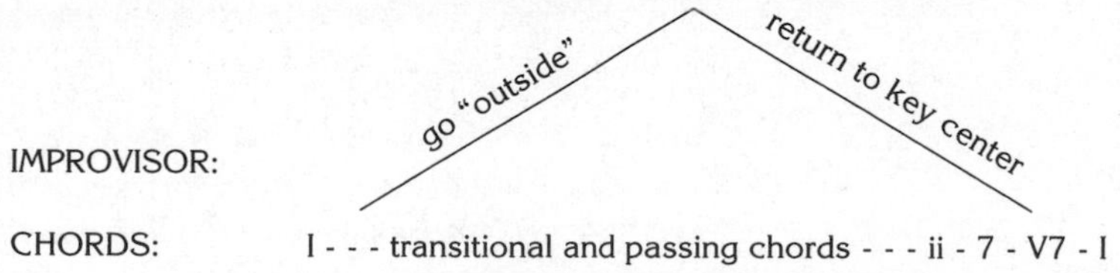

Playing "Outside" in a Tonal Context

There are many possible combinations of four-note groupings, the most common ones being derived from the major pentatonic scale. The first four

[1] Howie Mandel, "Pat Metheny Plays It His Way," *Downbeat*, 62, no. 4 (April 1995), 18.

notes in the scale yields a 1–2–3–5 grouping, the second a 1–2–4–5 grouping, the third a 1–♭3–4–♭6 grouping, the fourth a 1–2–4–5 grouping, and the fifth a 1–♭3–4–5 grouping. The following exercises are based on the 1–2–3–5, 1–2–4–5, and 1–♭3–4–5 groupings and their various permutations. The 1–♭3–4–♭6 will not be used because, lacking a perfect 5th, it tends to be unstable and vague.[2]

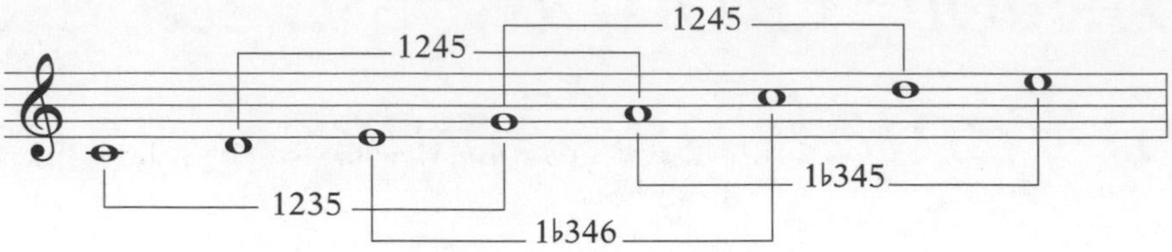

Four-note Groupings Derived from the Pentatonic Scale

Four-note groupings are frequently used by pianists, including McCoy Tyner, Hal Galper, Chick Corea, and James Williams, in part because they are idiomatic to the instrument. This concept, however, has influenced many contemporary musicians, regardless of their instrument.

Gaining Facility with Four-Note Groupings

Although the following exercises may be used to outline chord progressions, they are primarily designed to develop facility in "outside" improvisation. Therefore, there is no chord progression for this chapter. Practice the exercises with the metronome clicking on beats 2 and 4. All the exercises may be modified by extending their range, changing the rhythms, changing the order of notes, or putting a rest in place of a note. If you find yourself struggling with an exercise, slow it down, simplify it, or sing it while visualizing yourself playing it. After familiarizing yourself with the exercises, pick one or two to practice repeatedly, until you can play them without any conscious thought.

1. 1–2–3–5 Groupings:
 a. 1–2–3–5 grouping, with every other group inverted, ascending by half steps. Also practice this exercise ascending by whole steps, in two keys.

MM ______________

 b. 1–2–3–5 grouping, with every other group inverted, descending by half steps. Also practice this exercise descending by whole steps, in two keys.

MM ______________

[2]Hal Galper, clinics, San Jose State University, CA, 1978, and University of Southern Maine, Gorham, ME, 1991.

c. 1–2–3–5 grouping ascending by minor thirds. Practice this exercise in three keys.

MM ______________________

d. 1–2–3–5 grouping descending by minor thirds. Practice this exercise in three keys.

MM ______________________

e. 1–2–3–5 grouping ascending by tritones. Practice this exercise in six keys.

MM ______________________

f. A James Williams pattern based on ascending 1–2–3–5 groupings (live performance).

MM ______________________

g. A Chick Corea pattern from his "Matrix" solo based on descending 1–2–3–5 groupings (Chick Corea, *Now He Sings, Now He Sobs*, Solid State 118039).

MM ______________________

2. 1–2–4–5 Groupings:

a. 1–2–4–5 grouping, ascending by whole steps. Practice this exercise in two keys.

MM ______________________

b. 1–2–4–5 grouping, descending by whole steps. Practice this exercise in two keys.

MM ____________________

3. 1–♭3–4–5 Groupings:

a. 1–♭3–4–5 grouping with every other grouping inverted, ascending by half steps. Also practice this exercise ascending by whole steps, in two keys.

MM ____________________

b. 1–♭3–4–5 grouping with every other grouping inverted, descending by half steps. Also practice this exercise descending by whole steps, in two keys.

MM ____________________

4. Combined Groupings:

a. A James Williams pattern from his "Stretching" solo, which uses four-note groupings. He establishes the key and descends by whole steps, before resolving to the original key center (James Williams, *Flying Colors*, Zim 2005).

MM ____________________

b. A Hal Galper pattern from his "Spidit" solo, which uses a 1–2–4–5 pattern (Hal Galper, *Reach Out*).

MM ____________

c. A McCoy Tyner pattern from his "Passion Dance" solo, which uses four-note groupings (McCoy Tyner, *The Real McCoy*, Blue Note 4264).

MM ____________

5. *Creative jazz improvisation*:

a. Improvise on a jazz standard. At the beginnings and ends of the phrases, play within the chord structure; use four-note groupings to go outside in the middle of the phrases.

b. Improvise in a free manner, without any predetermined structure. Use combinations of four-note groupings combined with chromatic and diatonic scales.

6. Make up your own patterns and melodic ideas based on four-note groups.

a.

MM ____________

b.

MM ____________

Improvising on Jazz Compositions Using Four-Note Groupings

Four-note groupings can be used over virtually any jazz composition. For songs that lend themselves particularly well to this approach, please refer to the song lists in Chapters 13 and 19.

Chick Corea's Improvised Solo on "Matrix"

Chick Corea's improvised piano solo on his composition "Matrix" was transcribed from his album *Now He Sings, Now He Sobs* (Solid State SS 118039). It was recorded in 1968 and featured Miroslav Vitous on bass and Roy Haynes on drums. *Now He Sings, Now He Sobs* is considered one of the most significant piano trio recordings of its time, and is deeply rooted in the post-bop mainstream while exploring elements of free improvisation and the pentatonic modal style.

Chick Corea is a master composer and pianist who has embraced a variety of styles during his career. The influence of pianist Bill Evans is evident in his earliest recordings, but after the mid-1960s the impact of John Coltrane (or, more specifically, Coltrane's pianist McCoy Tyner) became pervasive in Chick's work, particularly in his use of *quartal* (stacked 4ths) voicings and pentatonic scales.

In the late 1960s, Chick began working with the Miles Davis during a period when Miles had begun switching from an abstract form of jazz to an electronic jazz/rock fusion style. Upon leaving Miles in the early '70s, Chick returned to acoustic music with the formation of his trio *Arc* (which he subsequently expanded to a quartet called *Circle*). Recordings from this time feature compositions with a twentieth-century classical influence, combined with extensive use of free-form improvisations. After a couple of years working in this genre, he switched to a more commercially accessible, Brazilian-flavored style with the formation of his group *Return to Forever*. Changes in personnel over the years transformed the group into an electrified jazz/rock fusion band. In the 1980s and 1990s, Chick led two separate groups, his *Elektric* and *Akoustic* bands [*sic*], which allowed him to alternate between the fusion and post-bop jazz idioms. He also made several recordings of extended compositions for large ensembles, which drew inspiration from classical music as well as fanciful themes, such as *The Mad Hatter*. Corea's investigations of the work of pianists Thelonious Monk and Bud Powell as well as his love of Latin-American music, also shaped his music to a significant degree. With his current group, Origins, he continues to forge new directions, primarily in the acoustic jazz idiom, as a composer, pianist, and band leader.

"Matrix" is a blues in F, but the solos are free from many of the conventions we associate with the blues form. The integrity of the 12-bar blues structure and the tonality are preserved, but the exact sequence of chord changes is not predetermined and does not follow that of a typical blues (therefore no chords are indicated in this transcription). The trio also plays in such a way that the three-phrase structure of the blues is often obscured. For example, in the transitions between his first and second and second and third choruses, Chick carries his ideas over to the following chorus, which has the effect of concealing the "seams" of the 12-bar structure.

Chick's melodic material is derived primarily from pentatonic scales, chromatic scales, diminished/whole-tone scales, four-note groupings and simple, triadic motives. Four-note groupings are prominent in bars 4–11, 15–20, 31–33, 52–54, 69–70 and 84. Frequently they are used as a means to depart from and return to the key center, as in bars 15–17, where he uses material derived from the minor pentatonic scale a minor 3rd above the key of F before resolving to the tonic key. Often they create polyrhythms or obscure the barline, creating a great deal of rhythmic interest, as seen in bars 9–11, 19–21, 52–54 and 69–70. Four-note groupings are also used in conjunction with chord arpeggios, as in bars 55–57, where they lead to major 7th chord arpeggios. The 1–4–5–8 grouping, derived from the minor pentatonic scale, figures prominently in bars 72–24.

Chick frequently uses chromaticism to set up a dominant to tonic resolution. Passages in which chromatic lines leads to a C diminished/whole-tone scale—which in turn resolves to an F minor pentatonic scale, occur virtually verbatim in bars 33–36, 45–48, 58–60, and 82–84. In bars 82–84, he varies this pattern by the unexpected resolution to the minor pentatonic scale a minor 3rd above the tonic.

Throughout, his highly chromatic and "outside the key" eighth-note phrases are contrasted with very simple, singable motives. Typically these "almost-coy" ideas are found at the beginning of a chorus and are developed sequentially, as in bars 1–7, 37, 49–50, 61–66, and 76–78. This transcription comprises approximately two-thirds of the recorded solo. After listening closely to the recording, practice it at different tempos with the metronome clicking on beats 2 and 4, and continue improvising on a blues in the same style. The tempo is brisk, at 𝅗𝅥 = 144).[3]

[3] The piano voicings to the first four choruses of this solo may be found in Ramon Ricker, *Pentatonic Scales for Jazz Improvisations* (Studio P/R Publications).

Treble-clef C instruments:

42
46
5
51
w.t.
B♭1235
A 1235
55
E♭1♭345
G♭Δ7
FΔ7
59
6
64
8va
G 1235
2
(8va)
C 1♭235
70
C 1458
7
75
(8va)
81
G♭1245

B♭ instruments (Trumpet and saxophone—8va where indicated):

42
46
5
trpt. 8va bassa
51
w.t.
C 1235
B 1235
55
F 1♭345
A♭Δ7
GΔ7
59
6
64
2
A 1235
70
D 1♭235
D 1458
7
75
81
sax. 8va
A♭1245

E♭ instruments:

42
46
5
51
w.t.
G 1235
F♯1235
55
C 1♭345
E♭Δ7
DΔ7
59
6
64
2
E 1235
70
A 1♭235
A 1458
7
75
81
E♭1245

Bass-clef instruments:

42
46
5
w.t.
B♭1235
A 1235
51
E♭1♭345
G♭Δ7
FΔ7
55
59
6
64
2
G 1235
opt. 8va
C 1♭235
C 1458
70
7
75
(8va)
loco
81
G♭1245

21
Intervallic Improvisation

"Sometimes you have to play for a long time
to be able to play like yourself."

trumpeter Miles Davis[1]

All melodies and chords are comprised of intervals. In tonal improvisation, these intervals typically imply a scale or a chord, but occasionally they are used to depart from or to avoid the implication of a predetermined harmonic structure. Like European classical music, jazz has become increasingly chromatic during its evolutionary history.

The chromatic scale consists entirely of half-steps and contains all twelve notes used in the Western musical tradition.

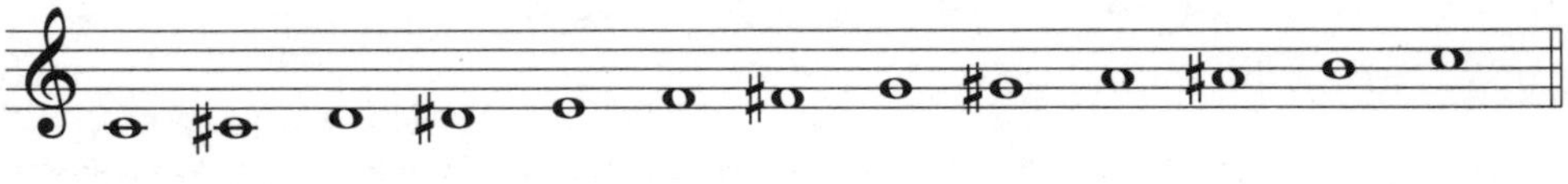

The Chromatic Scale

Many non-Western cultures developed scales and musical practices that are not based on the Western concept of dividing the octave into twelve notes, and much of the music of Asia and Africa (as well as the work of certain avant-garde classical composers) employs notes and *microtones* not found in the chromatic scale. In jazz, the influence of non-Western scales may be seen in the tendency of jazz musicians to bend notes and use falloffs and other dramatic devices. Some of the musicians of the free jazz school opted not to use the Western system of tuning, but most styles of jazz, particularly those involving the use of the piano, are reliant on the twelve notes in the chromatic scale.

Prior to 1942, jazz harmonies were based on triads, triads with added 6ths, and unaltered dominant 7th chords, and improvisers primarily used diatonic scales in their improvisations. However, intensive chromaticism may be found in some of the swing era compositions of Duke Ellington: "Mood Indigo," "Prelude to a Kiss," and "Sophisticated Lady"—all have highly chromatic, though strongly tonal, chord progressions and melodies.

The first phrase of Duke Ellington's "Prelude to a Kiss" (American Academy of Music)

The chord progression to the first phrase of Duke Ellington's "Sophisticated Lady" (Mills Music)

[1] "Miles Ahead," Public Broadcasting System.

The bebop era of the 1940s brought a high degree of chromaticism within a tonal context. In their compositions and improvisations, Dizzy Gillespie and Charlie Parker began surrounding chord tones with notes a half-step above and below (referred to as upper and lower chromatic neighbor tones).

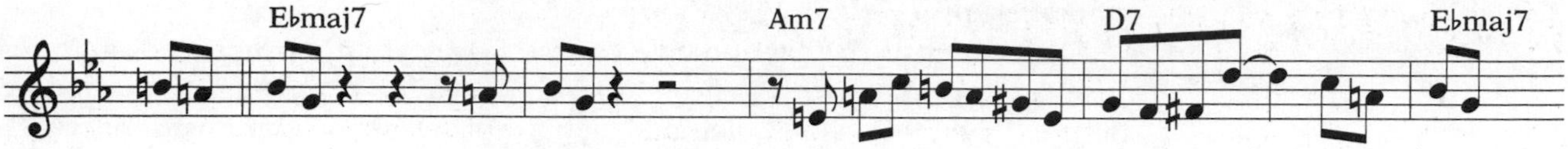

The first phrase of Dizzy Gillespie's "Groovin' High" (Leeds Music Corp.)

Dizzy also began employing alterations of the dominant 7th chord such as the ♯9th, ♭9th, ♯5th and ♭5th, in many of his compositions.

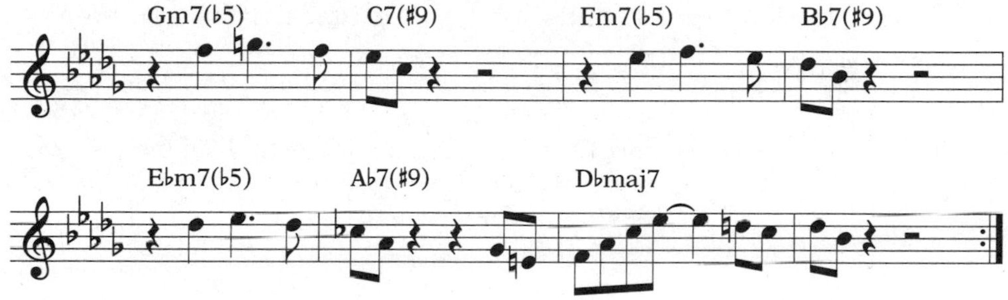

The 'A' section of Dizzy Gillespie's "Woody 'n You" (Charling Music)

Thelonious Monk experimented with a great deal of chromaticism, both in his melodies and in his harmonic progressions.

The third phrase of Thelonious Monk's "Straight No Chaser" (Consolidated Music)

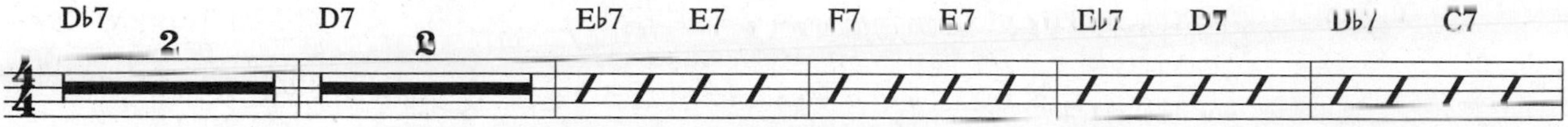

The chord progression to the bridge of Monk's "Well You Needn't" (Regent Music)[2]

Composer George Russell extended the chromatic implications of bebop into a style he referred to as *pan-tonal*, and his compositions frequently featured melodies played in two or three keys simultaneously. He also codified many of the concepts in his book, *The Lydian Chromatic Concept of Tonal Organization*, which is best known for making jazz musicians aware of the melodic and harmonic possibilities inherent in the use of diminished modes.

[2] Monk's original chord progression to the bridge of "Well You Needn't" begins on a D♭7 chord. Miles Davis's version of the tune (which is perhaps more widely known) begins on a G7 chord.

By the 1950s, the number of scalar possibilities for dominant chords had expanded to include the mixolydian, Bebop 7th, diminished/whole-tone, whole-tone, diminished (half-step), and lydian dominant scales. It should be pointed out that if you combined all the notes in the various dominant scales, you would end up with a chromatic scale. *Therefore, any note can potentially be used over a dominant 7th chord!*

The advent of the avant-garde or free jazz style introduced possibilities for greater chromaticism by eliminating the need for an underlying harmonic structure. In 1959 Ornette Coleman began improvising on compositions which were not based on predetermined chord progressions. This approach, which Ornette referred to as *harmolodic*, relied on the melody rather than the harmony, as a basis for improvisation. While Ornette's improvisations tended to be primarily diatonic, other musicians, particularly Cecil Taylor, Sun Ra, and the Chicago Art Ensemble, began basing their improvisations on more dissonant structures and raw sound sources. The work of these individuals subsequently persuaded established hard-bop artists, such as Sonny Rollins, John Coltrane, and Miles Davis, to experiment with compositions that did not use chords as a basis for improvisation.[3,4]

During the early 1960s, John Coltrane began extensive exploration of pentatonic scales. His work induced McCoy Tyner, Woody Shaw, and others to explore the use of perfect 4ths, an interval intrinsic to pentatonic scales. Sequences of 4ths and 5ths are used to depart from and return to the key center in this composition by Eddie Harris:

The third phrase of Eddie Harris's "Freedom Jazz Dance" (Hargrove Music)

Eric Dolphy, another Coltrane protégé, integrated perfect 4ths with extremely wide compound intervals. Combinations of minor 9ths and perfect 4ths are used in the following passage:

Opening motive from Eric Dolphy's "Gazzelloni" (MJQ Music)

The work of these pioneers and others opened up new possibilities for jazz musicians willing to embrace this chromatic universe.

Gaining Facility with Intervallic Improvisation

Intervals may be used over chord changes as connective material or as a means of obscuring tonality. There is no chord progression for this chapter. Practice the exercises with the metronome clicking on beats 2 and 4. Exercises com-

[3] Listen to Sonny Rollins's recording "Our Man In Jazz" or Miles Davis's "Miles Smiles," "Sorcerer," or "Nefertiti."

[4] Personal conversation with David Baker, Bloomington, Indiana, 1981.

prised of half steps are to be practiced in one key, exercises based on whole steps are to be practiced in two keys, and exercises that move by minor 3rds are to be practiced in three keys. If you find yourself struggling with an exercise, slow it down, simplify it, or sing it while visualizing yourself playing it. After familiarizing yourself with the exercises, pick one or two to practice repeatedly, until you can play them without any conscious thought.

1. *Call and response warmups*: Have another musician or teacher play short intervallic motives. Answer using the shape and rhythm of the motive, but not necessarily the identical pitches.
2. The chromatic scale, ascending. Also practice this exercise in a descending manner.

MM ____________

3. A chromatic pattern that moves down a whole step and up a half step. Miles Davis used this pattern in his "Petits Machins" solo (Miles Davis, *Filles de Kilimanjaro*, Columbia CS 9750).

MM ____________

4. A chromatic pattern that moves down a half step and up a whole step.

MM ____________

5. Minor 3rds ascending by half steps with every other 3rd inverted.

MM ____________

6. Minor 3rds descending by half steps with every other 3rd inverted. Jan Garbarek used a similar pattern, based on major 3rds, in his "Awakening-Midweek" solo (Art Lande, *Red Lanta*, ECM 1038ST).

MM ____________

7. Perfect 4ths ascending by whole steps with every other 4th inverted (Woody Shaw, private lesson, San Francisco, 1973).

MM ________________

8. A Woody Shaw pattern based on perfect 4ths descending by whole steps with every other 4th inverted (private lesson, San Francisco, 1973).

MM ________________

9. A four-note group of two consecutive perfect 4ths descending by minor 3rds.

MM ________________

10. An ascending line from Miles Davis's "Petits Machins" solo that uses chromatic and diatonic intervals (Miles Davis, *Filles de Kilimanjaro*, Columbia CS 9750). Practice this exercise in twelve keys.

MM ________________

11. An Oscar Brashear line from his "Begin the Beguine" solo that uses 4ths moving down by half steps, as well as chromatic and diatonic scales, to go outside the minor chord (Shelly Manne, *Hot Coles*, Flying Dutchman BDLI 1145). Practice this exercise in twelve keys.

MM ________________

12. A pattern that uses diatonic and chromatic intervals before resolving to a four-note group. Practice this exercise in twelve keys.

MM ________________

13. A David Liebman line from his "Napanoch" solo that emphasizes chromatic scales and 3rds before resolving to the chord. Practice this exercise in twelve keys.

MM ____________________

14. A Woody Shaw line from his "In Case You Haven't Heard" solo that use 4ths and 2nds to go outside of the major 7th/♭5 chord (Woody Shaw, *Little Red's Fantasy*, Muse MR 5103). Practice this exercise in twelve keys.

MM ____________________

15. An Eric Dolphy pattern from his "Fire Waltz" solo that uses 2nds, 3rds, and 4ths over a wide range (Eric Dolphy, *At the 5 Spot*, Prestige, NJ 8260). Practice this exercise in twelve keys.

MM ____________________

16. Creative Jazz Improvisation

a. *Going "outside"*: Improvise on a tune with chord changes. Over transitional chords in the middle of the phrase, passing chords, or turnarounds, use perfect 4ths, chromatic scales, or other intervals to go outside the chords. Return to the correct chord at structurally important places such as the beginning of the phrase, the cadence at the end of the phrase, or a major tonal shift.

b. *Free playing*: Improvise in a free manner, without any predetermined chord structures. Use perfect 4ths, chromatic scales, four-note groups, and other intervals to create lines that do not imply any given key.

17. Make up your own patterns and melodic ideas based on intervallic improvisation.

a.

MM ____________________

b.

MM ____________________

Improvising on Jazz Compositions Using Chromatic Intervals

Although intervals may be used to outline or to go outside a chord progression, compositions that do not have a predetermined chord progression or have long modal sections are particularly well suited for intervallic improvisation. For songs that lend themselves to this approach, please refer to the song lists in Chapters 13 and 19.

Miles Davis's Improvised Solo on "Petits Machins"

Miles Davis's improvised trumpet solo on the composition "Petits Machins" was transcribed from his album *Filles de Kilimanjaro* (Columbia CS 9750). Although the song is credited to Miles, it was actually cowritten by Gil Evans, and it appears on Evans's recordings under the title "Eleven."[5] *Filles de Kilimanjaro* was recorded in 1968, just as Miles's group was undergoing a change in personnel and style. During the 1960s, his music had been moving away from familiar standards toward increasingly abstract compositions by sidemen Wayne Shorter, Herbie Hancock, Ron Carter and Tony Williams, many of which featured new types of chord progressions and areas of free improvisation. By the time of this recording, Miles was also beginning to explore the use of rock rhythms and electronic instruments. The personnel varies on the album and the liner notes incorrectly list Shorter on tenor saxophone, Chick Corea on electric piano, Dave Holland on electric bass, and Tony Williams on drums in this selecion. Actually, the pianist is Herbie Hancock and the electric bassist is Ron Carter.[6]

"Petits Machins" has a written melody but no predetermined structure for the solos. After a highly syncopated, complex melodic line, the solos are freely improvised around a tonal center of F7. This transcription is notated in 4/4, but Williams accents the beats evenly, creating a rhythmic pulse which is free from traditional barlines and meter. The tempo is 𝅗𝅥 = 120 m.m.

Nearly every note in Miles's solo is derived from either a simple motive based on the pitches A–G–F and Ab–G–F, or a linking chromatic line. Note the many ways Miles varies this simple motive by altering the rhythm or expanding the pitch content, as seen in bars 1–15, 18–20, 27–29, 37–43, 51–52, 54–60, 63–64, and 73–77. He connects these episodes of motivic development with long lines of eighth notes consisting predominantly of chromatic and diatonic scales. Occurring in measures 17, 21–26, 29–32, 44–48, 65–67, 71–73, and 80–81, these chromatic lines serve to obscure the tonal center.

After listening to a recording of this solo, practice it at different tempos with a metronome. Then continue improvising in the same style. This transcription comprises approximately one-half of the recorded solo.[7]

[5] Jack Chambers, *Milestones II: The Music and Times of Miles Davis*, pp. 129–131.

[6] Ibid. Chambers points out that *Petits Machins* was recorded in June, 1968, while Dave Holland did not arrive in the United States until August of that year. Also, to this author's ears, the piano soloist sounds like Herbie Hancock, not Chick Corea. These facts were confirmed by a personal conversation with Ron Carter.

[7] The complete transcription, in a slightly different version by David Baker, may be found in *Downbeat* magazine, December 25, 1969.

Treble-clef C instruments:

42
46
49
55
60
hold back
65
69
73
77

B♭ instruments:

opt. 8va bassa
(8va)
(8va)
hold back
(8va)
loco

E♭ instruments:

42
46
49
55
60
65
hold back
69
73
77

Bass-clef instruments:

hold back

Appendix

I. Intervals

An interval consists of two notes which can occur successively (a *melodic interval*) or simultaneously (a *harmonic interval*). Names for intervals consist of two parts: a prefix (such as *perfect, major, minor, augmented* or *diminished*), followed by a number indicating the distance between the two notes. If that number is less than 8, the interval is called a *simple interval*. If the numbers is 8 (referred to as an *octave*) or more, the interval is a compound interval. Simple intervals have *compound equivalents*. For example, a 2nd plus an octave is called a 9th, a 4th plus an octave is called an 11th, and a 6th plus an octave is called a 13th.

To find the numerical part of the name, simply count the number of lines and spaces between the two notes, making sure to count the first note as 1. To determine the prefix portion of the name, either count the number of half-steps between the two notes or compare the interval to those found in a major scale. In a major scale, the intervals from the first note (*tonic*) to the 4th, 5th, octave or their compound equivalents are referred to as *perfect*. They are called *diminished* when contracted a half step and *augmented* when expanded a half step. The intervals from the tonic to the 2nd, 3rd, 6th, 7th and their compound equivalents are called *major*. They are called *minor* when contracted a half-step, *diminished* when contracted a whole step, and *augmented* when expanded a half-step. When intervals have the same number of half-steps but are spelled differently, they are referred to as *enharmonic*. Develop your ability to recognize these intervals by playing them on your instrument or the piano.[1]

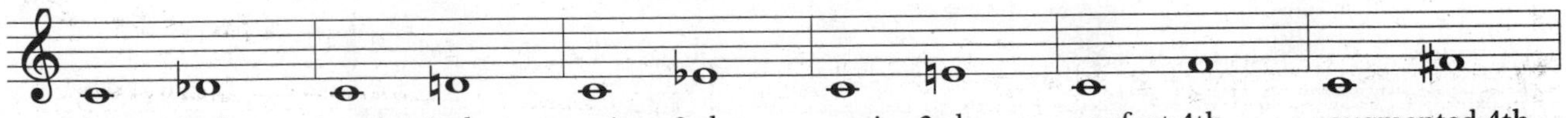

minor 2nd (♭2nd) | major 2nd (2nd) | minor 3rd (♭3rd) | major 3rd (3rd) | perfect 4th (4th) | augmented 4th (♯4th, +4th)

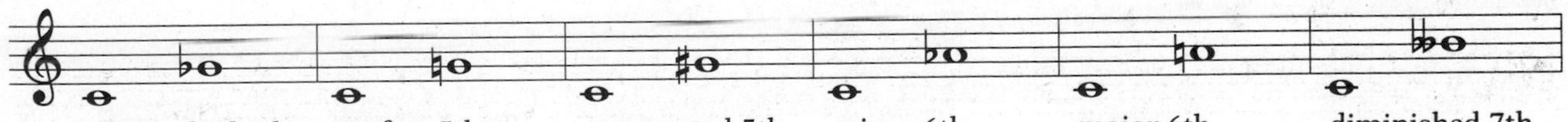

diminished 5th (♭5th) | perfect 5th (5th) | augmented 5th (♯5th, +5th) | minor 6th (♭6th) | major 6th (6th) | diminished 7th (♭♭7th)

[1] Scott Reeves, *Creative Beginnings: An Introduction to Jazz Improvisation* (Prentice-Hall, Inc., Upper Saddle River, NJ, 1997), p. 280–284. For much greater detail regarding basic music theory and jazz theory, please refer to Chapters 14 and 15 of *Creative Beginnings*.

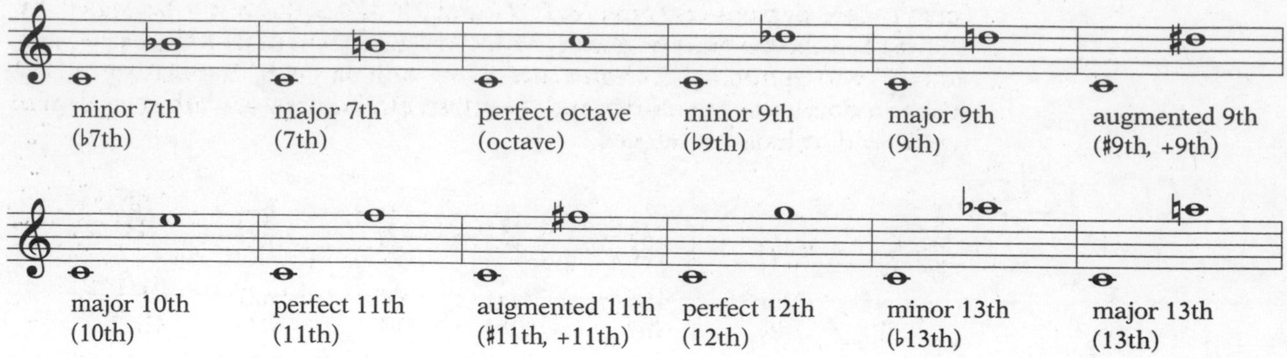

II. Modes in the Major Scale

Below is a chart of the modes contained in the major (or *ionian*) scale. By starting on each of the six other notes and continuing upward for an octave, the following modes or scales are created: major, dorian, phrygian, lydian, mixolydian, aeolian (natural or pure minor), and locrian.

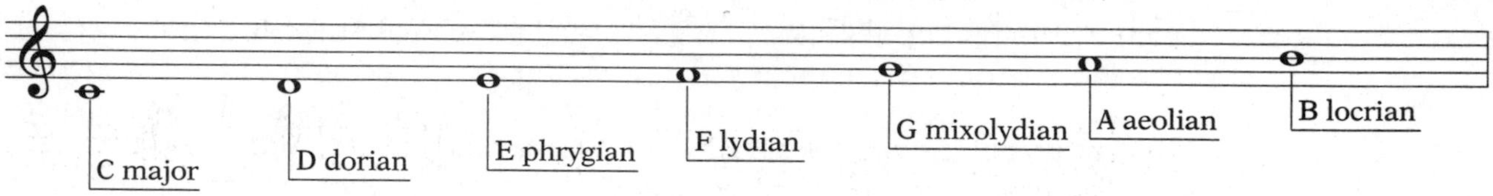

III. Modes in the Melodic Minor Scale

Below is a chart of the modes in the melodic minor scale. Of the seven modes found in this scale, only five are commonly used in jazz improvisation: the melodic minor, lydian augmented, lydian dominant, locrian ♮2, and diminished/whole-tone.

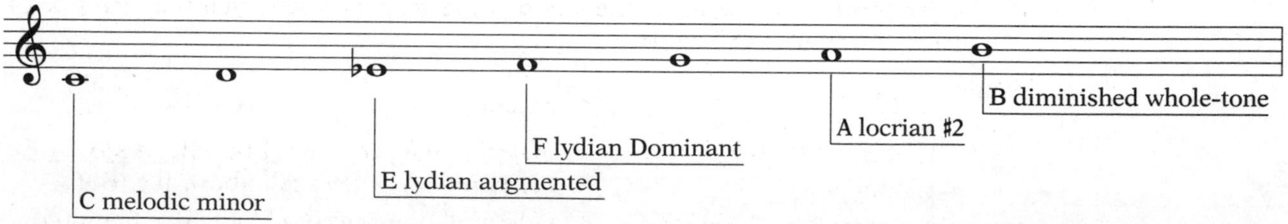

IV. Diatonic 7th Chords in Major Keys

Chords are formed from scales by stacking in 3rds on each scale degree, every other note in the scale. Chords that are derived from the same *parent scale* are called *diatonic chords*.[2] In any major scale, the chords built on the first and

[2] Ibid., p. 298.